Joseph Naeem Publishing Co.

Josephnaeem@aol.com

ISBN: 978-0-9896711-4-9

Book Design by D. Williams

Text is set in Microsoft Word Calibri

12 Font

Hear How it Goes

By D. Williams

Contents

ACKNOWLEDGEMENTS VI

INTRODUCTION VII

Halos or Horns 9

Cressey Street 10

Dennis 12

Morningside Hospital 19

PAB Furniture Company 22

Sears Service Center 23

"Why don't we get married?" 25

Why Teach 31

Teacher Corps 32

Tecate Mexico 35

Bullfights Beer & Basketball 42

University of Southern California & Student Teaching 45

Europe 60

Full Time Teacher 79

Marriage # 2 103

Move 115

Mr. Twichell & Mr. Hornbeck 118

Law School	129
Public Defender	135
Jail Time	138
Fieldsburg Elementary School	165
WCCUSD	175
Pittsburg USD	184
Life's Worst Day	191
Adair School	201
Sunset Continuation	207
Retirement	219
UC Merced	243
Cuba	258
Home Sweet	282
Monterey	288
Los Osos	296
Panama	298
Lost Son	3o3
No Free Throws	323

Acknowledgements

This is a work of fiction; all characters are imagined and any resemblance to actual persons living or dead is coincidence. With tears of joy and sadness this book is dedicated to the memories of Davis Chisulo Williams and Joseph Naeem Williams. The joy comes from the short time you spent with us and the sadness from your early departures.

With every waking moment, and sometimes even dreams; you are missed,

Love Pop.

D. Williams

Introduction:

Hear How it Goes

What kind of fool would want to teach school?

In most of the stories to be read you'll find that I mention several times that I was the 'only one' wherever I happened to be. Many of you will understand my meaning when you recall situations where you were the only white, Asian, Latino, black, woman, man, Jew, Christian, Muslim, Sikh, Hindu, atheist, etc. Reactions vary; some may have ignored the stereotypical statements and actions due to their presence; because there isn't much you can do about the opinions others may have about you your beliefs or ethnicity. As a teacher, most of my 'only one' situations happened in schools and colleges with a few in neighborhoods and apartments as well. At any rate I thought the following introductory poem might fit the situation; just replace Black, with Asian, White, Latino, etc

A Black Friend

Arriving late, I took the remaining seat, next to a very talkative person. Beyond the required introduction and handshake, I was forced to absorb his drama. Well you be the judge.

"Yes, hello, how do you do? Good to meet you, I've never had a Black friend."

"Reckon tht's me as you can

see."

"Are you sure you're Black? You don't talk Black, and you don't handshake

Black!" Where are the what-ups; the knuckle and elbow bumps; that's Black to me!"

"Well, you're white so you must be right. Who am I to question what you or

God intends; just an odd fellow trapped in Black

skin.

Dare I question my identity, when it's defined by you and wht you see on

TV?

Tell me who I am and define me right: How could I be real if I don't fit your stereotype.

Now you're a bit angry and some attitude may show: "How dare these uppity

niggers act contrary to what we all

know!"

"OOPs, nigger slipped out. Is that what I really meant to say? I'll just replace it

with the "N" word and hum a few bars of cum-ba-yah and all will be

OK."

If you live, work and interact with others on this planet I do suspect that you may have been exposed to the aforementioned 'only one' situations and faced the narrow minded and sometimes hostile scrutiny of others. As did I and so many others you tactfully dealt with it and moved on with your life; otherwise you wouldn't be here absorbing these lines. Enjoy the read.

D. Williams

Halos or Horns "The City of the Angels"?

Halos or Horns 'The City of the Angels'?

How do we get from here to there? Moving from a penniless cotton chopping "Colored Boy" in Arkansas to California universities took a lot of determination and hard work. Luck too played a large part as did much unacknowledged help from loving family and friends. Our family tradition was much like that of the many other Blacks who escaped active southern racism and poverty. Once out those escapees were counted on by other family members still in the south to lend a hand in bringing out the next family member. Then when a foothold was established by the newest escapee it was their turn to help another family member who had aged up and was ready to leave and so on. The process continued until all were functioning with jobs, homes and decent lives outside of the south. So it was with my family; the oldest brother CW moved to California with the help of Uncle Theodore and Aunt Irene. Once settled without question or conscience he helped the next oldest, Wally; by giving him a place to stay and finding him a job where he worked at General Motors. Brother Wally did the same for Lee Willie, the next oldest. But Lee Willie didn't last very long in the West; he hated California and General Motors. Cali was very different from what he was used to; Lee Willie missed that much slower life and his friends. He wanted to be in Gould, Arkansas; home near Mama Tang. Even before his discharge from the Army, Lee Willie wrote letters to Mama Tang weekly; begging her to get him out of the Army. Barely surviving until honorably discharged after his short time living in California; Lee Willie soon returned to Arkansas and the small town where we all grew up. After four years in the Air Force it was then my turn for California. No question for me, California had been my dream location since I was a small child and the dream came true. Could life be any better, I think not.

Cressey Street: Fresh out of the Air Force with a letter of acceptance to Pepperdine College I moved in with my brother CW his wife and five kids at 532 West Cressey Street Compton, California. The yellow 3 bedroom two bath stucco with a fenced yard and one car garage was small for 9 people but it was my new home. Just off Wilmington and Rosecrans, all the families in the neighborhood were Black except for the one Mexican family next door. Shunned by other Black neighbors, brother CW pointedly befriended the family. Having learned a bit of Spanish while stationed in Panama during his military service; CW enjoyed conversing in the language. That very same house at 532 W. Cressey St. with the chain linked fenced front yard I'd visited on numerous occasions when on leave from the Air Force. CW always welcomed me and my friends with a party after we had hitchhiked from Luke Air Force Base just outside of Phoenix, Arizona to his home. If the party wasn't at his house he would take us over to West 119th Street in Los Angeles to Uncle Theodore and Aunt Irene's house for the party.

Free drinks, good music and several single neighborhood young ladies were much better than the Elks Club back in Phoenix. My friends and I were pleased and impressed with our good fortune. But now as a civilian and college student, no longer a brief weekend visitor but living at my brothers house full time things were different. We still got along well as he looked out for me and was proud of his college student younger brother. But being there permanently on site one couldn't help but notice the relationship between brother CW and his wife Lois. He often called her"…a stupid, lazy fat bitch…" and occasionally slapped her around. Lois obviously wasn't a fan of housework as evidenced by the thick layers of dust and dirt visible on tables and floors. Flies swarmed around dishes with stuck on food piled in the in the kitchen sink. But all could have been easily remedied with a little organization. The older kids, one twelve and the other fourteen could have done some of the housekeeping chores as could I since I paid no rent. "That's her dam job!" was CW's response to my suggestion that the kids and I could help with the household chores. Other than being rent free, there were other bright spots just off the corner of Wilmington and Rosecrans on Cressey Street.

Cheryl: Unlike BIG sister Lois, Cheryl her younger sister was small and cute. Refreshing to see, smell and touch; she had a nice body, well developed legs, titties, ass and a good looking face as well. Cheryl, then a senior in high school periodically spent weekends at Lois and CW's house. I was still living with CW and family and occasionally when Chery visited we would borrow the car and take in a movie. After all, I was family znd was safe to go out with Cheryl. One night following a movie date Cheryl and I stayed up late talking. CW and Lois had gone to bed leaving us sitting on the living room couch. I do suspect that CW; seeing my eyes fixated on Cheryl's short mini skirt, knew what I had in mind. Although unspoken, that look in his eyes said "Luck and more power to you bro." as he ushering a reluctant Lois ahead of him said "Good night" and closed the bedroom door. Nope brother CW wasn't one to do any cock blocking. With the two of them out of the room Cheryl and I moved closer on the sagging brown pillowed living room couch. Kissing her, Cheryl let my hands roam over her soft places as she held onto me moaning and sighing with pleasure. Things were going good as my shirt and her blouse dropped to the carpeted floor fronting the couch. So into each other and doing what we were doing we were surprised at Lois's sudden reappearance. Wearing a long flower patterned flannel nightgown, hands balled into fists on her hips, in a loud mood shattering voice she said; "Cheryl, it's time for you to go to bed!" Silently, a warm hand on my chest pushing me aside, Cheryl picked up her black skirt and gray blouse from the floor. Barefoot, wearing only bra and panties Cheryl took that willing to kill for body into the adjoining bedroom and forever out of my life. Mesmerized I could only watch: Damm so close.

No thanks to sister-in-law Lois, there went my one and only chance to get next to Cheryl. She wasn't one of Lois's kids, but without question Cheryl obeyed older sister Lois. Later the thought of sneaking into the room where Cheryl was sleeping did cross my wicked mind. But the room was right next to Lois and CW's bedroom and I was fairly certain that Lois' married to my brother and knowing the family well; was awake and listening for me to make such a move into the room where Cheryl was sleeping. Further complicating matters Cheryl was sharing the room with a couple of the younger kids. Before another opportunity presented itself I had moved out and was living in Los Angeles near Pepperdine with brother Wally. But how could I not be saddened for having missed that one opportunity with fine ass Cheryl. On another note I couldn't keep my mouth shut and had several heated discussions with Brother CW about child raising. He wasn't one to listen to the opinions of others on any subject especially the opinion of a younger brother. As the kids got older the Crips and Bloods divided the Compton neighborhoods. So I suggested that it might be wise to move the family to a safer community before the kids now young teenagers were recruited. Cresseyu Street was Blood turf so they became Bloods and remain so to this day. Then and now it didn't take a genius to see that fewer gangs and hostile police were located in those communities outside of Compton and the city of Los Angeles. Suburbia meant nicer streets, better schools etc., it was safer. The inner city system with all attendant factors including education; was self perpetuating negativity. The best more experienced teachers refused to work in dangerous neighborhoods and schools with dwindling and often non existent resources. CW could afford to move, he was a supervisor and made good money out at General Motors. "Are you crazy, boy? I ain't going to live out there with a bunch of honkeys!" was his outraged response to my suggestion. In later years it was not surprising to see five of his six kids spend time in prison, all felons. Clearly their lives, the lives of their children and their children's children would be very different if raised in safer more nurturing neighborhoods without Crips and Bloods. Brother CW, maybe out of discomfort and fear chose to remain on Cressey Street. Unfortunately we had to witness the one son Dennis suffering the ultimate consequence of his father's stubborn attitude.

Dennis: It seems much later while observing the associates and conduct of his kids; CW began to suspect that I may have been correct in my earlier environmental analysis. The twins Dennis and Denise were babies when I lived with the family on Cressey Street. Always aware of the debt I owed my brothers uncles and other family members; when presented with the opportunity; of course payback was unquestioned. Sixteen years had passed since my Compton days and I was settled in a safe Northern California community; "With a bunch of honkeys." CW called and asked if I would take Dennis into our home.

Owing the debt and knowing that's what families did, of course I agreed. Dennis was a promising student and an excellent athlete, but Compton gang influence was beginning to hinder his performance in both the classroom and in athletics. Dennis was the baby, the last of the five sons. The other brothers too had started with much promise as fine students and athlete but ended up heavy into the Blood gang culture and all that that entailed.

Things went well; Dennis was an easy fit for my four and ten year old sons and the wife. Attending the flagship high school in town and a star defensive back on the junior varsity football team Dennis was soon moved up to varsity. Sitting in the stands watching the games with the family; our sons were so proud of him; it was easy to see that the coaches loved his speed and quickness. Both working in the school district we knew his coaches and classroom teachers. They also knew that Dennis was our nephew. Consequently, as the year progressed our teacher connections didn't bode well for Dennis. Too soon we started getting messages in our boxes at our respective schools about Dennis cutting classes and missing football practices. Knowing the pattern and wahta was coming next we began to brace ourselves for unwanted news. First came academic probation and then Dennis was dropped from the team. It was time for the family talk. Having dealt with such typical student misconduct over the years I didn't know what to say when family was guilty of such behaviors; so I was brief and asked, "What's up?" Head down, Dennis too was brief and responded, "Nothing." Things worsened. With an enrollment of more than 2,000 students there were only two very well known thugs and druggies at the school. It being a small town most kids knew and avoided the Trout brothers who spent an inordinate amount of time suspended or expelled. Somehow Dennis, the new kid in town found and befriended them. He even brought the Trout brothers home with him. He did it just once before I told him I didn't want them at our home. My younger kids looked up to Dennis and I was certainly worried about the example he was setting for them. Of course Dennis liked the kids but I am sure examples and modeling good behaviors never crossed his young mind. Once he started hanging out the Trout Borthers and doing drugs he was rarely home and had no time for the children. The family relationship was quickly deteriorating and moving toward its end when Dennis started staying out all night. Finding a baggie of marijuana in his jeans during the wash finished the Dennis experiment. I called brother CW and told him why I was sending Dennis home and put him on the very next Greyhound Bus heading south. The kids were very sad when I sent Dennis home and it took a while for them to forgive their "mean pop". A couple of years later we received an invitation to Dennis's graduation from Compton's Centennial High School. Overall Dennis was a good kid, who turned out to be a very nice young man. He visited the kids and the family often.

Sonoma County Airport

Ending the gang connections he had a fulltime job. Dennis would take the small commuter airline from LAX on weekend visitsThe kids were beside themselves with excitement the minute they sighted his plane.A refreshingly humorous chore was keeping them from running onto the tarmac. They couldn't wait to shower Dennis with hugs. Unfortunately, the last time I saw 24 year old Dennis was at his funeral. Not wanting to expose them to such a sad, sad occasion; I didn't know how to explain it to the wife and kids, so that trip I did alone. The funeral was quite a display with Bloods wearing their colors standing on the balcony and along both side walls of the church. In the latter part of the 80's Dennis had been driving a 1966 Chevy, that he had "freaked off" by adding a leather tuck n roll interior, lifts, whitewalls, a super sound system and other amenities. Early Wednesday evening Dennis was leaving Bible Study at his uncle's Compton church when he was approached by three Crips standing near his parked car. "Give me the keys." The shorter of the three said as Dennis opened the door. Dennis's "Hell no!" was heard by his uncle standing in the doorway as was the shotgun blast. They took the keys from his hand leaving Dennis to die on the church steps. At the funeral I was angry at the Bloods who found time to pose and stand around but never found the Crips who killed Dennis and also angry at my brother CW who just by a change in zip code could have saved Dennis. He could have easily shielded Dennis and the rest of my nephews and niece from that whole gang life thing. Storming from the church sadly, with those happy memories of Dennis visiting the kids and family I started that lonely 400 mile drive home. However, before seeing Dennis's sobering reality far into the future, I had to survive the early years with CW his abused wife Lois and the rest of the family. Although feeling completely welcome and at home in my brother's house, Mama Tang in our phone conversations constantly reminded me that it was "…his house."Having witnessed our mother Mama Tang being abused for years by a boyfriend it was very hard watching CW's abusive behaviors. But I had no other choice and I did see it daily.

His House: Yes, it was what it was, and that was my loving brother's pig headed stubborn attitudes. "Clean that dam kitchen! You're one fat ugly ass woman!" were daily comments. All was said in the presence of me, the kids and anyone else who happened to be on the premises. I wanted to speak out against the constant verbal and physical abuse; but as a visitor in his home with no other place to live; I remained silent. Always in the back of my mind was Mama Tang's reminder when I complained to her of CW's treatment of Lois; "It's his house."Daily witnessing the obvious conflict one wondered whether both he and the wife had other love interests outside the home. Remembering CW's visits to the family home in Arkansas when I was a child; on at least one occasion he brought with him a female companion. "Let's go downtown". I heard CW speak to the woman one afternoon, and he called her Gina.

Although never having met CW's wife at the time we in the family knew her name was Lois. So I said to Mama Tang, "I thought Gina was named Lois." Showing a sly smile, without explanation she said; "Lois is CW's wife." A naïve kid, still I didn't understand the explanation or the ensuing silence. Later, living in their house in Compton the major question of the many unasked was why marry a person you hated so much? How do you make love to someone you despise? Under such circumstance is it still called love? Just a 22 year old fellow from a small town in Arkansas, reckon I was too young to figure out such complicated things. Following each abusive day; nightly they slept in the same bed and kept having kids. How do you make love to someone who you despise? Strange, strange, drama. Maybe it was time for me to move on.

Old Friend: Transitioning from military to civilian life from Arizona to California took some getting used to. Finally moving from CW's house of abuse in Compton to brother Wally's home in Los Angeles was a welcome change. Living off Florence and Western Avenue in LA I was happy to be free of the daily tension and drama. Although rarely seeing the Compton folk after my move, the Compton address was remembered by my military friends from Luke Air Force Base. Terrance Wooten lived down the hall from me back at Luke AFB. He was now living off Adams Blvd in Los Angeles and selling insurance. The old road dog called Compton and got my new phone number and address from CW. Wooten called one Friday afternoon and invited me to a party near Venice Beach. Always ready to party but remembering Wooten from our time in the military, I was skeptical. Sure he had attended the parties, but I had never seen him with a woman during our years at Luke. Maybe he was just a shy fellow, but there was whispering among the troops regarding Wooten's sexual interests. Regardless, I borrowed Wally's car picked up Wooten and drove to his friends house for the party. Well kept lawns and vintage two-story homes covered the block. Parking on the street in front of the house, we could hear the sound of the Four Tops blasting from inside. All was good as we rang the doorbell stepped into the hallway and was introduced to most of the partygoers. Mason, a short bearded portly fellow shook my hand and slapped Wooten on the back as he guided us to the bar. Observing the room with rum-n-coke in hand I saw no other Black folk. Cool with that but more bothersome wasthe lack of women at the party. Fifteen or twenty dudes were present and there was only one woman in the room. Further, this being my first 'White' party; I thought it odd that folk enjoyed just standing around drinking and talking at a party with NO DANCING. Was no women and no dancing common at white parties? Glancing around the room, clearly Wooten and I were out of our comfort zone. This became especially apparent as we tried to keep from staring at Mason's wife. Wearing a light blue baby doll pajama outfit with a see through top; she was moving about the room serving drinks and snacks.

Pepperdine Then

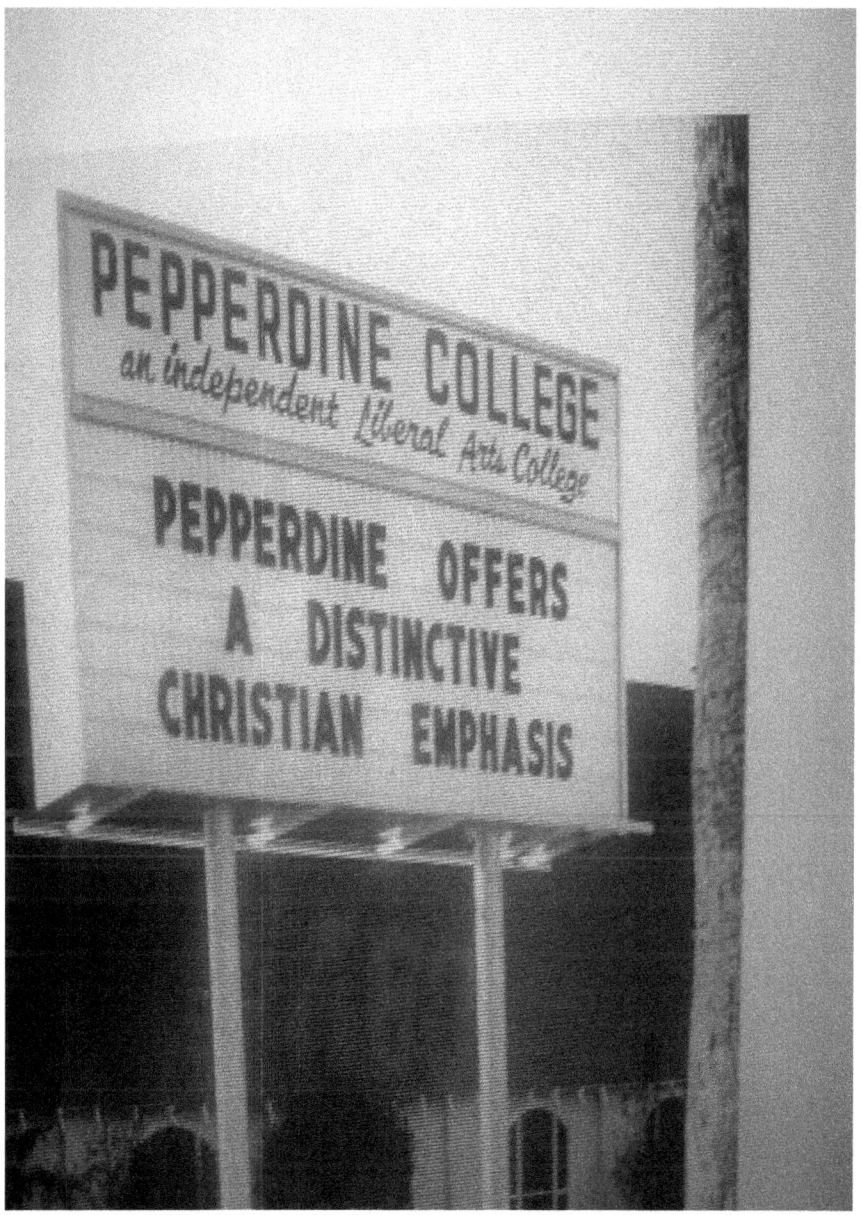

Pepperdine Now

Maybe a little over five feet, tanned legs, red nipples and a nice ass; who could listen or look at anyone else in the room?Damm, Wooten even whispered and pointed out strands of blond pubic hair peeking around the edges of her pajama bottom. Except for the two black dudes; Wooten and I; seemingly everyone else in the room was busy chatting and ignoring her. Not knowing what to do or how to act in a completely new situation we were in crisis mode.Sage didn't seem to mind or notice our locked on stares and our inability to stop staring at her embarrassing beauty. After a couple of hours spent trying not to get caught staring at Sage's tits and crotch, we said our goodbyes and wrote that party off as an interesting experience. It was certainly not like the parties we had attended back in Phoenix, South Central LA, or Cressey Street in Compton. At least his continuing lecherous stares at Ms. Body (Sage) may have dispelled any suspicions regarding Wooten's sexual preferences. Shaking off the unusual party, the coming Monday meant a return to my student reality. Living arrangements taken care of by my brother Wally, I still needed a job to pay for books and other expenses. The registrar's office; where part time job announcements were posted on the bulletin board was a good place to start. Students simply copied the information from the board and called the listing company or agency for an interview. Pepperdine being a 'Christian School', businesses were pleased to hire Pepperdine students. I saw that Morningside Hospital at 8711 South Harvard Blvd. needed an admissions clerk/cashier. Admissions, one of my jobs in the military it seemed the perfect fit.

Jobs

Morningside Hospital: Having worked hospital administration for three years while in the Air Force; I contacted nearby Morningside Hospital for an interview. Not interfering with my class schedule they needed an evening shift emergency room admissions clerk. Too soon I learned that working in a civilian hospital was different from an Air Force Hospital experience. First in the military on a fighter training base our emergencies most often involved weapons or engine malfunction accidents. On a training base where pilots were learning to fly jet fighters survivors was a rare commodity. Secondly, military discipline as well as the aforementioned reasons limited the number of arguing or fighting patients in the emergency room. Finally, the inner city location of Morningside Hospital I was to learn was also a major contributing factor to that difference as well. From a small town in Arkansas and into the military I knew very little about the inner city. Sitting just off the main drag at 8711 South Harvard Boulevard in South Central Los Angeles; appearance wise Morningside Hospital was reminiscent of Luke AFB Hospital. A squat one storied structure with long hallways separating the various wards, it was even painted the very same light green exterior with a darker green trim. The medical equipment, clothing and hospital odors were of course the same.

To say I felt right at home would be a stretch but I did feel comfortable at the new job. Smoothly coasting through the first few days was pretty much routine as I prepared for my first weekend. Slightly different from Luke Air Force Base Hospital; on Friday and Saturday nights patients with cuts, gunshot wounds and other evidence of violence were lined up wall to wall, bleeding in the emergency room. The doors locked automatically upon entry because it was not uncommon for patients to be followed by their cutters and shooters. Armed security patrolled 24/7 to quell patient on patient or patient staff fights in the parking lots and waiting room. It was eye opening to discover that patients and many workers at Morningside were dishonest, unstable and out of control. Considering the treaters and the treatees; all seemed a little bit shady, frantic and insecure. Also, unlike in the military there was no hazardous duty pay for the job. Respecting patient records confidentiality and securing finances; Morningside rules only allowed hospital personnel behind the admitting desk. But to the numerous scruffy looking non-hospital characters wandering the hallways and wards such rules didn't seem to apply. Admission clerks were prime targets for the scammers because they controlled access to the names, diagnoses, home addresses, phone numbers and other sensitive patient information. Those street hustlers paid $50 to $100 dollars per patient for information which they would resell to ambulance chasing lawyers. "Come on Williams you're not going to turn down this easy money are you?" I heard that and similar statements several times a day. A struggling college student, sure I needed the money but I never considered betraying the trust that goes along with the job. Maybe it was the way my momma raised me; but just the thought, the idea, felt very uncomfortable, unethical and illegal. How would I feel if I was a patient and my information was shared with unauthorized persons, not good? Consequently my four hours a day six days a week as admission clerk and cashier was worked with cautious care and observation. Name, I asked Weldon Crenshaw; "They call me Crennie..." he said while waiting. The large scruffy bare feet on his 6'4 inch frame hung off the edge of the gurney. Nurses Henderson and Sanchez, unfazed, continued chatting as Crennie's head wound squirted blood across the counter and onto the bulletin board behind me. "Uh, Henderson, you think you could take him back?" Giving me a hard "You're not my boss!" look she stomped out of the office, ignoring the blood spurting patient and snatched the front of his gurney. Then with a slow 'LA County General hospital walk'; Sanchez following, Henderson pulled Crennie through the examination room doors. Although nurses were questionably, authorized personnel in the admissions office; Henderson and Sanchez were doing what they often did during their shifts just hanging out. The admissions office was the most convenient place away from their work with patients on the wards. Collecting payment from the few patients who could afford to pay was also a part of my new job.

The locked cash box kept in my desk drawer was another reason why access to the office was restricted. During my hiring interview the human resources director told me that I was responsible for the cash and the only person with a key to the box. But on my very first night I noticed Senerey, a nurse's aide who sometimes filled in at admissions use a key to open the cash box. So I was surprised to discover the reason for my meeting with Human Resources. I showed up for work and found a note on my desk telling me to meet with the human resources director. For the 2nd time since my tenure at Morningside I entered the office of the suit and tied down white fellow with the Bradshaw nameplate on his desk. Not offering me a seat he said, "There was money missing from last night's cash box." "And what does that have to do with me?" I asked. "Well you're the cashier and you have the key." Taking the unoffered seat in front of his desk I responded; "I am sure you know there are others with keys to that cash box." Bradshaw then told me that another employee had seen me taking money from the cashbox. "Well that lying employee is probably the person who took money from your cash box. I am a veteran and full time student at Pepperdine, why would I jeopardize my future by taking petty cash from a part-time job, ridiculous!" That said I stood and walked out of Bradshaw's office. I was pretty sure that Senerey had taken the money; if any was missing. I continued working at Morningside but had lost any latent enthusiasm for the job. Soon I was again checking the jobs board at Pepperdine. Although only part-time; after giving two-weeks notice with mixed feelings I looked forward to the end of my first job outside of the military. Certain that there would be other jobs before the end of my Pepperdine journey, all were good. Telling my oft unemployed friend Charles that I was quitting I suggested that he might apply for the job. Yet I was surprised at how quickly Charles was hired. Pretty full of myself with three years of Air Force experience, two years at Phoenix Junior College, and being in my junior year at Pepperdine, it was unsettling to be replaced so fast by a man who with my help; just barely finished high school. Later, dropping by the old job for a visit it wasn't surprising to see the same shady characters hanging around admissions and lurking about the hospital wards. One would think that fat ass Claudell; hospital security, would do something, but he was friendly with them and knew those thugs and hustlers as I suspect did my friend Charles. Those low lifes were now dealing freely with Charles who had no compunctions about selling patient information. Henderson, Sanchez and Senerey disliked me just loved Charles; who at every opportunity bragged about how much money he was making selling patient information. Maybe the discipline made a difference; being ex-military and trying very hard to change my life, it took a while to realize that everyone didn't necessarily approach things as I did. Many folk were not willing to put in the extra time and effort to make changes. But who am I to judge others choices.

Pepperdine Reflection: Just twenty two years old it would have been nice to have some reminder telling me that all the experiences were just minor steps toward those life activities of my vague future. That eventual goal faced by all may become perfectly clear with age; which is to live life and die. But before that ageless wisdom there were absolute certainties. The first major certainty at that time was that I would NEVER return to live in Arkansas. Secondly, I would NEVER again work in the fields picking and chopping cotton. The US Air Force, Phoenix College, Pepperdine, and the part-time jobs were positive steps further and further away from that Arkansas dead end. It was comfortable knowing every step away was movement toward a positive California future. Knowing that whatever the job might bein California, it was comparatively easy.Following my stint at Morningside Hospital I prepared for an interview at PAB Furniture Company just off Slauson and Central Avenue in Los Angeles.

PAB Furniture Company: Mr. Davidovich was a nice man who seemed pleased to hire a young Black Pepperdine student. One of the first things he proudly told me during my interview in the back of the large showroom filled with couches chairs and lamps was that his was the only store on the block not burned during the recent 1965 Watts Rebellion (Riot). The two large front display windows remained unbroken during the chaos. Mr. Davidovich and his wife Talia, who did most of the in-house paperwork seemed very comfortable in the black community and unasked freely shared their kosher lunches. They shared of course after a long explanation of the meaning of the word kosher. Following a lifetime of cheerfully chomping on pig meat it was all new to me, so I was pleased with the commentary. Having been hired as a bookkeeper I couldn't help but notice that other than minor sales recording, Talia the wife continued doing the major book work. After a few weeks I was assigned an additional task, collections. Most of the collection work was done by telephone but sometimes I was sent out into the Watts neighborhoods to knock on doors. It never crossed my naïve mind that it wouldn't have been safe for a white face to knock on those doors in those neighborhoods at the time. "You're doing what?" was my older brother CW's reaction when I told him where I was collecting for PAB Furniture. He thought it very unsafe to work in that area. This reaction was coming from the brother who comfortably lived in Compton no less. Dealing with mostly black women, maybe it was my youthful good looks but I never had a problem out amongst the peeps. I was embarrassed, on several occasions when tactfully turning down offers of sex as payment for the money owed. Suddenly at PAB; I was spending more and more time away from bookkeeping, the job I was supposedly hired to do. Not pleased; yet again I remembered those sun up to sundown Arkansas cotton fields. Having not done such hard physical labor in more than five years, I certainly knew that working behind a desk was preferable.

Comparatively, needless to say salary was never an issue. Hey, this was California where even a Black man sometimes had choices. But then in a heartbeat at PAB furniture, there was no longer any pretense of bookkeeping. One day I showed up for bookkeeping and collecting work as usual wearing a coat and tie, but found myself assigned to the truck. Heretofore Odell in jeans and a t-shirt did the deliveries. Without warning or explanation Mr. Davidovich said; "I need you to help with the deliveries." Was delivery really the job he intended when he hired me; I wondered as days turned into weeks of hefting furniture. Although it wasn't chopping or picking cotton, the delivery job was reminiscent and much to close to thoughtless perpetual physical labor. Seeing no future changes I soon had enough of being a 'delivery boy'. Proper notice given, thank you and a sad goodbye, I was out of there. It was past time to move on and take another look at the jobs board in the registrar's office.

Sears Service: "Thank you for calling Sears Service, may I help you?" Those were my lines as explained to me by my new boss Ernie Engeron. That's it, talk about easy money. I was assigned a seat at one of two circular carousels, each with ten work stations. Better pay, better hours and I was working with nineteen others; all female, what more could a young single fellow ask? Lorna and Carmelita were the two black females of the nineteen working at the service center. There we answered phones and scheduled repair appointments for customers with broken appliances. A cause for minor concern, periodically an angry customer would threaten to come down to the service center and kick some ass, creating a few tense moments, but that never happened. Sears Service was an easy gig, where I remained for the following year and a half until my graduation from Pepperdine. But before graduation a number of major life changing events were a consequence of that Sears Service job. Still a shy fellow from the south I did manage to check out the two sistas working at the carousel. Carmelita was practically married; her boyfriend lived with her family in nearby Carson. Then there was Lorna, who stood a little above six feet a light chocolate brown body. Lorna returned my interest but she was an LA girl, born and raised. She shocked and surprised me moving from step one to step two much to fast for a country boy from Gould, Arkansas. Giving Lorna a ride home from work one day we stopped at the Sears Department Store on the corner of Slauson and Vermont Avenue. Returning to the car from the store I opened the passenger side door for Lorna. With no warning or preamble she got in the car lay on the seat, raised her skirt and beckoned with her right hand for me to get on top of her. More than surprise it scared me. An ex-military weekend road dog I'd been in some unusual bedroom situations but the Lorna action had never happened to me. Taking a very long look at those unblemished beautiful legs, white panties and demanding brown eyes; amazingly I shook my head, "No."

Sex, although I had been without for quite a while; early afternoon in a public parking lot seemed a bit much. Just the idea was very unsettling. I could see myself being arrested for indecent exposure or something worse. After that little incident Lorna made a point of avoiding me at work. I had hoped to finish what she started in the parking lot at a more convenient private place. Unfortunately, it never happened. A few years later I introduced her to one of my military buddies, Reginald Bell. They eventually got married had a child and I assume lived happily ever after. I lost contact with them when I moved to Northern California. But at the time I was cool with her attitude towards me; there were other interests.

Barbara Burns: While investigating possibilities with Carmelita and Lorna I couldn't help but notice the girl sitting on the bench waiting for her shift to start. She got off the city bus just outside the front door of the building. I sat with Lorna and Carmelita in the break room and she sat alone. Alone, but interested; I noticed her silently watching. Very light green eyes, with curvaceous muscle defining legs; standing a well built 5'9 with a blond ponytail, the girl was fine, fine, but white. It must have been written in the stars or something; one day I entered the break room and the only open seat was at the white girl's table. Barbara Burns, she introduced herself after I asked if she'd mind if I sat at her table. We talked about the things we had in common, school. She was about to transfer to UCLA from El Camino Junior College. During the conversation Barbara mentioned that she took the bus after work for an hour and a half ride to her home in Lawndale. Older brother CW had recently co-signed on a loan so I could buy a used car. The brown Dodge Dart now sat in the Sears parking lot. Of course I offered to give the most beautiful woman in the office a ride home after work. Soon I was dropping Barbara off daily. After a few drive in movies together I introduced her to my brother Wally and other family members. Wally had rented an apartment near Pepperdine which we shared; brother Wally was a good man. Warning me beforehand that her father wouldn't be pleased about her dating a black man Barbara invited me to dinner one Sunday afternoon. This was a big deal; I had never had dinner with white people; especially with the family of the daughter I was dating. Before Barbara there were no white dates; I'd never hugged, kissed or intimately touched a white woman. Yes those memories of Arkansas where such an act would have meant death followed me to California with other racial prohibitions. But hey; this wasn't Arkansas this was California, the perfect place to break out of those Southern racist fears. With wonderful thoughts about that beautiful woman and feeling positive about the relationship; I took the long drive down Crenshaw Blvd to all white Lawndale. Listening to the Young Rascals singing "Grooving on a Sunday Afternoon" I was ready, all was good. Meeting the father, mother, sister and the sister's Japanese-American boyfriend made for an interesting evening.

After that first of many Sundays the mother and father relaxed a bit. Maybe they expected me to break into some African dance or chanting but I didn't. Following that first Sunday's introductions sister Skye and boyfriend Stanley ignored us and the rest of the family. I was left to answer questions about my school, future plans etc. Later Barbara and I chuckled at her racist WWII veteran father's predicament; with two daughters who brought home non white boyfriends. Finally past the much anticipated Sunday dinner crisis we spent our time partying and hanging out with my road dogs from home Charles and Rosie Patterson. Whether at the Patterson's, the beaches, nightclubs or other places around Los Angeles; suddenly we were always together. Managing to find private places and moments, the sex was also very good. I was enjoying the experience, yet I was surprised the day Barbara said, "Why don't we get married?" Graduating from Pepperdine in the coming months was the main thing in my daily thoughts, even though being with Barbara made me very happy; until she mentioned it; I'd never once considered marriage. Sure I knew it would happen someday in my future but never imagined being asked the question, "Why don't we get married?" on that day, or any day. We liked each other a lot and had been intimate for months; but still I didn't realize, and had never considered that marriage was the step that followed. However, it must have been my youth and/or the times because without thought or hesitation I immediately responded; "Never tried that before, sure why not?"

"Why don't we get married?" Suddenly it was summer and just like that; the wedding was on. Barbara's friend Tessa was the bridesmaid and Tessa's boyfriend Homer did the ceremony. It happened on a clear bright Los Angeles summer afternoon in the backyard of a house my friends from high school; Charles and Rosie were renting just off Budlong Avenue. Fewer than ten people attended, so each got their own bottle rather than the usual glass of champagne. Both in rented tuxes Charles was my best man. Homer, also a professional photographer took the wedding pictures. My brothers CW and Wally represented my family but Barbara's family did not attend. She was very upset that her family had ignored our invitation. Barbara proceeded to drink a whole bottle of champagne. Later, literally carrying the drunken wife, we arrived at our place. First night of marriage, honeymoon night, how ironic I thought glancing at my new wife passed out on the bed at our home just off Adams and Western Avenue. There are times when participating in a new experience; you can't help feeling like an outsider watching yourself from a distance. Yeah, that's how I felt, a newly married man, sitting on the edge of the bed in my rented tux. The small one bedroom house, formerly the servants quarters sat at the end of a long driveway behind the landlords large Victorian. Just like that I was a married man with a house and responsibilities.

Both still in school and working at Sears Service we had to rearrange our lives. With the one car we now commuted to work together but on the days that Barbara had classes at UCLA I took the bus and she drove to school. Meanwhile we were working on getting to know each other as well. Things had happened so fast we'd never found time for a conversation about life, our futures or anything monumental or serious. We had yet to discover that marriage; a decision to spend a lifetime with another person was indeed a serious undertaking. Barbara, being a Theatre Arts major meant that we spent much time at numerous plays and other shows. A former beauty queen along with the major also meant that looks and physical appearance was most important to her. Seeing that faraway look, the glint in her eyes and hearing the excitement in her voice as she described the stars visiting and teaching her classes at UCLA; I observed firsthand the enchantment and fascination that attracts people from all over the world to Hollywood. In the break room one day at Sears where Rosie was now also working, she asked, "How is married life?" Of course I told her just fine. Rosie had been jobless for a few months after the birth of their 2nd child so I asked my boss Ernie if he could find a job for my friend from Arkansas Rosie. Sure enough after about a week he told me to bring her in for an interview. Rosie was hired in the lawn mower and small appliance repair shop part time. A hard worker in six months she was full time and by the end of the year Rosie was assistant manager. The following year she bought their first house, two years later she owned three houses. Rosie stayed with Sears until retirement as service manager for her department.

Children: Rosie was good friends with both Barbara and I. When I told her that I'd been thinking that maybe it was time for Barbara and I to have a child; wise beyond her years Rosie asked, "And what does Barbara think about that?" Thinking such a ridiculous question didn't deserve a response I just walked away. But later, that very same evening I brought up the subject with Barbara. After all that's what families, married people do, have children and carry on the family name etc. etc. isn't it? Remembering the ease of our decision to get married; I assumed the continuation into our next big decision and said to Barbara, "Don't you think it's about time for us to have a child?" Well nothing could have prepared me for the long pause and her response. "I'm in theatre; I can't mess up my body having children." Yep, that's what she said. Flabbergasted, I didn't know what to say. Barbara could have said something reasonable like wait until I graduate, or wait until we are more financially able, but she didn't choose either of those answers. Just the thought of never becoming a father was very upsetting. In my world as just mentioned, having children was a major reason, even when unspoken, why folks got married. This was serious business, at least to one of us. Then and there I knew that if I had known she didn't want to have children I never would have married Barbara.

UCLA

When a few days later I again mentioned having children; she laughed as if I was cracking a joke.Clearly Barbara was settled and comfortable with the idea of never having children. Obviously listening to that mythical 'different drummer' she didn't notice or take seriously my reaction to not having children. We continued with the routines of married life and school. Knowing how Barbara felt, although I didn't leave rightaway, as far as I was concerned then and there the marriage was over. Maybe there was more serious thought before the action, I don't remember but I do recall driving home one afternoon as usual. Barbara, then using a 2nd car loaned to her by her dad was at UCLA. Home alone I loaded books, clothes and a few other essentials into the car and drove away from that life we had together. Looking back, and never having had such a horrible thing happen to me; just the thought of coming home to an empty house not knowing whether I had been in an accident; or where I had gone with no notice or reason she must have felt awful. What a horrible, horrible thing to do. Many years later, today with just the memory I feel such great remorse, thinking what a mean thing, but on that day I only felt relief. Remembering those times, maybe it was the age but there is a long, long list of folk; including Barbara, if present I would fall on my knees and beg them to forgive me for being such an insensitive asshole. But time only goes forward to present events, going back is history. So what more could be said other than 20/20 hindsight is a mother.

Walking Away: Living can be hard work; homeless again, I was crashing on the couch back at Wally's house when I decided on my next move. Dropping by to check on my backbone and lifesaver; the jobs board at Pepperdine I saw a flyer that mentioned USC, UCLA and Loyola were looking for graduates of color for their law schools. If accepted to the program full tuition, books and a living stipend would be provided. It was the late sixties, so being a Black with a BA and riding that wave of white guilt, I applied. After the summer preparatory program with classes at all three schools I was accepted at Loyola's School of Law in Los Angeles. Not one to make excuses, but sleeping on the couch at my brothers house, a recently broken marriage, and a generally unstable life doesn't positively contribute to success in law school or any school. Not aware at the time but I needed a place to write and study daily. There were no time outs to take a break and catch up later. One had to be prepared for each class at each day. Once the semester starts actually before, nothing else should be on your mind other than Torts, Contracts, Criminal Law, Civil Procedure, Criminal Procedure and all the classes following. Looking back again with that legendary 20/20 hindsight I now realize that it took two attempts each time before completing advanced degrees following my graduation from Pepperdine A Masters Degree on my second attempt and so it was with my law degree. A wasted year at Loyola Law School and I dropped out to join The National Teacher Corps.

On the 2nd attempt I did finally get that sought after law degree but from New College of California's School of Law in San Francisco. Meanwhile back in the late 60's jobless again and freshly dropped out of Loyola's law school, what now? It was back to the Pepperdine registrar's office where I found a teacher training program similar to the law school program called Teacher Corps. There too they were looking for students of color and offering paid tuition and stipend through teacher training and graduate school. Upon completion of the program at the University of Southern California one would qualify for a teaching credential and a master's degree. Application complete and in a blink I was in the program attending USC and on the road to becoming a California teacher.

Teacher

Teacher, Teacher: Just trying to survive that 20th century slavery in Arkansas, I'd never dreamed that I would be able to say, I am a teacher. Having taught grades Kindergarten through university for more than 40 years, all in California yes, I am a teacher. Somehow, when still a bumbling younger man while contemporaries were involved in various other schemes; I found myself joyfully hooked within the educational system. A lover of books and reading as far back as memory; with periodic surprises, schools and teaching seemed most comfortable. So there I stayed, spending a lifetime attending schools or teaching, and oftentimes doing both. The stories may be familiar to many teachers with inner city experience but shocking to the uninitiated. Most names and locations of individuals and schools have been changed for obvious reasons. Many of the folk are still alive and disagreeable. One learns that truth may be much more offensive than a lie. An initial truth is that the public school classroom, as most imagine it to be is a comfortable myth. Past experience includes associating with some very scary folk in many unsafe places. Public schools are included as one of the scariest of places. At such times in such places showing hesitancy or fear would have been problematic. Fortunately, past teaching includes a few inspirational students and locales as well. Over the years the question was often asked, why teach? "You deal with a societal gamut, the best and most often the worst; yet your salary isn't nearly comparable to your education and training?" How does one put into words those inexplicable lessons learned from students, and parents and; with brief glimpses good and bad into the future of our society? Lest we not forget that reading and analyzing papers is reading and analyzing people. Like military discipline that stays with one for a lifetime so to does the lessons learned from checking and analyzing pages (people) in the classroom. Beyond the teaching stories that follow, the enclosed letter received near the end of a long career, transcends all; and best tells why I and many others chose to teach.

Loyola Law School

Why Teachers Teach

Heartfelt Thanks

5-10-2012

Dear Mr. Williams,

My wife Julia and I would like to thank you from the bottom of our hearts for the very positive and nurturing influence that you have had on our son Jose XXXXXXXXXX a freshman at UC Merced. He was fortunate enough to have had you as an instructor in his first semester history course.

You were also gracious enough to write him a supportive letter of recommendation which was of paramount importance in his successful application for the position of Orientation Leader. I believe he is one of only a couple of freshmen who were given that honor.

Above all else I want to thank you for accomplishing what gifted teachers do for their students: You convinced Jose to expect more of himself and you convinced him that if he really applied himself that he would discover abilities that he didn't know he possessed. Ironically enough the biggest turn-around came after Jose performed poorly on a history test and went to you for guidance.

You took the time to give him firm, corrective, but uplifting encouragement. This is probably the signature moment of his freshman year. The light came on. I believe it was Henry Brooks Adams who wrote, "A teacher affects eternity: he can never tell where his influence stops." Your teaching certainly meets that lofty standard and I hope you know this.

Please know that you have had an enduring impact on the personal and academic life of a young man looking to establish higher standards for himself, in everything he does. As the old adage goes, it truly does take a village to raise a child and we are happy that Jose moved into your neighborhood.

Perhaps one of these days Julia and I can express our gratitude in person. We wish you continued success in all your scholastic and musical endeavors, as I understand that you are equally blessed with the gift of rhythm and tempo. Have a blessed day.

Sincerely, XXXXX XXXXXXXXX

Preparation: On becoming a teacher; growing up in Gould, Arkansas attending and graduating from Gould Colored School I noticed that teachers were well to do and most respected in the Colored community. I say "well to do" meaning they didn't have to chop and pick cotton to make a living as did 99% of their students. I am thankful every day that I managed to get out. Teaching had been one of my first considerations upon graduation from Pepperdine but my G.I. Bill was about used up and I didn't want another student loan. So I looked at a number of programs. VISTA or Volunteers in Service to America didn't really offer a teacher training program although it did place interns in areas to work with men and women of color. Then too there was the Peace Corps but it seemed to white and to racist. The Peace Corps Interns I talked to even the ones volunteering to serve in Africa couldn't hide their nervousness and discomfort talking to an American Black man. Needing a job and wanting to stay in state and in country I looked for a California work-study training program. After a couple of false starts, one being Loyola Law School; with the help of the Pepperdine Registrar I stumbled upon the perfect opportunity; The National Teacher Corps at The University of Southern California.

Teacher Corps: was one of many federally financed programs which set out to bring teachers of color and the less represented into the educational mainstream. The plan was to show young teachers of color as active participants in classrooms where they were rarely seen. Much like Peace Corps rushing mostly young whites into third world countries; Teacher Corps sought to rush young Black, Latino and Asian teachers into neighborhood schools in the USA. Those neighborhood schools also included those servicing the often forgotten children of migrant farm workers. The idea was that a change in the administrations and teachers in the schools would positively change the hopes, aspirations and dreams of students in the schools. Student and parent attitudes toward, home, schools and themselves were targeted for positive change by the program. Crazy good, huh? Immediately one could grasp the possibilities and see the need for more teachers of color. But few of us realized or anticipated the many surprises, and that it was the beginning of a lifetimes work. Regardless of school size Teacher Corps trained teachers were most often the only ONE; that is the only teacher or administrator of color in the assigned school or district. Thankfully during and after Teacher Corps there was always a janitor of color in those colorless districts who would take the time on the QT to fill us in on the dominant realities and the racist ins and outs of a particular school. Then and today (2017) a new job in a new district meant integrating another faculty, even in districts where the majority of the kids were students of color. Being the first and only ONE again we of course remembered that without Teacher Corps we wouldn't have been there at all. Those teachers hired during that period of white guilt in the distant past have retired or are soon to retire.

Tommy Trojan

Here in 2017; a period of subtle and unsubtle racism with guilt long since past, retiring teachers and administrators of color are joyfully being replaced by whites. White privilege and white power unnoticed and unmentioned; even by many people of color is alive well and thriving. USC's Teacher Corps Urban Interns worked in inner city schools while Teacher Corps Migrant Interns worked in rural schools mostly in the San Joaquin Valley. The beginnings of the Teacher Corps program are divisible into several partsThe initial orientation after acceptance was held at USC. Following acceptance and orientation the program moved to Tecate, Mexico for Spanish language training. Following the summer in Tecate it was back to USC for classes and assignment to the various school districts where interns worked learning how to teach until the end of the two year program. At such time interns received the California Teaching credential and a Masters from USC. Three days working in school districts and two days in classes at USC was the typical weekly division of our time.

Orientation: Pre entrance interviews at the time weren't necessarily memorable but thinking back and remembering my associations with the people selected and their accomplishments during and following Teacher Corps I realized that I was working with a very special and talented group of people. But that specialness was to be seen in later years; however I do recall that very first social gathering of all the interns, team leaders and other functionaries downstairs in Phillips Hall. We had heard of the other interns; from the interviews and conversations with Teacher Corps administrators. The interns coming from various backgrounds and institutions; this was the first meeting of the entire group.There were all the people we would be working with the following two years. The first introductions were to our team leaders and the interns in our assigned districts. There were speeches, snacks, music, wine, beer and a plethora of interesting women. Maybe it was what I was smoking at the time or possibly just a combination of their youth and mine, but all were stop and pause good looking. Looks too must have been a factor; I must dig out some old pictures; or unspoken criteria for acceptance into the program. Head Teacher Corps administrators Annette Gromfin and Vida Van Brundt were unfazed by the mix of folk in attendance, but the USC professors seemed overwhelmed and a little uncomfortable around so many people of color; and soon beat a hasty retreat from the festivities. Dim lights, free drinks, fine women and good music: Would heaven be like this? Immediately forgetting names, I slow danced with as many lladies as possiblOne dance partner was especially memorable for things other than name and face. Feeling her legs and breasts pushing against my body as we barely moved to James Brown and the Famous Flames singing my favorite song from back in my high school days; "Try Me". It was dark in the room and I held on and still tried not to exaggerate my lower body movement as we turned.

Suddenly, over the sound of the loud music I could feel her mouth on my ear and her heavy breathing. Holding on with the strongest grip and letting out a long low furtive moan she pulled her lower body hard into mine. Unmoving, "uhhhhhhhhhhhhhhhh..." I heard as she locked me in an unbreakable breathless embrace until the end of the song. Then without a word she let go of me and walked from the room. Unfazed I moved on to the next dance partner.

Following the Teacher Corps years I always wondered, who was that woman? As time passed I got to know folks better and was still curious. Working with other interns over the two Teacher Corps years I had my suspicions. But people got married, divorced, moved, fell in and out of love, changed partners again and other things; yes, they lived. Life drama continued but I still wondered which one? Remembering, I wanted to hear and feel her panting in my ear and squeezing me again; but not necessarily in a crowded room standing on a dance floor. This time I wanted it all with the two us on a bed and me inside of her. Years later attending a conference in Anaheim I saw a number of former Teacher Corps interns. The woman who I most suspected as being 'the one' was there. Following several evening meeting I acted on those suspicions and invited Sasha to my room for after dinner drinks and conversation. Now divorced with a 20 year old son at Cal we'd always been friends. In the past we'd even lived together in a communal situation with her then husband and several others. Finding a music station on the television we danced just like before those many years ago. Undressed, showing no stretch marks, Sasha still looked pretty damm good. Finally, firmly inside of her, although I'd first heard it at the Teacher Corps Orientation Party I again listened to those very same orgasm sounds. Long overdue, now an active participant, with great pleasure the orientation mystery was solved; this way was so much better. But getting back to the times before the orientation mystery solution; following those welcoming activities we were off to Mexico for a summer of Spanish language training.

Tecate Mexico, Baja California: Traveling south from Los Angeles to San Diego and into the mountains southeast of the city we soon arrived at Tecate, Mexico. Some of us had reluctantly made the Tecate choice. We were considering another summer gathering on the other side of the country at a place called Woodstock. So instead of the open fields of Woodstock the Eldorado Motel in Tecate Mexico was our home for that summer of 1969 where we attended Spanish Language classes. The mornings were spent in class and our afternoons were free for study and to prepare for the following days lessons. Hah! To us 'free' meant time to drink beer, listen to music and study in that order. That very first afternoon, sitting in the doorway of my room textbook and notes in hand; I heard "Purple Haze" coming from across the way. On the 2nd floor Eldorado Motel balcony I saw Chauncey, Lorena and others dancing to the music.

Welcome to Tecate

The Eldorado Motel

Feeling 'Purple Haze' and Jimi Hendrix; instantly books and notes aside, I rushed over to join the dancers. Always, the beer and the music seemed more important and it probably was☺ Beyond, Jimi, Janis Joplin, Pharaoh Sanders, and Cream, Teacher Corps and the isolation of Tecate was hard on some folks. It was especially hard without a language. The language school rules required all communication be in Spanish. Students who broke the rules were penalized. Sooooo we could learn Spanish or be silent. Silent isolation wreaked havoc among our group of colored folk who had over the years changed their lives with learned verbosity. The loneliness seemed an extra burden on those with families and loved ones back in Los Angeles. Folk reacted to those Tecate conditions in a variety of ways. Alan slept in all day, rarely leaving his room. He didn't even come out to attend classes. There was talk of kicking him out of Teacher Corps but he was Black so it never happened. He wasn't the only one manifesting odd behaviorsI attended classes but rarely participated in classroom activities.The Latino guys who didn't speak Spanish not only found it especially hard and embarrassing because the Latina instructors seemed to enjoy showing a patronizing disdain for their lack of the native language.

Mureen: An older Black, I say older, she must have been late thirties to early forties; which was ancient to most of us in our 20's. A graduate of Texas Southern University, she cried in her room daily and talked incessantly about how much she missed her husband and kids back in Los Angeles. Stuck, courteously listening each afternoon because Mureen refused to talk to whites or Latinos; I thought how simple it would have been for husband and kids to come for a visit. Unless, maybe, somehow I got the feeling that she was worried about the husband and kids enjoying themselves to much during her absence. Many of the interns had friends, girlfriends and relatives visiting. Some even stayed beyond the weekend. But what do I know about relationships? Mureen never finished at Tecate, she dropped out of Teacher Corps and returned to Los Angeles. A few years following the Teacher Corps experience I ran into Mureen at a party in Baldwin Hills. She was divorced from the husband of Tecate times and teaching for LA City Schools. I also ran into Alan and he too seemed quite stable and was working as a Psychologist in New York City. Don't know how it happened, maybe my being older and ex-military had something to do with it but I found myself the unofficial representative of the Black Teacher Corps Interns. When there was a problem or a complaint, regardless of whether it was Teacher Corps related, they told me about it. A private person, I told no one of my past or my personal life. Consequently I was somewhat taken aback by some of the very personal stories of lives and families shared by Black interns. Usually silent and alone, I didn't hang with a lot of folk so I guess they figured I was discreet and a good listener. Finance, mental breakdowns infidelities, parenting, they told it all, nothing was sacred.

Listening, without showing surprise or judgment and never sharing their very personal information was an assumed truth. Francisco Garcia, also older and ex military seemed to fill the same position among the Latino interns.

Migrants & Race: There were other issues: I still carry the scar on my chin from hitting the pavement chin first in the parking lot of the Eldorado Motel. We were supposedly playing 'touch' football but this big white guy from Teacher Corps Migrant tackled me. Bloodied and up from the pavement, "That wasn't touch motherfucker!" Backed by my fellow interns from Teacher Corps Urban the fight was practically on. The tackle was just a ready excuse; there were already tensions in the program between urban and migrant interns, whites and blacks; and also between whites and Latinos. Blacks and Latinos were in agreement and many were pissed because whites were in the Teacher Corps program at all. The question was often asked, why in a program supposedly to train Black, Latino and Asian educators were whites allowed to take slots that rightfully belonged to people of color. What was up with that? So how was I going to deal with the motherfucker who tackled me, and any Migrant assholes willing to back his play? Well the guy was really apologetic and the asshole who backed his play was a girl, a white girl. Turns out she was the girlfriend of one of our Teacher Corps Urban road dogs, Guzzie. Peggy and anomaly was a white girl in the Migrant program who spoke fluent Spanish. She vouched for the tackler saying he was a nice fellow who taught kindergarten and "...wouldn't hurt a fly." So I let it slide and headed for the local doctor who gave me 5 stitches to the chin. Well Migrants **were** different and backward country folk, or so we believed. When most of the white Teacher Corps interns dropped out of the program the mostly Black Urban and Latino Migrant interns were left to deal with each other. Teacher Corps Urban interns were as named reflecting that certain hint of hardness common to young survivors of color from a variety of colleges and universities scattered among the cities of Los Angeles County. Cal State LA, Long Beach State, Cal State Fullerton, Cal State Dominguez Hills and Cal State Northridge; were feeder schools for most of the urban interns. The few teacher corps urban interns who did not graduate from a state college suffered some good hearted teasing from fellow urban interns. Teacher Corps Migrant interns were mostly from the San Joaquin Valley and graduates of Fresno State. Woodlake, Cutler-Orosi, Allensworth and other towns in the valley were places they called home and where they would eventually work. As mentioned earlier, there were strong Latino Black divisions among the Interns. Abel, a migrant intern who claimed to be a Brown Beret, when around blacks; I saw that same old 'hate stare' reminiscent of my days growing up in Arkansas. Obviously a racist, but weighing maybe 120 pounds soaking wet he knew I would kick his ass on a whim if need be, Abel kept his distance.

Anne Marie: For many young men and women during that so-called love generation, sex seemed to supersede all other issues. Anne Marie, a good looking single white female in Tecate was under great pressure from black and Latino males to "Give it up!" She was the youngest intern in the program, only 20 and very shy. When approached or 'hit on' Anne Marie quickly walked away. Consequently, although exhausting his very limited knowledge of Spanish; Frank (Francisco) Garcia gave Anne Marie the nickname. "conehita", little rabbit. Looking for reasons to ridicule and put pressure on conejita to stop running and give in to one of us; it was not surprising how quickly word of one of her verbal gaffes spread. Standing around outside the cafeteria after breakfast with Anne Marie Frank, Guzzie, Pablo, Greg and I cracked up laughing when she said; "Tecate would be a nice place if there weren't so many Mexicans around." So many Mexicans in Tecate, Mexico; who wouldn't laugh after hearing such an honestly bizarre absurdity? Of course Anne Marie's statement was merely a reflection of the unspoken thoughts and feelings held by many of us trapped in the isolation of our English language; but we didn't say it. Teacher Corps forced our group of thirty or more into an environment and situations with people from Mexico and the United States, with whom we would otherwise never acknowledge or interact. Then we add place to the mix. Place took us to Tecate's Eldorado Motel, sitting snugly on Benito Juarez No. 175, Centro, B.C. 21400, Mexico. Mexico was a foreign country to a group who in which most had never been outside the United States, and did not speak the common language, Spanish.

The Federales: Early one fall evening I was surprised to hear an authoritative knock on my room door. Setting aside the remnants of a Tecate Beer I was met by two burly brown shirted well armed Federales in the open doorway. Much like police around the world, they stood well balanced with right hands resting on their guns. One sobering look at the closed doors of my fellow students and teachers brought on additional concern. Although less than a hundred miles to the US Border, it seemed a thousand miles away. Having little or no fluency in the language here was I a Black man with questionable credibility facing police in their home country. Where were the program administrators who brought us down there? Such absence during that time of crisis was noteworthy. Stepping further out onto the balcony now the other Black male interns could be seen standing just outside the open doors to their rooms watching. Saying not a word to me the heavyset Federale spoke to the little girl accompanying them. He pointed his well worn brown finger just inches from my face. After a long look in the heavy silence that seemed to take forever the child shook her head "No." Still, only the brothers, without even their white or Latino roommates remained standing in their open doorways watching. They too, the other Black men, I discovered had already had their turns.

Mine was the last 'Black' room to be questioned. Later, talking to the motel staff they told us that "... a dark man..." had fondled the little girl downtown in the plaza. We being the darkest men in town and foreigners, naturally the Federales came to pay us a visit. Listening closely to the conversation between the Federale and the little girl; picking up a word here and there and noticing her gestures, the very poised kid said that the man who touched her wasn't quite as dark and didn't have an 'afro' which we all wore. What would they have done if the Federales had decided to take us to jail? It rankled that no team leaders or administrators stepped from their rooms to assist during the crisis even if only to act as translators. Reckon the answer is obvious, Nada! Not that day, the following, or any time thereafter did others mention or acknowledge that the incident occurred. It was a topic of discussion only among Blacks.

Fortunately, many positives happened in Tecate as well. The community as a whole went out of their way to entertain and accommodate us. Entertainments also included the bullfights one Saturday afternoon. Peering through the cultural divide, witnessing the foot stomping and cheering; clearly our Latino Teacher Corps interns and administrators thought the bullfights were wonderful. The bullfights were identified as a physical manifestation of their heritage. Yeah that was all well and good, but the Black and white interns and administrators weren't favorably impressed. Many sided with the bulls saying that the bullfights were not entertaining just cruel and gory. The horror of the bullfights when balanced against the following trip to the Tecate Brewery was soon forgotten. The brewery trip, from the moment we discovered that as much free beer as we could drink was part of the tour, was a guaranteed success. Paying little or no attention to Tecate Brewery tour leaders or explanations of the assembly line and brewing process; we concentrated on sopping up as much free beer as possible. Few remembered how we got back to the motel, what a day! Painfully hung over the following morning; our demands for a menudo breakfast at the Eldorado Motel café were unmet. Although unspoken the hefty, "No!" and disdainful reactions of the kitchen staff suggested that they would never serve such low class food. Undaunted, we did find menudo; that hangover healing soup at the dirt floored mom and pop restaurant next door. Although they had to prepare extra soup, the owners were quite pleased to have eleven new unexpected cash paying customers, Another great morning south of the border in Tecate Mexico; Baja California. On another occasion Frank arranged; I use the term loosely, he told us he had arranged it; although we all had our doubts about him giving prior notice. We put on a Teacher Corps intern music performance one Saturday night in the Tecate town plaza. With utmost courtesy, wonder, and seemingly little enjoyment; a small group of locals listened as we pounded on several bongos and tambourines for at least a couple of hours.

Bullfights, Beer and Basketball:

Overall, with looks and hints our Teacher Corps administrators let it be known that they were thankful for the general safety and goodwill granted by Tecate residents as we wandered about their town at all hours. Yes we were out there but what could we say; except that we were actively curious inner city road dogs unused to such safe quiet environments.

There too were several athletes among our group, even a few basketball players. Looking for a place to play we found a gym in Tecate, however unlike back in the states it wasn't open for general play. But several members of the Mexican National Basketball team happened to live in Tecate. When they asked if we would play them in an informal scrimmage, we all agreed. Comfortable in our stereotypes we were sure we could beat them. "Mexicans are short. And they know nothing about basketball." "Basketball is America's game!" An easy win was guaranteed. In our arrogance, not once did we consider that those guys were professional basketball players who had been playing for their national team since childhood. We also didn't account for the altitude. Los Angeles sat at 233 feet above sea level while Tecate was 1700 feet above sea level. Fools rushing in, we were all ready for that easy win. Jump ball at center court, 6'8 Tom Myers tapped the ball to me and I quickly passed to Greg who passed to Guzzie. He returned the ball to me for a shot from the corner. The bulky 6'6 Mexican center rebounded my missed shot and made a bullet pass to their streaking point guard; the Mexican fast break was on. Running rings around us, they scored at will. Tom Myers, hitting several sweet corner jumpers didn't seem to be affected by the altitude, which we blamed for our overall poor performance. After the first few minutes, they were far ahead. Seeing us dragging slowly down the court and not getting back on defense following missed shots; the Mexican players felt sorry for us. They pulled their starters and substituted their practice players. Then a much slower game we managed to score a few baskets. Beaten and embarrassed at the end of the game we shook hands and wished that excellent team well. Soon after that Mexican drubbing it was time for our goodbyes to the Eldorado Motel and Tecate. Having enjoyed a great summer experience we were more than ready to leave, it was time. Anticipating the next great adventure we were already looking forward to our teacher training classes and student teaching. Packed into several cars for the return trip from the mountains of Tecate, we were soon rolling down the grade toward San Diego, Los Angeles and the University of Southern California.

The following picture of the author was taken a few weeks following Tecate by Romie, a female intern who I watched swimming in the Eldorado Motel pool in Tecate daily. She had an expensive camera and took several pictures; I managed to salvage just one.

The Author D. Williams, then

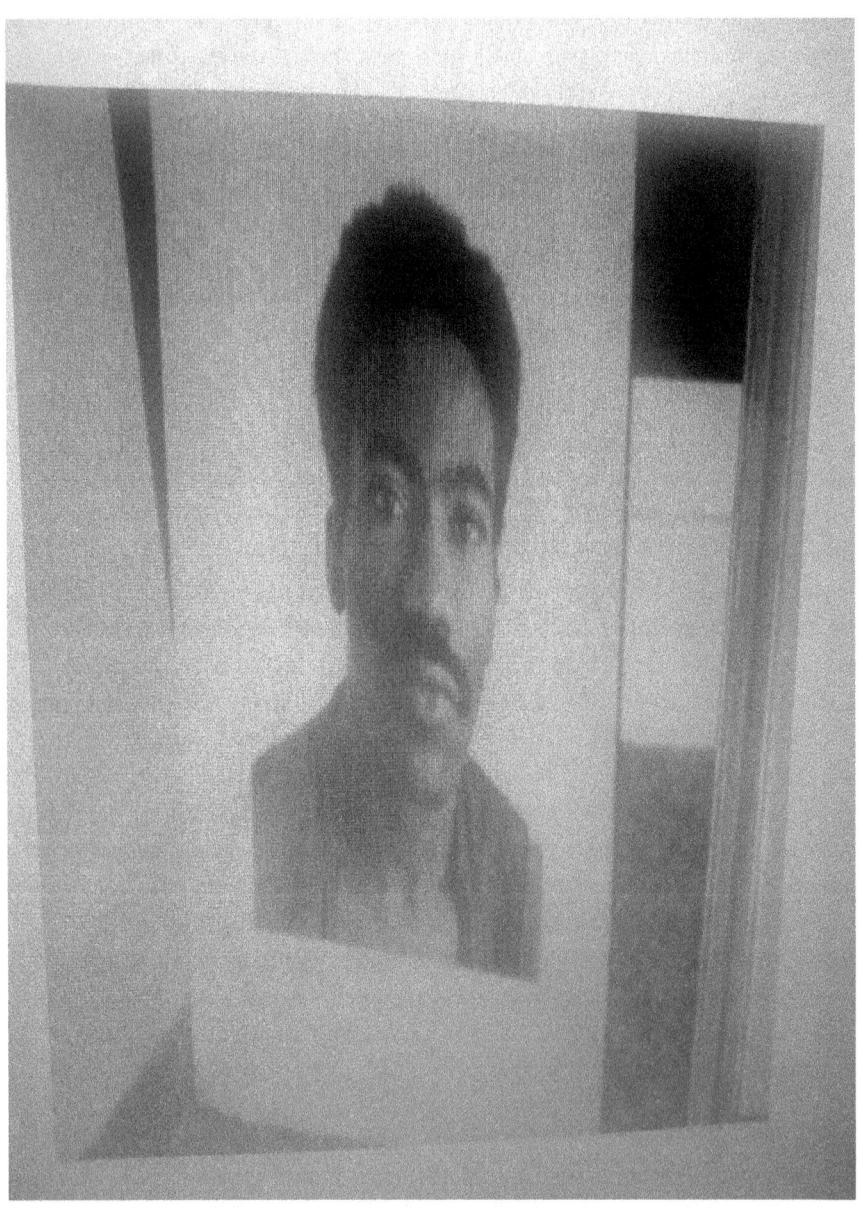

Maybe staring would be the more accurate word than watched, she looked that good. Consequently I was pleasantly surprised to discover that she had noticed me watching (staring) during that time.

The University of Southern California & Student Teaching Classes at the University of Southern California and actual work in schools followed our summer in Tecate. Beyond the habitual partying, we were all familiar and comfortable in university classes but awestruck at that other reality. Now we were actually working in our own classrooms full of kids! We were assigned to Rubidoux School District just outside of Riverside, CA for on site teacher training experience while attending classes at USC's Phillips Hall. Regardless of previous divergent experiences so began our new lives. We all felt it, there was a growing uneasiness, this was major, a big, big deal. Without discussion or group contemplation, suddenly things changed.

Rubidoux: Frank Garcia, Chauncey Noel and I and several other interns with high expectations and excitement moved to Rubidoux District in Riverside County. Hadn't worn one for years, but on my first day of work; I found myself wearing a tie, slacks and a sport coat. Meeting with our Rubidoux Teacher Corps group after school I saw something I had never seen and thought I would never see. Those beer drinking, head band wearing roughneck Teacher Corps interns from Tecate; including myself, were all noticeably scrubbed and kempt. Teaching did that! Soon we discovered that the regular teachers in our assigned schools were happy to have us. We assumed in our arrogance that our youth guaranteed superior knowledge in all areas, including teaching. Grudgingly, with time in the classroom we discovered there was much to learn. Fondly, I remember the first class I taught, Kindergarten. With the help of an observant, wise and tactful Master Teacher; it was a fantastic experience. New at the job, making mistakes and screwing up lesson after lesson as I learned to teach; those kids never failed to greet me with anticipation, trust, warmth and enthusiasm. Daily those little guys started my day by yelling the morning greeting; "Hi Mr. Williams! Looking back over more than forty years, those kindergartners, that classroom at the beginning is one of my most refreshingly enjoyable teaching memories. They kept me going, day after day giving me reason not to throw up my hands in frustration, say the hell with it and walk away. But as one of a group of Teacher Corps interns young enough to still wonder about the many things not yet tried, I was also interested in those new adventures outside of the classroom.

Exotica: Beginners, of course the classroom situation from the front of the room was new to us. New, as were the looks and other reactions from white teachers and administrators suggesting that our presence was a uniquely rare..

Much like today, 2017, most of those teachers and administrators, outside of TV and movies had never seen or associated with people of color; so they couldn't ignore us as we walked past on campus. The school kids, mostly Latino and black; after the first welcoming high fives didn't seem to notice. But being the only teachers of color in the school district or the entire county at the time wasn't necessarily a bad thing for us or the white folk. The extra attention was kinda nice, especially when the ladies were looking. At our weekend gatherings, the older white teachers who worked hard at being hip or cool, and the younger teachers all wanted to be invited to party with the blacks and Latinos. A new and unexpected surprise, a touch of the exotic, us, was suddenly added to their school district. Most of our parties were pretty routine with conversation, drinks, food, music; a little ganja in the back room and dancing. But one party in particular we restricted attendance to Teacher Corps interns and their guests only. I don't know who came up with the idea for that party, probably Frank. None of us had ever attended a nude party, but Frank; maybe he had heard of or read of such a party; decided that we should throw one of our own. Strictly word of mouth invitations, we put a box by the front door of the apartment for placing clothes upon entry. Then it dawned on us that answering the door nude might be a problem. Problem solved, we decided to wait until everyone was inside and then disrobe together.

Nervous, unsure of the details or whether anyone would actually show up; too soon Friday evening was upon us. The first arrivals found it hard to undress until they saw us undressing along with them. One of our first discoveries was that sex does not necessarily follow nudity. Undressed and wandering among the smoke, drink, music and all the party props; folks still found it difficult to loosen up and relax, I know I never did. Once the clothes came off then what? Where was the wild sex and bizarre behavior? Roommates, Brad and Jim, two of the seven male interns in the district were although closeted; known to be gay. Jim attended the party without his partner Brad. Loosening up a bit the naked people started playing cards, dancing and some were sitting on the back patio; while others just wandered about looking at the variety of body shapes, sizes and colors. For whatever reason Molly a young teacher in the district decided to show us that she could stand on her head. Well she could; with her back touching the wall and enormous breast nipples resting on the floor Molly looked odd; so I took a picture. If I could find that picture it would be on this page☺ Getting Molly off the wall Frank came up with this great idea that he thought would be funny. Knowing that Jim the gay fellow was alone in one of the rooms lying on the bed, Frank convinced Molly to agree with his plan. "A present for you Jim" Frank said as he opened the bedroom door and shoved the naked Molly onto the bed with an unclothed Jim, and locked the door.

Hurrying outside to peer in the window we saw Jim's male instrument of satisfaction, limp as that proverbial dishrag as he and Molly lay side by side naked on the bed not touching but talking. Frank thought the situation hilarious, but weird me I thought it was boring. What was to be expected; we knew the guy was gay and wouldn't be attracted to Molly, a WOMAN. Molly also knew he was gay, that's why she readily agreed to hop in bed with him. Not complicated thought or so it seemed to me. The following day Molly told us that she tried to get Jim to "…do something." But not surprisingly Jim wasn't even a little bit interested. Overall maybe the party was such a bust because as amateurs we didn't know how to accentuate the nudity. After a few pictures the boredom really set in and folks started getting dressed and heading home. However, that wasn't the end of the nude fascination for some. Although not particularly interested, the rest of us followed along as Frank led us to our next nude stop, San Carlos Mexico.

San Carlos: No, Exotica weren't the end of Frank's fascination with nudity. Typically out of touch and just following along for the ride, I thought if you saw one nude body you'd seen them all, unless the body belonged to someone you were interested in. This Teacher Corps hang had me associating with people who were not Black which was a new learning experience. So in most situations, many of them new to me, even the ones seemingly odd or strange although cautiously observant, I went along. Consequently on numerous occasions I found myself asking, "What the fuck am I doing here?" San Carlos was one of those occasions. Frank decided that we should visit this place in Mexico, San Carlos, Baja California "… with these really neat hot natural sulphur baths." By the time I heard of the trip my lady friend and I had already been penciled in as drivers. No one questioned participation; again maybe it was the times. For a small fee groups were allowed to soak in the natural waters. Frank never mentioned that shorts, swimsuits or other clothing was not allowed in the baths. None of us were sick or injured but Frank kept on raving about the healing aspects of the sulphur and natural heat. I worried that some of the ladies might be uncomfortable getting naked among strangers, but all were game. Soon we were seated on low stone benches carved from the red brown rock around the edges of a ten foot wide reddish clay pool in maybe four feet of water. Thankful that we had our own vehicle and didn't have to crowd into "The Van" for the ride home we absorbed "…the healing vibes" for about an hour and chalked up another of Frank's nude experiences. Simple me; while sitting in the healing waters; I kept thinking of the long drive we had taken for such boring nonsense; Frank's kind of fun. I never said it but the thought did cross my mind that the bathtub at home was much more comfortable. White Folks! And Frank wasn't even white, go figure. The green and white Dodge van was one of several Frank owned over the years.

By the time he got rid of this one to buy another he had logged well over 500,000 miles. Even then the engine and most importantly the SPEAKERS remained top notch. When traveling and using the floor along with the seats; eight or ten passengers were not uncommon. Frank wasn't comfortable, unless the van was packed with lots of folks. Since I had little or no interest in alcohol I was most often the designated driver. Before even starting our trips all were as drunk as that proverbial skunk. Beyond the metaphor I'd be willing to bet that none of us have ever seen or really imagined a drunken skunk☺

Golden Gate Park or Bust: On this day we were headed for San Francisco early one Saturday morning. Crosby, Stills and Nash were playing a free concert in Golden Gate Park the following day. It was a beautiful morning moving along the 101 north and Greg had brought along some 'killer' weed. I didn't mind smoking a little ganja. With all the windows closed there was so much smoke inside the van, I had trouble seeing out the front windshield. Then too, the smoking of that 'killer' weed may have had something to do with my limited vision. "Well you know we're riding on the Marrakesh Express…" blasted loudly from the six speakers as I controlled the vehicle at a little over 80 miles an hour while sucking on a roach. By the time the highway patrolman was spotted in my minds eye, I had slipped past and forgotten he was there on the side of the road. So seeing him close on my tail with lights flashing a few minutes later was quite a surprise. Checking the right shoulder, there really wasn't a good place to pull over. Finally, I bounced off the side of the road and parked with the vehicle hanging near the edge of a deep ditch. Remembering to turn the music down I watched as the patrolman walked cautiously alongside the van trying to peer inside. I then yelled impossible instruction to Frank and the boys "Get rid of the joints and beer cans." We certainly couldn't throw anything outside since that's where the cop was. Seemingly, after an eternity the patrolman signaled me to roll down my window. Reluctantly, I complied. Enveloped in a massive cloud of marijuana smoke pouring from the open window, the patrolman dropped his head and coughed. Recovering and reaching for the license I handed him he asked, "Where are you fellows headed?" "San Francisco" I said while wondering why he kept staring at the dash board. Without another word, shaking his head in disgust the patrolman handed me my license, turned and walked away. Thinking what an odd fellow, I pulled onto the freeway listening to the guys in back yelling, "Close the fucking window!" as they lit another joint. Thanking God for out luck; I thanked him again when I noticed what the highway patrolman must have been staring at on the dash. There in plain sight was the smoldering roach I was smoking when he pulled me over. Oh well, what could I do but take another hit, turn up the music and keep on rolling toward the Golden Gate.

The Van

After an interesting night greeting old friends and meeting new ones; the following day we spent in Golden Gate Park enjoying the concert, which seemed secondary to the activities among the crowd watching. A few thousand people were camped out in tents, vans and various other contraptions. All were sharing food, assorted drugs, music and general good will. As mentioned earlier, Frank loved to travel and hang with large groups of people, reckon that's why he always owned a van. Yes, he was in high heaven; as were the rest of us. Anyway, by late Sunday afternoon, having to work on Monday we started getting the folk together and preparing to head back to Southern California. We all climbed into the van as did Frank; with a woman we didn't know. Greg asked, "Where did you find your new lady Frank?" "She was with the people in the tent next to ours, they put her out."Wordlessly, moving like an automaton the woman slowly climbed into the front passenger seat. Then the shit got really weird, "Frank, what's her name?" "I don't know her name she hasn't spoken. Her friends gave me a Riverside address where she lives." Needless to say the ride home was odd. Everyone was subdued as a sober Frank; a rarity in itself, drove with the automaton sitting next to him. When we made pit stops she wordlessly climbed from the vehicle found the bathroom and returned. Having decided that the chick was a deaf mute we nearly fell of our seats as we approached the Riverside city limits when she said "Take the next exit."Dropping her off at her house, standing in her front yard as we prepared to leave the loquacious one gave Frank a big hug. He smiled and climbed into the van as we looked on with wonder and awe. Who was that Chick? And what's with that strange, strange silent shit? She certainly turned a great trip to the bay area into quite a bummer. Good riddance, thank God we were home and hello Betty.

Betty: Some former Teacher Corps interns claim that the parties were the most memorable part of the program. Maybe, but when speaking of parties Betty is the first who comes to mind. During the Teacher Corps era a new group of interns started the program each year. So with each year came a new cycle and ours was cycle IV. Betty was a year ahead of us, cycle III and in her last year when we started cycle IV. Introducing herself, Betty let us know right away that we were always welcome at her apartment. She literally meant that welcome. Living in LA's Crenshaw District, Betty never locked her front door. Any time of the day or night even when she wasn't home Teacher Corps interns walked into the apartment, kicked back, grabbed a beer from the fridge; got stoned, watched TV etc. Go-Go Boots mini skirted; outspoken and loud with a gigantic afro and an even bigger heart; Betty was impressive. All relatively new to Teacher Corps; several of us were sitting on couches, chairs and the floor in Betty's living room about 2AM one Sunday morning. Pharaoh Sanders was making music, Betty was talking and all were feeling pretty good, loaded to the gills. In walked a twelve or thirteen year old kid.

Golden Gate Park

The following day we spent in Golden Gate Park enjoying the concert, which seemed... A few thousand people were

Jimmy kissed his mom on the cheek; "Night Betty" he said before stepping over the reclining bodies on the floor and continuing down the hall to his room. So the question was asked, "Betty who is that kid?" "My son Jimmy, he spends a lot of time at his girlfriends'. Robert, stop hogging the joint" She said. "He has a girlfriend?" I asked. "Yeah and a six month old son, can you believe it I am a grandma." Betty smiled as she passed the joint. So was she saying that her son, barely old enough for junior high, maybe thirteen just walked in the door at 2AM? He had just arrived home from visiting the mother of his child, and Betty his mom was cool with that. Hey, it was what it was, their drama, or not. So I was comfortable on the floor and cool with that too. Betty was much like the women we preferred at the time, ready for anything. After that first year's association Betty graduated from Teacher Corps and disappeared into the work force. I never saw her again but heard rumors of her getting married right after Teacher Corps, good for her. Unfortunately not all the women we met at that time were like Betty, those unlike her were to be avoided until far into the future, maybe when looking for a wife. Eva who I met before Betty was quite different.

Eva: A caring, thoughtful, no nonsense kind of person was one of the first people I met following orientation. Recently divorced she was living in an apartment near Cal State LA where I visited on occasion. We went for walks and had tea and lunch a few times. Right away Eva tactfully, let it be known that she wasn't a 'quick lay'. Nope she definitely wasn't a 'hit it and quit it' kind of woman. Eva was so straightforward and nice one couldn't help liking and respecting her. Smart, wise and very attractive Eva wouldn't let me rush her. Although feeling the closeness, I put her on a back burner thinking maybe something might develop later. But through orientation and Tecate we never hooked up. One weekend Frank suggested that we make a run up to Woodlake, a small town in the San Joaquin valley and visit some Teacher Corps Migrant Interns. Thinking nothing of it, we had driven up before for migrant parties. Having seen her at those migrant parties, I knew Eva lived in Woodlake. But it never crossed my mind that Frank had her address until he mentioned that we would be stopping to visit Eva and her roommate. Later, after dinner prepared by the ladies, unaware of how the evening was going to play out, but knowing our histories I felt comfortable because Frank only dated white women. Eyes on Eva as the evening progressed; and she was looking back at me. Frank may or may not have been oblivious but I began to wonder about what may have gone on between Eva and Frank in the past. After all it was his idea to come to Eva's house. So with no positive sign from Eva, I silently avoided conflict and/or confrontation. Retrospectively it becomes so easy to see what so many have seen; how a single action or inaction may change lives forever. Maybe I should have been more aggressive, more demanding instead of wordlessly watching.

Walking into her bedroom with Frank, she turned eyes on me again as the door closed behind them. Surprised, I wondered whether Frank was suddenly having a 'Roots' moment, Eva was Latina. Regardless I was left sitting with the dirty dishes and Marjorie, Eva's overweight white roommate.

There are forms of expression much more poignant than words, always check the eyes; they may tell the deeper story. A new day, although Eva and I had never had the experience, it felt odd waking in different beds. The bacon, eggs, juice and coffee breakfast; was shared by the four of us sitting at the kitchen table. An open windowed beautiful fall morning in California's central valley; feeling the sunshine and the curtain moving breeze we listened to Janis Joplin singing, "...freedom's just another word for nothing left to lose..." My bedmate sat with her large naked leg touching mine as I glanced across the table at Eva; who dropped her eyes refusing to look at me. Knowing something monumental and life changing was happening which I did not fully grasp; again I chose a habitual response; watchful silence. Tearing into his breakfast, gulping coffee and typically ignoring any subtlety, Frank didn't notice the visual exchange. Snug beside me, Marjorie noticed and did not smile.

Of course following that night in Woodlake, marriage and three kids later Frank and Eva were definitely a couple. Over the years I'd gone down to visit them in Pomona and Claremont and they in turn would visit the wife me and our two kids in Northern California. Frank was the godfather to my oldest son and I the godfather to his youngest daughter. Remembering that evening in Woodlake, Eva never looked at me again with such poignancy, until the very last time I saw her. On that day watching the mannerisms of Frank and the kids it was pretty clear that they had mentally moved on from the crisis. They were seeing Eva's impending death as a relief from her constant pain. She was dying of cancer and traveled with Frank and the kids to my home; it being the northernmost stop on her final visits to friends and family. No longer able to sit, Eva traveled lying on a mattress in the back of the van. Nearing time for departure on the long trip back to Claremont the sadness was overbearing as they prepared to leave. Knowing this was the last time; on Eva's face I saw no fear, but maybe a hint of regret. Momentarily locking eyes, remembering that time at Woodlake and the words from Janis's song' "...freedom's just another word for nothing left to lose..." I kissed her on the cheek and slid the van door closed. Closing, endings, death, most often quite common, so long as it doesn't happen to those we love or US. For most, life becomes routine and we never anticipate its end; even as we age and the body slowly deteriorates. But death, that uninvited surprising visitor comes at any age. After Eva's death I did think how horrible it would have been to have my wife die at such an early age leaving me with three kids to raise, alone.

However, it has been said that we all have our unique life burdens; still, I don't know how I would have handled that. Soooooo, maybe it was all for the best. Possibly Eva choosing Frank made life as it was supposed to be. But getting back to the times before Eva died, before I moved to Northern California, found a wife, kids and a different life; there were other Teacher Corps moments.

Rosa & Lucia: It could possibly be age related but during one's youth and early adulthood too many, inexplicable, unplanned events occur. Sometimes you may see it coming, yet you remain a spectator intently watching it happen to you. Rosa and Lucia were the teachers and administrators in the Spanish Language Program in Tecate. Having grown up and attended schools in Latin American countries; Argentina and Mexico; possibly that may have contributed to their attitudes regarding classroom conduct and discipline. In Tecate I never once commented on their curt militaristic commands in the classroom, but maybe they noticed my looks of disapproval. Always together, back at USC I had seen them on campus a couple of times but much like in Tecate; had never spoken to them. The very last time I saw them I was walking across the USC campus very loaded as was my wont. Rosa was driving a small Volkswagen with Lucia riding shotgun. It was raining and Rosa stopped, Lucia rolled down the passenger side window and asked. "You want a ride?" Knowing they knew I wasn't particularly fond of either of them, I was reluctant to say no to their obvious gesture of goodwill. Quandary, the cigarette I was smoking was filled with marijuana, what should I do? Should I throw it away before getting into the car? Hell no, I just couldn't bring myself to throw away perfectly good weed. Silently, I kept smoking in the small enclosed vehicle for the five block ride to my apartment. They didn't say anything but they certainly could smell it, although I don't think it got them high. That was a fitting goodbye to Rosa and Lucia, I never saw them again during my remaining time at USC but there were many other lurking ghosts of Tecate on campus. Single and active; surprisingly sex became an issue. Being the naïve person that I've always been; I assumed sex was a simple, natural, experience enjoyed by all. How could I be so wrong? Why wasn't I aware of various complications within that sexual simplicity?

Carol: She had the smarts, an athletic body and an admirably innate fearlessness. Both student teaching and living in the ultra conservative San Bernardino/Riverside area; when hanging out together we got some stares. Carol a young white woman was the first to suggest that we go dancing at this or that Country/Western bar. Ignoring the hostile looks from the cowboy boot wearing crowd; we had great times dancing to Credence Clearwater's "Willie and the Poor Boys" Beyond those good times I soon discovered that Carol had some serious problems. During sex I worked hard thrashing about and thoroughly enjoying myself.

But I couldn't help noticing Carol as she lay there quietly unmoving; with utmost patience, until I finished. The first time it happened I thought maybe it was timing or some other minor problem. But after the 2nd or 3rd time I asked; "What's wrong?" "Well I don't mind doing it but I've never had an orgasm." Carol said. Whoa! Too much! I asked and she put it out there! What to say? What to do? It felt so weird having sex with a woman who showed no movement or expression of pleasure. Carol had silently watched me panting and thrashing about having my way with her. That was worse than having some stranger sit in the room watching you during sex, unless of course that rocks your pleasure boat. Anyway, although we cared about each other Carol was hurt that I couldn't handle things; it seemed too weird for me. Before I left for good Carol hinted that she had some abuse issues as a teen. Again too much information, maybe a bit cold hearted but I didn't want to deal with a psych case, keep it simple please. One would think that if you found the right person and you were attracted to each other, the rest would come naturally. Not so! Why must I be the one to find a woman with sexual issues? Maybe I needed a change and so it was. Near the end of my first year in the Teacher Corps Program at the University of Southern California I transferred to Teacher Corps at San Francisco State University, goodbye Carol. About the same time several other mostly white interns after that first year; completely dropped out of the program. Possibly they finally succumbed to the negative pressures from the Latino and Black interns complaining about Teacher Corps slots being taken away from people of color, who knows. Whatever was in the air it seemed to be affecting us all. Annette, the program director at USC wasn't pleased with my transfer request. Wise beyond her years; most assuredly mine; she tried to talk me out of it, but tiring of my persistent hard headed whining, Annette finally agreed to the transfer.

Suddenly in the bay area and finding an apartment just off 40th and Telegraph Avenue in Oakland, things looked good. Cal Berkeley was just down the street as was the perfect outdoor basketball court at Shattuck and Rose Street in Berkeley. With those important bases covered, things seemed to be working. I didn't own a car, but public transit was timely and convenient as was hitching. Having pushed hard and offended some folk to transfer; almost immediately I noticed the uncomfortable disorganization of the San Francisco State program.Most irritating was the fact that no one else seemed to be bothered or aware of the chaos. I dared not complain because complaining got me to that place. This was a place where both the staff and students thought I was crazy to leave, "...that fantastic program at SC." They were right, reckon I had been spoiled and brought unreal expectations with me from that "fantastic program at SC" It was bothersome that the classes at San Francisco State were often cancelled without notice, The student teaching assignments were also unpredictable and changed weekly

San Francisco State

Also, San Francisco State was way out in the avenues shrouded in a foggy gloom day after day. Unlike the bright sunshine of USC; the intrusive daily San Francisco State gloom out in the avenues merely added to my mental fog. Not having the time or thetransportation; and double dipping in melancholy, I never really got a chance to see any other parts of San Francisco. San Francisco State assigned me to Havenscourt Junior High out on 66 Ave, in Oakland for my student teaching. Yeah, it was the ghetto.

66 Ave and Havenscourt Jr. High looked much like other California schools in Black neighborhoods. South Central LA, Rosecrans and Wilmington in Compton, Centennial High School, all came to mind. Havenscourt was "déjà vu all over again". It was unlike the country schools in Riverside County with a mix of mostly poor whites, Latinos and a few blacks. Havenscourt was a full time inner city experience. There, it was not uncommon for adults to wander the hallways and the school grounds during school hours. One day while on yard duty a young adult male about my age approached and started a conversation. He was much too old to be a student and fairly well dressed so I assumed he was a teacher. Laughing and pointing to a group of kids huddled by the basketball courts he said, "I just sold those dumb fucks a bag of green tea." "The little fools think its weed." He was an adult on the school grounds selling drugs to twelve and thirteen year olds and bragging about it, to me! Maybe he saw the look in my eye; God I wanted to hurt that man. "Mr. If I see you on this campus again, provided the police don't get to you first; we will have issues."I said to his back as he turned and hurried to a Black Cadillac parked just outside the fence. Drug dealer, Cadillac, it never crossed my mind what else he might be carrying inside that car. The fellow didn't shoot, he just drove away. What happened to me, just a little over a year before I was a marijuana smoking, fiend. Now a non smoker I was ready to go to war with a dealer. Damm, teaching changes attitudes, it does things to you. Beyond the everyday street drama, inseparable from student teaching and campus life; I was forced to see that the San Francisco State, Havenscourt Junior High experience could negatively affect my future. Things got a little strange inside my student teaching classroom soon after the drug dealer confrontation. On the day in question, Ms. Tranell; the woman in charge of my student teaching; weighing well over 300 pounds while suggestively resting a 100 pound arm on my shoulder said, " Sugar, if you want me to sign off on your student teaching forms we gotta spend some time together."

Talk about the proverbial 'last straw' that was it; nope wasn't doing that chick. Under no circumstances was I having sex with that extremely obese woman. I had had my one obese woman experience when I was an undergrad simply because it was a new experience....but that's another story.

Anyway, after two days of frantic calls to Annette the director of Teacher Corps back at USC I was out of there. Years later I decided that Annette must have really liked me to put up with my bullshit. By the start of the semester I was settled and back at USC to finish Teacher Corps where I started. Being back felt good but also kind of weird. Annette was a magician, she reassigned me to my old student teaching district, scheduled my classes and prepared me for upcoming graduation; she fixed everything. However my fellow interns, especially my 'friends' weren't so forgiving. Awkwardly keeping their distance; Frank, Pablo, Greg, and Guzzie avoided me at work and during class at USC. They treated me like a stranger and acted as if I had betrayed them by transferring to San Francisco State. But all were not so unforgiving; Dave and John who transferred to USC from a program in the south offered their couch until the end of the semester. Suddenly having returned to Southern California with no place to stay their offer of assistance was a very nice thing to do. Great to be back and one of the first most noticeable people in my classes upon my return was Romie, alone.

Romie: She was a Tecate legend. I along with the other male interns lined the upstairs balcony at the Eldorado Motel to watch Romie swimming laps every afternoon following language classes. Wearing the smallest red bikini with a smooth freestyle and matching body, Romie was quite an attraction. Tall, thin of face with dark hair and lashes, her very fit golden legs were especially noticeable doing flip turns at the end of each lap. Fully aware of her daily balcony audience, with a knowing smile, Romie ignored us. Like many of the folk in Tecate who found companions in the crisis of language learning, she coupled off with a young rock climber. Squat, strongly built with long arms and big hands he rarely spoke but offered patronizing smiles in class and the dining room. The fellow didn't use the stairs; he climbed the banisters and poles to their 2nd floor apartment. We also watched his daily dives from the 2nd floor balcony into the deep end of the pool. But before the end of that summer in Tecate, he was gone, having dropped out of Teacher Corps never to be seen again. Since Tecate, back at USC Romie too was rarely seen as were most of the interns; student teaching in school districts all over Los Angeles and neighboring counties. Until my return from San Francisco State I hadn't seen her since watching her in the El Dorado Hotel pool in Tecate. It never occurred to me that Romie noticed my interest until she agreed to spend some time with me. We did lunch, dinner and movies a few times before she stayed over at my new found apartment a couple of blocks from campus. Very pleased, I was finally where I and the many other lecherous Tecate Teacher Corps males dreamed of being; in bed with the Tecate Goddess Romie. Deep in the sheets and inside of Romie; looking into her eyes I saw pain, and more. Not wanting to stop, thinking pain, pleasure; there is a thin line maybe that was her way of enjoyment, I kept on working.

So happy about being with Romie without comment, I put the odd occurrence out of my mind. The 2nd time with that same painful expression on her face Romie pushed me away and quickly pulled me back. The very next time she showed that same pain but additionally started thrashing about and pounding me with her fists. Sheets on the floor along with the pillows, mattress and a broken lamp; that was it we had to talk. Was it just my bad luck or what, I'd done this crazy sex talk with Carol and now Romie too. At the time I thought the Carol situation was just a rare occurrence, but maybe such bizarre sex problems are commonplace. During the following conversations with Romie it all came out. She told me that during her very first sexual experience she had been raped by a black man. Wait a minute, that was to much information, some folks just put it all out there; should I get the hell away from this woman? Although unsaid, listening to her explanation it became immediately apparent that Romie wanted me, a Black man, to join her in reenacting her first sexual experience. She was asking me to rape her and that's how she would get her sexual pleasure. The woman wanted me to hit and hurt her during sex, now wasn't that some crazy shit? Looking at that body, Romie was still quite fine but most certainly not worth such absolute insanity. Again, whatever happened to simply enjoying sex? How many people are out here carrying such gargantuan burdens? Much too much drama, Romie didn't need me; she needed some heavy duty counseling. Graduation and the end of Teacher Corps just around the corner, hastily I ended another relationship. Romie moved to Berkeley and I took off for Europe. I saw her once more after returning from Europe when interviewing for a job in the area. Needing a place to spend the night before my interview the following day, Romie agreed to let me stay overnight in her room at her commune. In the same bed again, I of course wanted to see if she had grown sexually, actually I just wanted to get some. Unfortunately, Romie didn't want to get laid; pushing me away she turned her back and fell asleep. At breakfast one of her roommates pointed out her angry partner who had slept on the couch while I shared Romie's bed. That explained the dirty looks the woman had been giving me and the reason for her sweeping dust from the upper patio onto Romie and I as we talked below, before breakfast. One look at that angry morning countenance and I knew; if that woman thought she could kick my ass she certainly would have. Romie's partner was pissed! How was I to know that Romie was Gay? At any rate I still had Europe to do before that final Romie experience.

Europe

Europe This was a trip planned while I was at San Francisco State by Pablo, Greg and Frank as a reward to themselves for completing Teacher Corps. It took me a while to realize it but they were much closer to each other than any one was to me.

Ignoring that minor detail, I decided to go along. Frank and Greg showed little enthusiasm for my joining the group but Pablo was more visibly displeased. Remembering his times around Blacks in Teacher Corps Pablo seemed fidgety and nervous and this time was no exception. So I handled the situation as always and thought, "Fuck Him!" With my round trip ticket and knowing to be skeptical and watchful, having survived two years with them; two weeks should be easy. Leaving from LAX for the 8+ hour flight over the pond, typically they were all quite drunk long before the east coast. By the time we reached Heathrow, embarrassingly they could barely stand. I had hoped the trip would be different from hanging with those guys back home where they were usually drunk when not working.

London: Going through customs I made my first mistake, or maybe my second; the first being deciding to travel with those assholes who were supposed to be my friends. When the customs agent asked why I was visiting and how long I was going to stay I said "Maybe a week or so unless I find a job here." It seems job was the key word. "We have no jobs here for foreigners!" The agent angrily said as he stamped my passport for entrance and exit only at Heathrow; so much for me and my big mouth. Officially I was allowed to spend no more than two days ONLY to pass through London going to and from the airport. So it was. Hitting all the tourist spots in London we listened to Greg, the white guy, talk about the wonderful past of England and its contributions to world history. Of course I the history major and the black guy was thinking of England's rapacious exploitation of the third world.

"Homeland"

California to New York to Heathrow, a long way: now England and a listen to what my white traveling companion had to say.

I heard words like homeland; "This is our history, can't you feel it?" I could have said yes, but one look at my face such a lie any fool would see.

Silence was the comment from me, thoughts overflowing with a different

history.

Thoughts of those folk in their "homeland" dragging my ancestors from their

homes

to a place stolen from other people of color; to work lifetimes for free

Exploitation, the rapes, the cutting lash; unending hard labor, with no

cash.

Anger was my memory; however my Latino brothers with similar historical pasts, accepted the "homeland" analogy a little too

fast.

But then too we are free to choose what we see.

So the tour began. Approaching Westminster Abbey one couldn't help but notice the height of some of the ancient doorways; reckon those humans of the Middle Ages were shorter folk. The sign fronting the grassy lawns surrounding Westminster Abbey not only said "Stay off the grass" but also said that the grass was blessed by God "...Holy". Looked just like any other green grass seen on front lawns all over the world, so we walked on it before hurrying away.In October of 1805 in what is said, especially by the British, to be one of the most decisive battles in naval history, Admiral Nelson and the British Fleet defeated a combined French and Spanish fleet off the coast of Spain at Trafalgar. And so began British dominance as a world power for more than a hundred and fifty years. Surrounded by the statues and other artifacts in Trafalgar Square we decided to climb one statue and pose for pictures. The Bobbies didn't think posing on the statue was a good idea and chased us from the square. A friend from London recently told me that there are now barriers around the statues. Piccadilly Circus on London's West end we found some time after midnight; it was much like a mini Times Square with lots of lights, shops, theatres, and people on the streets, it was busy. Frank, Greg and Pablo were drunk; what's new, but upright and walking as we checked out the area. A very pregnant black woman standing on a street corner heard our conversation as we walked past and asked, "Are you blokes Americans?" Frank was cracking up laughing at her heavy English accent; what does one expect in England; as I said earlier he was drunk. He asked her if there were night clubs nearby. She agreed to show us where they were. Supposedly leading us to the nightclubs I noticed that we were moving away from the lighted areas and down deserted darkened streets. Thinking they were walking alongside me and the Black hooker I just happened to look over my shoulder and saw Frank, Greg, and Pablo stopped, standing about a block behind whispering among themselves. Feeling the setup on both fronts I left the sista and rejoined my 'friends'.

Trafalgar Square

Westminster Abbey

Morning found us sitting on a downtown sidewalk; ignoring the dirty looks from Londoners heading for work; eating a tasteless breakfast purchased from a street vendor. Never would we have dreamed of sitting on a downtown sidewalk back home in the states, but here in London, for the moment we were playing that 'hippie' role. The one thing that stuck in my mind at the time was that London, England was very white. So far the sista working the streets was the only color we had seen; or should I say the only color I had seen. I suspect I was the only one in the group noticing the lack of color; where were the black folk? Much like back in the states, being knee deep in white folks and their patronizing assumptions got a bit tiring. Well later we found the black folk when we took the underground to the coast. At the station and on the train I met several "Coloreds". The trains, buses and transportation jobs; the drivers, operators and other workers were "Coloreds". In England regardless of origin or ethnicity people of color were lumped into one category and called "Coloreds". It was nice to see that unlike in the United States where South Asians avoided Blacks and worked hard at trying to be white; there the South Asians (Indians) and Blacks seemingly shared a feeling of camaraderie and brotherhood. Regardless of my American roots; with words attitudes and courtesy they readily accepted me into that brotherhood. It was a very nice feeling, there in the "homeland" ☺ I got used to being called a "brother" by Indian (South Asian) dudes as well as Blacks. Of course my traveling companions having spent the time finding a place to buy two fifths of scotch were oblivious to my newfound cultural awareness. The beginning of a new day, we arrived at the coast and boarded the ferry for the trip to Ostend Belgium. From Ostend we were scheduled to take the train to Amsterdam.

Soon after boarding my three companions passed out on the sun drenched deck. Standing alone I watched as we sailed past the hundreds of sea gulls surrounding those historic "White Cliffs of Dover". "How do you think those cliffs got so white?" I was asked by a fellow passenger noticing my interest in the cliffs. "I have no idea." "Well the cliffs are covered with sea gull cack." He said. I had to ask, "What is cack?" Looking at me as if I was mentally incompetent, "Cack, poo!" he responded. Ok so sea gulls fly over and crap on the cliffs I think I got it. Maybe the guy was kidding me, but I listened to a more reasonable explanation from an English friend later. She said that the cliffs are white because the rocks are chalk not cack. Truth is good; now on to Ostend. Early afternoon at Ostend Belgium we moved quickly toward the customs lines. The plan was to take the train from Ostend for the three hour ride to Amsterdam. Amsterdam was on the travel list because they had such liberal marijuana laws. Smoking marijuana in public was not a crime in Amsterdam. Oddly enough at the time, regardless of my past; maybe it was the teaching thing but I wasn't interested in marijuana, drinking or any other drugs.

As we approached the customs counter Greg whispered. "I brought along some marijuana for us to smoke when we get to Amsterdam." Listening to him I thought that was the most bizarre, craziest thing I'd ever heard. Me, the one black guy on the ferry was about to go through customs with a group of drunks smuggling drugs across an international border. No, not going out like that way.I immediately moved to another line, far away from my 'friends' the drug smugglers. Once past customs I looked for hours but couldn't find Frank, Greg and Pablo. I decided that they found the time convenient to hide out and finally get rid of the touchy black guy. Good riddance, they were drunk and irritating most of the time and I didn't trust them. Again, finding my comfort zone, alone as usual I set out for Amsterdam. I never saw those guys again until years later at a party back in the states. They of course treated me like a long lost friend, and I didn't mention Europe or their mysterious disappearance during customs check at Ostend. Consequently amidst the back-slapping and Teacher Corps memories it was like those things never happened. Smiling and shaking hands. I remembered it all but for whatever reasons said nothing. But before all that I was headed for Amsterdam.

Belgium: Riding past the many windmills alongside the tracks I knew I was in the land of the Dutch, the Netherlands. Now I just needed to see that young fellow with his finger in the dike☺. The brief stop at the city of Haarlem reminded me of my American history as I remembered the Dutch were some of the first European settlers in New York where America's Harlem is located. However this city of Haarlem with its ancient churches and cobbled streets obviously was much older and very different from it American namesake spelled with one 'a' Harlem.

Amsterdam: my first task was to find a place to stay. In the visitor/ tourist section of the train station on a wall mounted bulletin board were price postings for room rentals with addresses and phone numbers. I soon found a place near downtown Amsterdam and just walking distance from the train station. I was welcomed by a middle aged man, his wife, daughter and young grandson. After a good night's sleep in an upstairs bedroom and breakfast with the family the following morning I hit the streets. Those streets were overflowing with new lessons. Standing on the curb I couldn't help but notice men and women much like in other cities of the world formally dressed for work. They were sitting with their vehicles bumper to bumper waiting for the light to change. All closely aligned they reminded me of the morning rush hour in Los Angeles; except when the light changed they pedaled away. Yep, shock a farm boy from Gould, Arkansas, not a car in the bunch; the morning commuters were all riding bicycles. Amsterdam is a city with many museums and other sights; most in walking distance to major transportation hubs. The Van Gogh Museum, Anne Frank's House and many other tourist attractions are nearby.

The White Cliffs of Dover

When traveling, if possible I try to blend in with the native population, that was at first difficult in The Netherlands and Amsterdam because most folk are white. Getting used to the place riding the bus one afternoon, I happened to glance up from my habit of scanning the feet of the native inhabitants. A major task in Holland, I wanted to see if anyone still wore wooden shoes. It was disappointing not finding one person wearing those wooden shoes. I did happen to see a pair in a store window, but I think they were for decoration only. Anyway on this particular afternoon I couldn't help but notice a man standing in the aisle near the front of the bus; giving me that look. That 'look' recognizable in any language needed no translation. Remembering we were in the city that killed Anne Frank, I sized up the fellow staring with eyes so full of hatred. .Just in case he wanted to start something to get ready; I stood holding onto the overhead handrail. Both rocking gently with the movement of the bus as he maintained his hate stare I noted that Mr. Racist was at least a foot taller than my 6'3. Wondering what I would have to do to take him; maybe I'd have to strike first. OK there was my stop; walking past the unblinking stare while watching his hands and feet I was ready for some hostile move from the seven foot fascist. Without incident I got off the bus at Dam Square. Back in the states hippie types, far left magazines and newspapers spoke glowingly of the laid back atmosphere and of the freely flowing legal marijuana in Amsterdam. Centrally located with many restaurants and shops Dam Square is a gathering place for locals and tourists alike. Many older residents sit on nearby benches around the square feeding pigeons. On the day of my visit there were no exceptions to the routines except for certain tourists easy to spot. Typically they were talking and laughing loudly and openly smoking marijuana; white Americans. Also standing alongside the square were several frustrated uniformed Dutch policemen. Very much like the police in Los Angeles or any major city; faces etched with anger they paced, circling the square slapping their long batons into their open palms. A foreign country; regardless of the so called freedom and openness of the laws; no way would I consider possessing or smoking marijuana in that place. Seeing the marijuana situation as just another tourist attraction with a heavy police presence was enough for me.

My quiet observations were interrupted several times by folks I didn't know approaching and speaking to me in several languages. Guessing at the languages I possibly recognized Dutch, French, Arabic, Russian and Spanish. Why were they talking to me I wondered? Consequently I decided to move from my comfortable seat alongside the square. Relieved to see an American Express office, I hurried inside and asked the clerk working the counter, "Why do these people in the square keep asking me questions in different languages?"Glancing up at me he said, "You're black, they think you're a drug dealer."

Ostend Belgium

He said it as if he was stating a fact that was common knowledge. Flabbergasted I thought, thousands of miles away from home, the good old USA; on another continent, yet the black stereotypes follow. So be it, in country for nearly a week now seemed a good time for the Black American "…drug dealer…" to look at other sites from the tour book. I picked up the free book at the train station when I first arrived in the city. Thumbing through the booklet I couldn't help but notice the listing for the Canal district.

The Canal District: It seems as was marijuana consumption; prostitution too was legal in Amsterdam. The working women were housed in buildings fronted by well lighted sidewalks alongside several canals. Here tourists and customers strolled along the sidewalks shopping for sexual goodies. Each of the houses had a large front window where women sat in chairs comfortably on display. Conservatively dressed, wearing gray, black or brown suits with knee length skirts; some cigarettes dangling from red lips smoked while waiting for customers. All sat in lighted windows with varying colors. Blue, red, orange and green were most common. Interested customers chose from the women on display and knocked on the side door and talked to the chosen until they worked out a price. If the deal was made of course they would disappear inside one of the rooms behind the display windows. The information regarding proper etiquette with the women on the canal was outlined in the tour booklet. No I did not nor did I see anyone else go inside, reckon they were all tourists as was I. The Canal, outlined in the tour book was just another site in Amsterdam to be seen. Actual participation never crossed my mind I say feeling the thoughts of many readers saying. "Sure buddy." Even though they seemed without stress and bored sitting there on display awaiting customers, it seemed an unusual way to make a living. Besides they really weren't that good looking, I saw better looking women on the streets and at the bus stops. However, I did want to take some pictures, but the minute I pulled out my camera a policeman suddenly appeared and loudly said in English, "No pictures!" Oh well back to the local homestead.

The Room: Living in a home with a traditional family was sometimes awkward. From my room at the top of the stair, daily interaction with the family in the small home was a necessity. They seemed to be nice people who showed no discomfort at having a Black person living in their home. Although all spoke English, they were fluent in French and Dutch as well. The linguistics was especially noticeable as we all sat around the breakfast table each morning. They flowed from Dutch to French as they spoke to each other and to English when I was included in the conversations. Daily in English the father embarrassed me and his young daughter by praising her positive attributes. Yet he never failed to mention each day her major misdeed; an early pregnancy and baby son. "But we all make mistakes in life…" he said.

Dam Square

The Canals

The repetitive conversation about his daughters "...mistake in life..." the wife, daughter and I didn't want to have. Staying in 'his home' very embarrassed; without comment I listened. A well defined body with short black hair and a cute face the daughter was a fairly good looking lady. But only on a brief visit to the country I would be a fool to get into a relationship with his daughter or anyone else. Daddy obviously wanted to hook the daughter up with a well to do, or any American, me. Much too much drama; a wife and a baby in another country and the necessary paperwork and expense to move them, having no love and a child; I didn't want or need any of it! Further, they were nice but I didn't know anything about those people. But I did know several nice women back home in the states without such complications, so why would I or anyone else in their right minds consider the foreign wife baby option? Sitting silently at breakfast each morning listening to the various creative ways the dad broached the subject; my thoughts of the absolute absurdity of the situation remained unsaid. The beginning of the 2nd week; always on the lookout for; but having seen not one person of color; realizing that Europe was overwhelmingly white; I was thinking it was about time to head for home. Out for my early evening walk a BMW suddenly stopped at the curb. Peering inside I noticed the pleasant brown color of the driver and passengers. But with disappointed faces they soon drove away when the driver said something to me in Arabic and I responded in English. Arabs, but still they had color maybe there was hope in that white land. Later after meeting the 'brothas' my new found black friends I told them about my encounter with the Arabic speaking folk. They said there was a large population of Moroccans living in Amsterdam.

The Brothas: The day following my Arab encounter I saw an amazing sight. Walking past the train station and crossing the bridge over a canal approaching me was a group of six black dudes with big afros. Wearing bell bottoms and headbands they were in deep conversation in Dutch until they saw me. With about three feet between us I was addressed in Dutch, Arabic French and Spanish. "Damm is everyone multilingual in this country?" I thought. "So how are you brothas doing?" I said in English. Abram, the tallest of the group, standing about 5'11 said "Ohhhh, and American." With big smiles all was talking at once asking question after question."What are you doing here?" Where in America are you from?"California I responded to Abram who seemed to be the leader of the group. "That's cool." He said and asked "Have you had lunch?" They asked me to join them for lunch and the instantaneous free flowing conversation. Suddenly I felt at home and comfortable with those guys. It was like being in Compton, Baldwin Hills or on Crenshaw Blvd in Los Angeles. Instead there I was walking down a street in another country talking about music, Amsterdam, Suriname and California among our crowd of seven brothers. Enjoying the ambiance I was in for more surprises.

Stepping inside the street side café I couldn't help but notice certain identifying smells. Hard to believe at first but there I was in a soul food café, in Amsterdam no less. Over ham hocks, beans and a dish I didn't recognize with even more questions we continued our conversations. "What the hell are you guys doing here and why is there a soul food café in Amsterdam?" Those were a couple of my first questions. It seems the brothers were Dutch citizens from the former colony Dutch Guyana. Later to be well known for the infamous Jim Jones; the country is now called Suriname. As natives of the colony of course Dutch was their first language, hence their fluency. Hanging with those guys for the remaining few days in the country I discovered a part of Amsterdam most tourists are unaware of. Sitting in a nightclub in a black neighborhood in the city listening to the music of Marvin Gaye, Gladys Knight, The Temptations and the Four Tops I saw faces similar to those seen in jook joints in the states. Kicking back with my friends it was easy to forget about the rest of Europe and enjoy the welcome feelings of home. The brothas told stories of joblessness and racism in Amsterdam similar to those heard back home in the USA. Although Dutch citizens they were treated differently when job hunting and in schools because of their color. Much like the Black drug dealer reference in the square it was uncomfortable listening to their very familiar reality. Martin Luther King, Malcolm X, Rosa Parks, and others from the American Civil Rights Movement were common household names and their heroes. Hanging with them in the neighborhoods and looking at the 'dark side' was a once in a lifetime experience. Too soon promising to stay in touch and visit each other in the future it was time to leave my new friends and head for home and Liz. Amsterdam to Heathrow and the eight hour flight home from Heathrow was inconsequential. There are those who would prefer not to hear it but yes as on the trip over, I was the only black on the flight home. Persons of color may understand without further explanation. Annnnny way; gone for more than a couple of weeks, wherever the destination, Cali is always a welcome sight. Yeah being home again in LA felt soooo good.

Home Sweet, Back in the USA: Now it was time to see Liz again. We had met in language school in the mountains of Baja California, Tecate, Mexico. Having noticed Liz from the very beginning of the program I finally convinced her to talk to me. For practical reasons we kept our relationship a secret from the program administrators and my fellow interns. All residents at the Eldoraado Motel discretion was difficult. Liz was a Team Leader and a program administrator, consequently fraternization with lowly interns like me was frowned upon. Using forbidden time together on the patio of the dirt floored restaurant next door to the Eldorado Motel, simply holding hands was very special. They were looking from the open kitchen at the two of us sitting at a table in the shade of a large tree with mangoes on the ground around us.

Suriname, Presidential Palace

The café owner and his wife exchanged knowing smiles; it was a memorably nice feeling in a nice place. Looking forward to the end of the Tecate experience we were anticipating our return to Cali and a time when the need for secrecy would be unnecessary. Sharing a vehicle on the ride back I didn't really know what to expect. While continuing to touch, Liz followed my lead during the return and on our first night at a friend's house. Waking skin to skin after a night of exploring bodies it felt so good. Liz, Liz; sensual, a word which normally would suffice, but she was so much, much more. Words regardless of meaning didn't begin speaking to the excitement felt from the happy anticipation of just the sight of her. All those feelings were brought to a cauldron like boil at the sound of her voice speaking to nearness in spite of distance. The smell of her perfume was electric because then I knew she was close enough to see, hear and touch. Liz's presence unfailingly created a paradise of joyful pleasure with warming smiles and other re-explorations. Love, like a bright burning candle in a darkened room touching all aspects of that space is an experience, if we are lucky, felt at least once in a lifetime. Considering the depth of what we had shared the first night after Tecate; in that small space in Long Beach; and the following morning, simply sitting on and old living room couch still holding hands watching two astronauts walking on the moon felt so special. Such relationships should never end, but like life and all other aspects thereof they do. On our return we didn't have that expected freedom; Lis was still and administrator and that certain distance between Administrators and interns was expected by the Teacher Corps directors. She was also assigned to a school district in Los Angeles County and I was out in Riverside County. The separation and distance mattered. So while biding my time and hoping for a Liz future I found other interests. But after Europe Liz was still around and no longer a Teacher Corps administrator, so it was time to follow up on her magic.

Nor-Cal: Having dreamed of living in California as a small child while listening to the stories told by my uncles and older brothers on return visits to Arkansas, finally getting to Los Angeles was very special. As a relatively new resident and student; Pepperdine College, USC, UCLA, Cal State LA, Long Beach State, San Fernando Valley State, Loyola Marymount and other area schools were all a part of my associations and interactions. Snug in Los Angeles County the only place I had lived for a reasonable time in California; it was easy to feel content with the knowledge that there was no better place on the planet. Of this I was certain until just at the right time in my life Liz was there to help me ease thorough some challenges. Again I found myself in the middle of endings and change; is that not life? Graduate coursework at USC was completed as was my student teaching at Mission Junior High School. My lady at the time, Shawna was moving out and on to a job at RAND.

Now I was spending more and more time with Liz, who said to me one afternoon; "Los Angeles is not a true representation of the state, this weekend I am going to show you the real California." What the hell was that woman talking about,"...true representation of the state."? Early Friday morning she picked me up and in no time at all we were rolling north on US 101. Kicked back in the passenger seat I was seeing everything as we rolled pass the mission bells along the historic El Camino Real. Nowadays US 101 but back in the day it is said to have been the route used by the Spanish Missionaries; walking the California Coast who claimed to be walking for King Jesus hence the name in translation "The King's walk or the walk of kings. It was a bright clear California day, the top was down on her green Austin Healey Sprite and we were moving north on The King's Highway. Her voice, windblown brown hair, dark blue eyes flicking from my face to the road and back again; thigh muscles flashing in the short brown mini- skirt, relaxing and rolling with a fine, fine woman on that perfect sun splattered afternoon, what better could life offer? Legs tightening as she worked the stick shift; then and there Liz was pure beauty and the sexiest woman alive. Focused on her body and those slim, shapely tanned legs; I didn't remember or hear much of what was said and I missed most of the beautiful Pacific shoreline. Sure I had briefly spent time in San Francisco before, maybe it was the Liz magic; but nothing like this.

The Golden Gate: Arriving in San Francisco during the early evening hours reminiscent of Sandburg's "...cats feet..." close enough to touch, we watched the puffy soft, slow moving clouds of fog rolling into the Golden Gate. Driving past Victorian Houses, up and down steep hills; with fleeting glimpses of Alcatraz, Treasure Island, Berkeley, the east bay and all three bridges; line and sinker I was hooked! The weekend spent with her closeness in the foggy San Francisco cold and her friends and their kids out in the avenues, I found myself adjusting to a slower, quieter, gentler way of life. The 32 automatic that I had been carrying since moving to Los Angeles years ago became an unnecessary anomaly. Surrounded by courteous, trusting friendly folk; I didn't need weapons. Golden Gate Park, Fisherman's Wharf, Alcatraz, Sausalito, Mill Valley, Stinson Beach and numerous other tourist haunts made for a grand experience. Impressed, I vowed then and there to do all in my power to find a way to return, to move; to work in Northern California. Soon after our perfect San Francisco weekend, Liz and I ended up going our separate ways. What happened, maybe some of us are just meant to live this life thing alone. Selfishly I wanted to have kids, a house with a white picket fence and all of that. Cool with the marriage part, Liz didn't want to have kids. I'd certainly heard that before. Yep another sexual problem, why me Lord? Liz said she had a defective gene that would cause birth defects in her children

The El Camino Real

And so it was that Liz returned to her home state of Kansas and I was left to find a way to live in Northern California without her. Immediately I began sending out job applications and inquiries to school districts in Northern California. Sifting through prospects in and around San Francisco I found a high school in a small town north of the Golden Gate that seemed a perfect fit. After several conversations with the district superintendent I flew up one day for interviews and immediately signed a contract. Probably the age or youthfulness, but things were moving fast and just like that, in a blink another life change. The very next weekend I rented a car, packed in my few possessions, mostly books and moved to northern California. It is amazing to remember that everything I owned fitted into a mid sized rental with room to spare. After two days lying low at the local Motel 6 reading the classifieds I found a small apartment. Having no friends or relatives within 500 miles and never feeling lonesome or the need for them; thanks to Liz for the introduction to the area, the North Bay was now my home.

Full Time Teacher, Drummond: Yep, a small town about an hour or so north of the Golden Gate with two high schools, four junior high's and three elementary schools. I was assigned to Drummond, the larger of the two high schools and was scheduled to start work in late August, it was now early June. The new apartment was near downtown and walking distance to work, life was grand. I even found a nearby store that sold 'hot links' what more could a brotha ask? Well there was more, the one thing that first attracted me to teaching; I was free for the rest of the summer to do a couple of things that I especially loved. The first being to use the work free summer to read books; and the second was the daily freedom to play pick-up basketball games. The RA Expeditions, Something Wicked This Way Comes, The Coming Fury, Terrible Swift Sword and A Stillness at Appomattox were on my summer's reading list; and then there too was basketball

Summer B-Ball: Pick-up basketball games had been a part of my life since before high school, wherever I lived, especially on weekends. Saturdays and Sundays, it was not uncommon to find me playing 3 on 3 or 5 on 5 basketball, all day. If there was an open gym the games often went on into the nights. Even when stationed at Luke Air Force Base just outside of Phoenix, Arizona friends and I managed to find pick up games in the neighboring towns of Avondale, Glendale, Litchfield Park, Scottsdale, Phoenix and other cities. There were a few anxious moments playing on strange basketball courts with and/or against people we didn't know. Especially tense were those times playing without your usual friends and teammates.

One afternoon before moving to Nor-Cal I was playing on a basketball court just off Avalon in South Central Los Angeles, and feeling it; I couldn't miss.

The Golden Gate Bridge

It was one of those days when my jumper was unstoppable. Jogging down court after faking left, dribbling behind the back and swishing another shot from the right corner we all noticed the maroon Model T with whitewalls and lifts pull up onto the grass. A short chubby fellow, barely 5 feet tall hopped out of the front passenger side wearing brogans and overalls. I couldn't help but smile; I hadn't seen brown brogans and blue overalls since leaving the cotton fields of Arkansas. Without preamble, "Which team am I on?" he said. I just looked at the little fellow and was about to tell him to fuck off and wait his turn when I glanced at my teammate Tucker who anticipated my carefree recklessness and shook his head, "No!" He discreetly pointed towards the car. Peering through the open windows I saw two guys sitting in back dressed like the short fellow who wanted to play with bib overalls and dark sunglasses; intently watching our reaction to their friend. Also easily seen were the upright double barreled shotguns resting comfortably between their legs. What the hell? Standing well over 6'6 and weighing over 250 pounds plus, "You can take my spot man." Tucker said as he stepped off to the side. 'Big Tuck' stepping aside, never seen that before; we all took notice. Obviously out of my element we continued playing, and now without 'Big Tuck' my team was losing badly. Dropping several soft passes and dribbling with both hands; clearly the short fat guy was not a basketball player. After about thirty minutes of action; "Good game fellows" the intruder said as he walked off the basketball court and climbed into the waiting car. Twelve guys staring, "Who the fuck was that?" I asked. "Those dudes are The Farmers and this is their turf." Tucker responded. Farmers, turf, whatever happened to a simple basketball game, do they own the fucking park? Most of my outdoor court experience in Los Angeles had been played with my older brother Wally and his friends there at Avalon Park. They were fairly well known and didn't expect any shit from other players. "Are you Wally's brother?" A yes answer insured my safety from the local basketball playing thugs. Of course after a while it became easy to discern the safe neighborhoods and gyms for pick-up games. Open gyms at Dorsey, LA, Hamilton and other high schools were good for most weekends and sometimes university gyms too were open for public play. Here at Drummond, thankfully not a major city like Los Angeles, learning the ropes, I was on my own. A small town; all the black families knew each other, especially the basketball players, but they didn't know me.

Summer B-Ball at Drummond: That first summer my time was spent playing on the outdoor courts a couple of blocks behind my studio apartment. The games were very physical with varying levels of talent. While standing on the sidelines listening to the players while waiting my turn I picked up bits and pieces of information about my new community. There were only two outdoor public basketball courts on "...this side of the highway."(Highway 80).

The one downhill from my apartment where we were playing in a mostly white neighborhood was one and the other court was located in The Crest. Blacks came from all over the city to play on the court in my neighborhood. Except for me and my upstairs neighbor everyone else in the neighborhood was white. Those neighboring whites often stood in their front yards angrily staring, but wisely not commenting to the large numbers of cussing blacks playing basketball. I certainly could understand why parents living near the park wouldn't want their kids listening to the constant stream of loud cussing. Knowing that The Crest was my only other basketball option in town, I felt their pain, remained silent, and kept on playing basketball with those loud cussing brothas. On another note, the strangest thing happened on those courts by my apartment. One afternoon I saw this fellow standing waiting for the next game. I thought he looked familiar and gave him a holler. Sure enough it was C-Dub from my earlier years in the US Air Force. We both had been stationed at Luke Air Force Base and hung out on weekends at the Elks Club on 7th Avenue in Phoenix, Arizona. As I write this in 2016 I am reminded of a fairly recent article I read from the Arizona Republic newspaper in which numerous visits to the Elks Club by local police are mentioned. "The Phoenix Elks Lodge has been cited repeatedly for liquor license violations and is a magnet for illegal late night activity..." All of that, the illegal late night activity and liquor license violations included me C-Dub and our friends back in the day. Eighteen and nineteen years old at the time; we visited the Elks Club every weekend and it would have been shocking to be asked to show ID. More shocking would have been a police presence in that part of town. Even when C-Dub was involved in a shooting incident at the Elks, mentioned in my book, *There Are Times When* police weren't expected and didn't show up. But that was there and then.

Anyway I was pretty surprised to see him or anyone so far away, mentally and physically removed from that other seemingly distant time and place in my life. C-Dub was unimpressed and just like he had seen me the day before; gave me the same old greeting; "What up Will?" that he used to give me years ago back in Arizona. C-Dub had grown up in Chicago and I in Gould Arkansas, so how the hell did we both end up north of California's Golden Gate in Drummond; a town that I stumbled upon by chance? I never got around to having that how you got here conversation with C-Dub. I felt the same but I reckon times had changed; it was no longer like our days of drinking Thunderbird wine outside the Elks Club. C-Dub heard that I was a teacher and the few other times I saw him he started treating me with embarrassingly absurd formality. Absurd because this was a guy I saw most days at work when we were in the military. On weekends comfortable in our element we had often shared cheap wine and cheaper women; both we could just barely afford. What changed? I was the same person inside, or so I thought. Too soon, with real and memorable faces from the distant past, new information, a new place and new job, another summer of basketball and reading was ending. Finally, I was taking the next major step after having completed an unimaginable preparatory journey. Incomprehensible to most Americans, the journey began at Gould Colored School in Gould, Arkansas. Gould Colored School where we learned in our free time to balance books on our heads as we walked to and from school. This we learned after reading about and seeing pictures of African tribe's people carrying water, wood and other objects on their heads. Gould Colored School where after reading about and seeing drawings of the "founding fathers" using quill pens to sign The Declaration of Independence we realized that quill pens were feathers. Having chickens at our homes we too began using quill pens made from sharpened chicken feathers dipped in ink for our school writing assignments. After such great physical and mental distance traveled; again change was afoot. Just a few years removed from the hopelessness of those Arkansas cotton fields, and later military training at Lackland, Greenville, Montgomery, Luke and other Air Force bases, already things were so different. Beyond the military, school continued being a major life focus at various California universities. Now it was September; and still feeling the tension and expectation that students and teachers feel every fall, it was time for the culmination of this new beginning as a full time high school teacher in the great state of California. Yes, beginnings and endings, is that not the simplistic, easily understood totality of life, and death as well? Here we go. Looking back to a time when nervously preparing for a special date, party or job; I am sure we can remember the thoughtful pauses before putting on a dab of a favorite cologne or perfume, selecting just the right tie, belt, scarf, dress, or jacket. With adventurous anticipation, I hurriedly dressed for the first day of school. With three English and two American History classes, I couldn't wait to start. Grabbing my windbreaker, backpack and new bicycle, I was out the door and coasting downhill; past the basketball courts toward Drummond High. The roads were slick form a morning drizzle, but in no time at all I was rolling up to the front of the school. Several students gathered on the imposing front steps waiting for the first bell; glanced up at my approach. A black man wearing a tie may have caused some consternation. Having no black teachers at the school some wondered whether I was security or just maybe, possibly, a new teacher. Regardless, they all laughed uproariously when I hit my brakes did a sideways skid and tumbled off the bike; splashing into a big puddle below the steps. Picking myself, my backpack and bicycle up amid the loud guffaws from the students and a few curious teachers; I dragged everything to the nearest open bathroom to prepare for my first period class. Paper towels are good for soaking water from shoes and wet socks. They work on wet pants as well, although my bag lunch was a total loss.

Day 1: Not exactly the start I anticipated, but it was certainly noteworthy. Still feeling a bit disheveled at my first teachers meeting at the end of my first day; I listened as the principal introduced the older and we new teachers. The oldest and largest group of teachers was composed of mostly gray white women nearing retirement age. The seven new teachers including myself were all under thirty years old. Sitting there among the new hires, Jerry got quite a laugh from the group as he described my early morning "...grand entrance..." and fall in front of the school. However, Jerry's comments weren't the only faculty meeting surprise; thinking that I was the only 'one' (Black teacher) at the school, lo and behold I found another right there in plain sight. Stepping into the teachers lounge for the first time following the faculty meeting, I noticed off to one side the coffee maker, vending machines, refrigerator, and then the folks. With a quick glance at all the white faces, my momentary pause when looking at Ms. O'Neal went unnoticed. It seems that most judge race by skin color, Ms. O'Neal was very light skinned, almost albino with distinctive hair, nose and lips. I immediately recognized her as a 'sista'. I was probably beginning to stare a bit as Ms. O'Neal smiled and winked at me. Returning the smile I realized she was passing and thought, "That's her business." Having worked at the school for several years, passing for white was more than likely the only way she could have gotten the job in the first place.

Son of a gun, they didn't know she was black. Later in the teachers lounge I couldn't help but laugh as the most renowned racists at the school sat huddled at their all white tables during breaks and lunch deep in conversation with Ms. O'Neal. Power to the people. Fitting comfortably into my first full time teaching experience I began noticing what I thought were interesting and quirky things about teachers and teaching. **Math** teachers were mostly loners and not very talkative; **Art** teachers also loners but were talkative when approached and attracted to the unusual with little or no classroom control. On any given day one might find the art teacher with her 30 or more students outside under a tree. Or she might be downtown, at the fairgrounds, a local park or some other locale. They tried but maybe it was an art thing; they too were loners. **Science** teachers, although not necessarily by choice; few teachers wanted to hang with the uninformed not very socially skilled scientists. **English** teachers were the most outgoing and social and got along well with all groups. History teachers were second only to English teachers in sociability and with a hint of reluctance, got along with all the other teacher groups. English and History teachers most often hung out together. **PE t**eachers only hung out with other PE teachers. All, including students treated PE teaches as if they weren't very bright; and with few exceptions they weren't. Typically in the faculty lounge teachers usually sat with folk in their discipline.

Drummond Senior High School

Except as mentioned earlier history and English teachers being more mobile and might be found sitting out of discipline. The aforementioned observations, judgments; were made during my first year of full time teaching and seemed to resonate truthfully throughout my long career. Those habits, rules, associations and attitudes seemed to apply from Kindergarten, through junior high and high school, college and university teaching. But back to a typical day at Drummond high school; Thump Friday.

Thump Friday: It took but a few days to see the most important reasons why we younger folk were hired. Friday morning a student in my first period history class just happened to say; "Teach you new, do you know its thump Friday? I didn't know so Buddy explained that thumping meant fighting and that two or three times a month during lunch on Fridays there were fights between "...The brothers and the honkies..." Sure enough later that very same day hearing shouting below the 2nd floor faculty lounge we looked out to see a gathering of black male students at the edge of campus facing the street. I along with three other new teachers hurried downstairs and to the sidewalk fronting the school to find a group of older whites with chains and baseball bats in hand approaching. We recognized many of the black kids now facing the whites; they were students in our classes. We encouraged our students to start heading towards their afternoon classes. We also reminded the whites with the baseball bats and chains that they were not students and had no right to be on the school grounds. Glancing over my shoulder towards the school building behind us, easily seen; holding onto their coffee cups and leaning out of the windows of the faculty lounge and classrooms were the principal and the other white faculty watching the show. Surprised, I said to Barbara, Jerry and Russ; "What are they doing up there watching, they should be down here with us, especially the principal. Then things got a little dicey, suddenly the police were on the scene. Wearing faceguards and riot helmets, nightsticks in hand, lights flashing, four cops hopped out of two vehicles. Walking quickly past the white adults on the school grounds with baseball bats and chains, they approached the black students. Unafraid, about 50 strong, assured by their numbers, the black students stood watching the approaching cops. Suddenly Barbara our young Italian-American teacher, red hair in a conservative bun, standing barely five feet stepped between the approaching cops and the black kids; we followed suit. She was the only one of us with any local street credibility. Her mother having been an elementary school teacher in the district for years had taught many of the parents and some of the black students in the crowd. Barbara also grew up in the city and knew many of the older brothers and sisters of the black kids. But typically talking to the cops was like speaking to that proverbial, "...brick wall." Not listening to anything said nightsticks in hand they kept trying to step around us to get at the black kids. I said;

"These kids are students at this school and have a right to be where they are, here on campus. Maybe you should be arresting those people standing in the street and on the school grounds with weapons. Breathing a sigh of relief as the bell sounded ending lunch and our students slowly turned away; heading for their afternoon classes. Wordlessly, swinging those heavy nightsticks in frustration the angry cops strode past us and the white thugs with bats and chains; climbed into their cars and screeched away from the curb. Show over, the principal and the watching teachers moved away from the upstairs windows. Quite naïve and knowing nothing of the trapping of power; foolishly, a few days later I dropped by Principal Higgins office to discuss the incident. Our first meeting up close, I couldn't help but notice the heavy bags under the drooping eyelids, his large graying head and the smell of alcohol permeating the office. Then I understood why Principal Higgins was never seen outside of his office walking the school grounds. Remembering him hiding upstairs with the rest of the white faculty during the Thump Day confrontation I wondered if this white man was a drunk because he was a afraid of the black kids at this predominantly black school? So I asked without mentioning his name or position; "Why didn't the other faculty and staff help during the confrontation between our students and those white outsiders?" "Outsiders, those were former students; these little dust ups happen once or twice a month at the beginning of school." As he talked I noticed his trembling hands moving papers back and forth across his glass topped desk. "Well I just wanted to know what should be done when things like that happen." Before I finished speaking Principal Higgins bounced out of his chair, grabbed my hand and started shaking it in dismissal while I was still sitting. "You did a great job out there and thanks for dropping by."He said as he escorted me from his office. With so much to think about on this new job, easy came the decision to deal with educational issues and avoid Mr. Higgins and his problems. The students themselves created enough drama that we as teachers generally were prepared to handle. It also helped to remember that those concepts and actions facilitating the education of our students were why we were there and the basis of our teaching. Monitoring or educating an alcoholic principal was not a part of the job. Later I mentioned to my fellow teachers Barbara and Jerry my visit with Principal Higgins and both said that was not wise, Higgins should be avoided. "Principals have long memories and they don't like to be questioned by teachers." I was told. Incident forgotten we began to enjoy working with our students.

The Travel Club: The few white students at the school were in the AP college prep classes sometimes with as few as 13 students as opposed the norm of 30 to 35. Of course those classes were taught by the older white teachers. Getting to know the students in our classes was an 'eye opener'

Less than hours drive away not one student in any of our four classes had ever been to San Francisco. Most had never been outside of the city limits of Drummond. Many had only been outside of their neighborhoods to attend school. Another surprise, I was finding that 'real' teaching was nothing like Teacher Corps and teacher training at USC. Clearly, beyond the reading, writing and arithmetic, there was more serious work to be done. How would our students react to the discovery of new places and situations outside of their school, city, state and country? Jerry mentioned that he had started a travel club at one of the schools where he had previously worked. During spring break and other holidays faculty volunteers and parent chaperones had used their cars to travel with students to neighboring cities states and countries. Sounded like a great idea and an excellent hands on extension of our teaching. And it would fulfill a major need for most of our students. So the Drummond Travel Club was launched. On weekends our travel club students,, mostly from our classes, with parents and faculty chaperones fanned out across the city going from door to door collecting cans and bottles to be resold to recyclers. The money from sales to the recyclers was used to buy gas for the vehicles and food for our trips. A few years before the advent of Google and Mapquest; with a little help, students using free paper maps from the auto club of The United States, Canada, Mexico, California, Oregon, Arizona, Washington and other states mapped in advance each planned trip. Using the number of miles per gallon of gas each vehicle could travel students then calculated the number of gallons of gas necessary for each vehicle on the round trips. They also looked at the average cost of gas per gallon in the areas traveled. Thereafter we had a rough estimate and could match the amount of money on hand to the anticipated travel distances. Travel times and scheduled stops at chosen campgrounds were also a part of the pre travel calculations. Counting the cash on hand, after a few months we were ready for our first trip. Heading north, reservations had been made at campgrounds in Northern California, Oregon, Washington and B. C. With five teacher chaperones, four vehicles, food for seven days; tents and other camping equipment; the seventeen students, as did we; prepared for the trip of our lives. Excited, we were ready!

Culture Shock: Arriving at our first stop, a campground in Southern Oregon, we began preparing meals on our outdoor camping equipment. This was a new experience for most of our students and as mentioned earlier, so was being away from home. Then too I noticed that the black kids, seemingly very nervous; found ways to be near me, the one black teacher/chaperone as much as possible. Keisha, an 11th grader; peering from underneath her gigantic afro asked, "Mr. Williams is this Oregon moon the same one we see back in Drummond?"

Turning to face the questioner, I immediately hid my smile when I realized that she wasn't joking. Keisha listened intently to my mini lecture regarding the moon, stars, planets, etc. She listened as if she was hearing it all for the first time. Things like that kept happening during the trip. A breakfast stop at a restaurant, for the very first time the black kids discovered waffles, bagels, and French toast. Quickly we learned to accept without judgment; questions about things that seemed unbelievably common and simple to us. The kids didn't know directions; north south, east and west, states, cities, or oceans; not even the Pacific which they had lived on the shores of all their lives. Only about an hours drive away from Drummond, they had never seen the Golden Gate Bridge, the Bay Bridge, Oakland or Berkeley. We had anticipated that the Travel Club would add new knowledge and awareness to our students, although we were very surprised at the unanticipated depth. We couldn't help but be pleased at the numerous opportunities for enlightenment. Big smiles each day when we asked ourselves, is this not what schools and teaching is all about? As adults and teachers we looked upon our students as one group, just kids from school. But they were looking at a new world being introduced singularly, and from specific points of view. In Oregon and Washington the black kids voiced only to me, certain concerns. Daily I was asked with an irritated tone;"Mr. Williams where are the black people?" I didn't say it but thought; "I never promised you black people." I tried to explain that black people really did live in Oregon and Washington but not very many. By the time we reached British Columbia the black kids had stopped all associations with white kids and chaperones. Rolling even farther north and crossing an international border, outside of the United States for the first time in their lives I suggested that this was a monumental occasion. In response to my enthusiasm at least the complaining ended but was replaced by a quiet unease. My cousin Bobby from Bakersfield was among that group of young blacks.

Cousin Bobby: I mentioned in my first book, *The Killing of Mr. Floyd & Other Stories*. He does seem to be a constant just on the outskirts, in the shadows of my life. Even today, more than forty years later he still lives close by in a neighboring town. He often thanks me facetiously for teaching him that life is much simpler and safer outside the ghetto. Proudly declaring that we are the only two blacks in the county, I still find time to avoid him. When he was a junior in high school he came to live with me to attend Drummond Senior High. His mother was my mother's first cousin and best friend. With money being scare and six other kids in the house when his mom asked I said it would be fine for Bobby to come live with me. Bobby's hometown of Bakersfield then and now is an odd place reminiscent of the South. Blacks and Latinos in the city seem to believe in and ascribe to that racial inferiority propaganda dumped onto them by the ruling whites.

Without thought of other spaces or complaint, they live in a specified area of Bakersfield just off Cottonwood Road. Fearfully avoiding other major areas of the city they shop only in certain stores and eat out in certain restaurants. They attend only the movie theatre (Police patrol the parking lot and inside the theatre) in the neighborhood. Beyond the culture shock, living with me and attending the school where I taught may have been uncomfortable for him. When Bobby was screwing up in his classes I reminded him that it put me in an awkward position on the job. It was especially irksome when he reacted by placing me in the same category as the white teachers at the school. "You teachers don't understand a brother." What the fuck do you mean YOU TEACHERS, those teachers are white, I am black and your family asshole!" Facing an insurmountable communication problem, still I asked what was there to understand about his empty seat when he was cutting class. Not his father and just a few years older with no parenting skills or experience, the on-the-job training with Bobby was hard work. But then too there were moments of great humor shared with Cousin Bobby. It was not uncommon for folk to step outside and fire their weapons, not at any particular target but skyward, at midnight to welcome certain holidays like Halloween, Thanksgiving, Christmas and New Years, or simply to satisfy the need to hear the sound of gunfire. In towns and cities throughout the country the stroke of midnight on the aforementioned holidays sounded like a battlefield with all manner of weapons being fired. On this occasion Bobby and I stepped outside with my 32 caliber automatic. Following four quick shots skyward we returned to the apartment. The following day I noticed that the phone wasn't working and called the phone company repairman. Checking the wires out back he soon returned to the apartment and checked my phone. It was now working. "What did you do? "Well I replaced the phone wire because there was a hole right through the center of if it." He said. Cousin Bobby looked at me and started smiling. Giving Bobby a hard look, I asked the repairman what could have caused such a hole in the phone line. "Seemed to be a bullet, you wouldn't know anything about that would you?" He said with a knowing smirk. "It was New Year's; there were a lot of crazy people out shooting last night." I said as Bobby struggled to keep from busting out laffing as the repairman walked away. Having spent much time alone sometimes it was kinda nice to have family around, but not the drama. Bobby lasted most of the year and enjoyed several trips with the travel club. But early during the 2nd semester I began noticing money and other valuables missing from the apartment. The absolute last straw was the day he walked into the neighbors fenced back yard and started picking fruit from their tree. I told him to stop and get out of that yard; Bobby looked at me and smiled and continued stealing fruit. Such a bold act, maybe he was tired of my rules missed his family and wanted to go home. Accommodating, I called Cousin Vera that very night and the next day Cousin Bobby was on the Greyhound Bus headed back to Bakersfield.

Reflecting on his life more than forty years later; Bobby said to me that I lied to his mother when I told her that he was stealing fruit from the neighbor's back yard. Looking directly at me he said I lied when we both knew he was lying. How, why does a person do that? I could have reminded Bobby of his life following the fruit stealing incident. He is a felon, in and out of jails and prisons for theft, drugs and other crimes; but I did not. I could have mentioned to him that I was prepared to finance his college education following graduation from Drummond, I did not. Maybe Bobby's flashes of anger paints a clearer picture. On two occasions when I was wearing a Pepperdine Alumni shirt he commented; "Why you always wearing that ugly shirt?" Possibly his anger comes from knowing his life may have been very different if he had remained at Drummond. Unfortunately, I do suspect that the deck may already have been stacked against teen aged cousin Bobby. Some argue that educational training should begin before age two while others say it should begin while the child is in the womb. Needless to say Bobby missed all of that. Bobby's table was already set, the pattern established by the time he got to Drummond. Helplessly, I could only watch him follow his environmental educational pattern. Returning to Bakersfield Bobby never finished high school. Somehow he managed an admission to California State University at Bakersfield. Character unchanged, he applied for and got student loans, spent the money and never attended classes or repaid the loans. Having lived through and knowing his past; at family gatherings family members listen to Bobby who with a catch in his voice, a shining tear in one eye tell made up stories suggesting that he actually attended college. He goes on to say that he had a 4.0 GPA and that he actually graduated. What a character! Marriage too was just another Bobby life scam. By chance chatting with one of his former wives in the grocery store line, I asked how the divorce worked out. She said that Bobby told her he didn't get a divorce the last time he was married and that there was no need to waste the money. "No one checks such things." He told her. Truly, 'the proof is in the pudding'. But before the future Bobby events, there in Canada he was just another one of several black kids. Far away from home, he too wondered, "Where are the black people?" Little did they know that literally, relief lurked just around the next corner?

The Lone Canadian Black Man: Early one afternoon the issue came to a head as we left Stanley Park and drove through a suburban Vancouver, British Columbia neighborhood. In a caravan, the black kids were riding in two lead vehicles. Suddenly the first car stopped and we did the same. For no apparent reason; flinging open the doors they jumped out of the first two cars, ran across a busy street and into the yard of a man watering his front lawn. Watching from our parked cars in front of the house we witnessed an incredible sight, the kids were talking to and hugging the man.

He dropped his still running water hose as the greetings continued with handshakes and introductions. A bit taken aback, who wouldn't be; but the 'brotha' was a trooper; he smiled and responded to the kids' excited chatter. Soon several of us were standing on the sidewalk watching. They told him that they were from California visiting British Columbia with their high school travel club. "How long have you lived here? Do you have kids? Are there other black people living here?" Typically those were the questions asked by the kids. Finally with big smiles and final goodbye hugs the kids returned to the cars. Without to much detail I tried to explain to the 'brotha' that "The kids live in black neighborhoods in California and haven't seen another black person, other than myself for the last four days. They insisted on stopping and talking to you because they were so happy to see yours or any black face." I later wondered whether he understood or even listened to my explanation of the students' behavior, or did he just shake my hand and smile to get our group of California crazy people off his lawn. Barely noted by the teachers and kids but he too became a part of the Travel Club experience for children outside the neighborhoods, city, state and country for the first time in their lives.

The Canadian trip was the ice breaker; figuratively and literally. Having left sunny California a few days before Easter, it never crossed our minds that our Northern British Columbia Campground would be covered with two feet of snow. After all the careful planning and preparation, somehow we all forgot to check and/or anticipate the weather in Northern British Columbia. Reckon those campgrounds in that part of British Columbia was cheaper for a reason. Somehow we managed; sleeping in cars and building huge campfires the kids adapted to the cold and enjoyed playing in the snow; many seeing it for the first time. There too were other snow issues. Being Californians none of the drivers had any experience driving in snow, so not surprisingly two of our cars, including my own, got stuck. At a loss; pushing and pulling nothing seemed to work until Dieter, our German Exchange student suggested that we put blankets under the back tires for traction. Germans know snow, it worked! Other outstanding travel adventures followed, some as memorably humorous as the Lone Canadian Black Man incident. Local colleges and universities and San Simeon's Hearst Castle were included in our travels. Hearst Castle was especially memorable not for the numerous animals and artifacts but for the guards. Ignoring the other (white) tour groups; furtively staring at the black kids they paced back and forth nervously past them time after time; especially when we were in the room with the gold art work on the walls. One of the parent chaperones mentioned that racism too; a part of the American travel experience; was alive and well, thankfully the kids didn't notice. Griffith Park in Los Angeles, Venice and Venice Beach, Baja California and many other notable destinations were a part of the Travel Club experience.

Stanley Park, Vancouver, British Columbia CANADA

We may have even ruffled some presidential feathers on one of our trips to Los Angeles and the southland.

Nixon Turf: When on our trips if the drivers and chaperones had friends or family along the route they were visited by 20 or more members of the travel club. We would spend a night in their homes when convenient. On the 600 mile trip to Ensenada we stopped for an overnighter at my friends Charles and Rosie's home. Nineteen mostly white kids and chaperones was quite a shock for the neighborhood and their five year old son Junior. The two bedroom house in South Central Los Angeles had sleeping bags in the living room, kitchen, laundry room, and hallways. After breakfast the following morning neighbors stood outside watching as we waved goodbye to Charles, Rosie and Junior. For most of the travel club kids it was more black people than they had ever seen and for the neighbors, it was more white people than they had ever seen in that neighborhood. All became part of travel club lore as we rolled toward the Mexican border.

Continuing south toward Ensenada Mexico on the Baja Peninsula we passed through San Clemente, the location of President Nixon's West Coast residence just off I-5. Those were the days when the exclusively white press, there were no black or Latino reporters; never mentioned police hostility and overreaction to people of color. We stopped to gas up at a Chevron Station just off the interstate in San Clemente. Suddenly we were surrounded at the pump by four hulking Black Crown Victoria unmarked cop cars with dark tinted windows. They sat engines idling watching while we gassed up. Then one after the other they pulled out following us onto the freeway. With one car behind, one in front and on each side they traveled with us to the San Clemente city limits. In later discussions with our students about the San Simeon and San Clemente police reactions to their presence; they were not surprised and thought us very naïve and unused to police realities. As a parent looking back to that time; there is no way in hell I would have let my children be exposed to so many uncertainties traveling thousands of miles inside and outside the country with a bunch of teachers. However, only a few years older than the students ourselves, somehow we managed to effectively deal with several unanticipated situations.

Run for your life: During our trip planning we always assumed that we had covered the basics, food, gas and lodging. Although traveling great distances; foolishly, important things like latitudes, longitudes and the weather we never considered. Weather played a major part in our Canada trip and our Ensenada trip as well. It never crossed our minds, mainly because we knew there was no hurricane season in California; we never considered Baja California☺

But our very first night in our Ensenada, Baja California beachside cabins a major storm blew in as did the tide. We spent the night on our bunk beds looking down at the foot deep water covering the cabin floors. The following bright sun lightened morning the tide receded and we could see the brown, now squishy dirt floors. Also attractively visible was the waterless bottom of the slightly down sloping ocean floor out to nearly a mile from shore. Having never seen the tide out so far and thinking; "How many chances will I have to run on the bottom of the ocean in this life?" I grabbed my running shoes; three of the students decided to join me for that morning run. The ocean bottom was flat downhill and clear; so in no time at all we were looking back at the cabins and the shoreline in the distance. While so doing, that is looking back, I just happened to glance to our right and left sides and got the scare of a lifetime. Inexplicably, I could now see the tide with splashing whitecaps moving back toward shore and quickly closing in on both sides. "What the hell, we were nearly a mile out on the ocean floor!" Not much of a swimmer myself, I also knew that two of the kids couldn't swim at all. Starting a slow jog toward the cabins I explained the visibly growing crisis. "We are quite a ways out and the tide is coming in on both sides of us. We gotta run fast enough to reach the cabins ahead of the tide or be trapped out here in the ocean." Before I could finish my explanation the kids were well ahead of me making a wild uphill dash for the shoreline and the cabins. With the ocean lapping at our heels and closing, that was without question the fastest and most desperate mile any of us had ever run.. Remembering Moses and feeling just a hint of the story about the parting of The Red Sea; its closing and drowning Pharaohs' Army added biblical proportions to our panic and fear. Just seconds after clambering up on the beach the two sides of the ocean did close up on the middle where we had been running with a splash as we lay panting on the sand. "Were you scared Mr. Williams" Oscar, out of breath and breathing hard asked. "Hell yes, but I still couldn't keep up with you Oscar!" The smiles of relief were welcome as we ended a frightening and unexpected travel club experience. Knowing it's a part of the process, parents trusting their kids to teachers, schools and other responsible agencies, still I am certain my life would have been very different had I lost one of those children. But then too they were receiving an education typically not found in schools that would carry them for the rest of their lives .God was with us.

USA Rules: Traveling around the western states and other areas we never ceased being very surprised and uncomfortable with our students' lack of geographic knowledge. They all knew they lived in California, but disregarding other important factors; they didn't know what it meant. The kids didn't know that California was one of several states joined together to make what we call a country or nation; The United States of America.

Ensenada Mexico

Most had no conception of statehood or nationhood. Back on campus, one day while walking across the wide section of blacktop in the quad area I was struck by a grand epiphany, and the very next day began implementation. Listening to their complaints about having done the very same assignment in elementary school; I had every student in all four classes; about 120 kids, using the wall map as a guide draw pictures of the United States Map. The maps were to include each state and its' capital city. All of the students were given credit for completion of the assignment, but Marcelino's map, by far was the best of the bunch. Talking to him after class I showed him the quad area and asked if he could draw his map on a scale to cover it. "Absolutely!" was Marcelino's response, so the project was on. I figured if all the students at the school walked across those states and capitals painted on the quad area several times a day changing classes; they couldn't help but notice and develop a basic knowledge of the states, their locations, shapes and sizes. They would also develop knowledge of the general makeup and shape of the United States as well. So that was the general plan. For the remainder of the semester during American History class; using paint, brushes and other materials borrowed from the custodian; Marcelino worked on the US map in the quad. Upon completion of the project, like the true artist he signed at the bottom of his map. For his outstanding work inside and outside of the classroom Marcelino got several free lunches and an A+ in history. Many years later I happened to be visiting the newly remodeled school and noticed after thousands of footsteps across the quad area, Marcelino's US map remained, looking as good as the day he finished it. The drawing foreclosed one problem, but there was at least one other major personal issue to be dealt with.

Learning NOT to carry: Returning for a visit from the north to Southern California, rolling along the familiar streets of Los Angeles had brought back memories of me as a different person in my recent past. Using a variety of excuses including, maybe it was just the folk I hung around with; because much like them my gun was always with me. It was such a common thing that all of my jeans had the design of a 32 automatic pistol worn through the fabric of my right back pocket. Much like my compatriots and the millions of others in the various hoods; of course I had no legal permit to carry a gun. However, I did keep enough charge space on my Master Card for bail if needed. Living in that city, in Los Angeles; I knew with utmost certainty that the folk with whom I interacted, even in the most innocent circumstance were strapped. So, for my own safety and well being I thought it necessary to be strapped at all times as well. But my time in Los Angeles soon ended and I found myself in places where a gun may have been an encumbrance. Generally, teaching was a profession where armaments were unnecessary. Explaining an assignment to one of my students; "Now do you see how it works?"

I asked and stood to move on to the next student needing help. Pointing to the seat I'd just vacated, Kasim said; "Is that your gun Mr. Williams?" My 32 automatic slipped out my pocket and was lying on the seat in my high school classroom. Realizing the seriousness of the situation I thought, "Don't panic, and handle this." Casually, lifting the gun from the chair and putting it into my front pocket, I said to Kasim; "Thanks, It's my starters' pistol that I use coaching track." Busy, heads down working on the assignment other students didn't seem to notice; and Kasim, a sprinter on the 4X100 Relay Team took me at my word. Whew! That was kinda uncomfortable, but the future held other uncomfortable occasions.

Cal Berkeley: Teachers with the most graduate level earned college credits/units made more money than those with fewer units. Consequently, during the summer months many of us took classes at the local colleges and universities to earn extra units which would translate into higher pay at the start of the school year in the fall. On the very first day of my summer class at Cal (University of California Berkeley) I couldn't find a parking space, so I the only person of color in the class was late, CPT (Colored People's Time?). Walking into the classroom of 60 or more teachers enrolled as students; a tall 20 something young white instructor with a bushy white guy afro gave me 'the look'. Recognizable was that very same look that I had given so many times to students who came into my classes late. Hurriedly finding a seat the quiet was shattered by the sound of the 32 automatic falling from my shoulder holster and landing on the highly polished tile floor. Sitting about five rows back, I watched helplessly as the gun slid silently towards the front of the classroom. The instructors gaze too was fixed on the small pistol now moving toward him. All listening in the poignant silence, the other students stared as the gun coasted to a stop, just inches below the teachers' desk. Raising a quizzical gaze he observed as I stood, walked to the front of the room, picked up the pistol put it in my shoulder holster and returned to my seat. Nervously, I sat waiting for some reaction or comment; like maybe a question from the instructor or even a fellow student; "What the hell are you doing with a gun in class?" But not a word was spoken or questions asked, nada, nothing. I heard nothing at the time of the incident or later. Although I had prepared for their reactions with a bogus explanation; after several weeks there was no mention of the incident. I just wrote it off as some people being very strange. Of course that strangeness didn't include me, the guy with a gun in a college classroom. So, oblivious to other realities; life continued in that vein as I moved on to the new school year at Drummond High School.

Apartment Living: That continuing life was one of a single young black male living in a small Northern California town.

32 Caliber Automatic

Comfortable in my studio apartment; this was the first time I had permanently lived outside of Los Angeles County since moving to California more than five years before. My apartment was located a short walkway and two steps down the left side, below a duplex facing Capitol Street. Quiet in the back where a long shaded alley led to the neighboring grocery four blocks away; it worked well for me. Not owning a car with the basketball court and new job also in walking distance was another positive. Blankets and an open sleeping bag on the floor; what did I know of or care about extra comfort, it all seemed good and right. Right until the day I arrived home to find my front door wide open. The cops came after I reported the break in and asked what was missing. A very hard question; I couldn't answer, having so few things I really didn't know what or if anything was missing. No luck for that burglar in my place, he didn't even take the TV. At one time I forgot and left it on top of the heater and a large hole was melted into the bottom. It looked ugly but still worked. After the initial shock and surprise having lost nothing, with nothing to lose; I soon mentally moved on forgetting the intrusion. Living just north of San Francisco I maintained several old Teacher Corps contacts. Anne Marie and I got together on occasion at my apartment and at her commune in San Francisco. I may have mentioned this before but the weirdest thing; when I wanted to see Anne Marie and thought about her, within a day or so she would show up unannounced at the apartment. It seemed to work both ways, when she wanted to see me inexplicably I would find myself on a bus heading for her place in San Francisco. Although we enjoyed each other, she made it clear that the relationship wasn't going beyond the good sex. Cool with that; I also happened to meet Bernice at work. She was a recently hired black woman who worked as a Speech Therapist for the school district. Bernice was a good looking sista with a short afro, nice legs and body. Those years during college and teacher training, the women encountered were all white with a rare Latina. So Bernice at Drummond was a unique experience that I especially looked forward to. Although Bernice was fine, there was reason for concern; she was also a Seven Day Adventist. But I found out about her Adventism afterward. At first I just thought her very religious before deciding those Adventist folk were kinda crazy. Seeing those tits and beautiful legs while ignoring the hints from Bernice, only later would I discover the depths of her fanaticism.

Bernice, Bernice: But before those discoveries, an intense mutual attraction was on. She would catch me staring at her as she walked past my classroom and always gave me a welcoming smile. Young and foolish, I was certain that if I could make a woman smile I could easily convince her to have sex with me. Yup, that had worked so many times I thought it foolproof. Sure maybe they had other reasons but on numerous occasions; first came the smile later the sex.

Anyway, I talked to Bernice for several weeks; minimizing her religious misgivings before convincing her to come to my place for dinner. "You should only have sex with the person you marry." Bernice had told me this on several occasions when sex was mentioned, .but dinner at my house was on! Unable to hide that shapely body, wearing a knee length black skirt with a sleeveless black top, the woman looked good. We sat on the floor eating filet mignon and sharing a bottle of zinfandel. Leaning over to kiss her after clinking glasses; there was no stopping. Soon we were clawing at each other as we discarded clothing. While undressing I did notice that Bernice's cute afro that I so admired was actually a wig as she took it off and placed it beside the sleeping bag. Hmmmmmmmmmmm; that could have been a turn off for some folk but it was not for the wild man. Moving on those perfectly robust brown breasts, tongue encircling the firm dark nipples, we both moaned. Bernice spent the night and suddenly we were and item around the school. Thinking that we just had very enjoyable sex I continued living my life as before; so I was surprised to hear that Bernice was telling folks that I was her man. I liked being with her but she seemed a little to religious and old school for any long term relationship. Thinking back to what she said about only having sex with the person you are going to marry I got a little nervous, did she think I was going to marry her? Having made no marriage guarantee, that certainly wasn't my belief. Besides I had seen that Bernice wasn't a virgin, she had been with men before and didn't marry them. Is that a male chauvinist point of view? Maybe, but it was truth. Well things came to an explosive head one evening when Bernice showed up unexpected and unannounced at my apartment. Maybe I shouldn't have been surprised, I hadn't seen Bernice in more than two weeks, it was a Friday night, the lights were on and Cream was blowing "…in the white room with black curtains…"Bernice must have known I was inside and not alone. There were reasons other than Bernice's religious quirks that I chose to continue living my life as before. There was Anne Marie. I saw no reason why I couldn't have them both, Anne Marie didn't mind but I was certain that Bernice wouldn't go for that. Naked making love in the apartment; Anne Marie was surprised as was I; when we heard a forceful knock on the front door. Ignoring the knocking until it stopped, we continued having sex. But then it resumed; except now there was banging and kicking the door. Peering through the peephole I saw the tightly closed tearful eyes, and the frowning angry face of Bernice. Black boots, pounding and kicking hard she was very noisy; the pounding and kicking must have hurt her hands and feet. Not knowing whether the crazy woman was armed or what else she might do I picked up my 32 automatic as Anne Marie and I moved from the bedroom and huddled naked in the kitchen, waiting. A scary thought, would I have to shoot her, I didn't know. Guess that would depend on how crazy she got and whether she had a weapon, which she didn't seem to have. Looking at her face, if Bernice had a weapon she certainly would have used it.

I wondered when she would go away; it seemed Bernice had been pounding there forever. She didn't go away; after more than a half hour of pounding things got even nuttier. Wondering what the upstairs neighbor must be thinking and hoping she wouldn't call the cops; I noticed that Bernice had moved to the front window. Anne Marie and I still unclothed, peering around the refrigerator by the kitchen door, watched Bernice sitting in the dirt below the window crying as she started scraping and pounding on the glass. Something had to give, hopefully not the window. Breathing sighs of relief we watched Bernice, head down tears flowing with dirt streaks on her pants and sweater; stand and walk slowly toward the street and her car. Some would have freaked at so much drama, but Anne Marie was cool and we soon got back to our activities. A few days later I saw Bernice at work and she walked right past me, said hello with a smile, as if nothing had happened. Thereafter she treated me as any other stranger working at the school. Regardless of Bernice's coolness toward me, life continued at the apartment. Walking by the upstairs neighbor's apartment one afternoon she called me aside. I thought she was about to confront me about the Bernice incident but she did not. Sitting on the large shaded Victorian porch with a ½ gallon of rum and two large colas; Mindi, a pale, thin, balding forty something black woman; wearing a loose fitting satin robe and showing a lot of leg; introduced herself and invited me to sit. Declining the offered drink I sat listening as she told me about her life. Chain smoking from a pack of Salem's as she talked, Mindi spoke of her recent lung cancer diagnosis and life without a man around. Recently divorced she said her former husband Harry "...was fucking everyone in town but me..."; Yeah, much too much information. Getting a feel for where the one sided conversation was headed, I put some thought into a tactful exit. Mindi seemed to be a nice person but she was sick and very old, my God she was over forty. In my mid twenties, just the thought of dating someone so old was incomprehensible. Knowing she was home during the Bernice craziness; Anne Marie and I heard her clumping about upstairs, but not once did MIndi mention the incident. After courteously listening for a reasonable time I made my excuses and left. Reckon her come-on was just a part of apartment living. She never approached me again so I assumed she knew I didn't want what she had to offer. Life goes on and not surprisingly there were other issues. About midnight one Saturday night, I was awakened by pounding on my front door. Groggy, half asleep and hoping not Bernice again, I heard excited male voices outside. "Is Tyler in there?" The shortest of the three scruffy fellows peering through my screen asked. "No, I don't know a Tyler." "He ran down this alley!" Shorty said, and snatched my latched screen door. When he grabbed my screen door and tried to come into my apartment; I knew things were about to get out of hand. Silently, from behind my leg I casually raised my right hand holding the cocked, one in the chamber, and safety off, 32 automatic.

Not pointing directly at the three intruders I held the 32 at chest level. Did they see the weapon? I'll never know. Would I have used it, absolutely; I had already planned the shot pattern to take out the three of them quickly if they tried to force entry. Were they undercover cops or drug dealers, I wondered? In retrospect, my thinking leans more toward undercover cops, even though they looked and moved like meth heads. "Let's check the alley." The leader of the group said as they turned away from my door and ran down the walkway towards the back of the building. And so it was on Drummond's Florida Street at years end.

Marriage # 2

Wedding & Things: The new school year would be quite different. Finding the love of my life at the workplace, no it wasn't Bernice; would add some semblance of stability. There were two very attractive women working at Drummond; one was married and Barbara, the brighter of the two. Not that looks was paramount, but she was quite fine and unmarried. A slight problem was her friend Jerry. They spent much of their off time together attending plays, movies and other functions. So it was a pleasant surprise to discover that their association was strictly as friends, I had to ask. Much later it came to light that Jerry was no competition at all. We were invited to a party at Jerry and Thomas's new house. Jerry's sister Maddy just happened to mention that "If Jerry and Thomas truly love each other they should stop fighting all the time." As Barbara looked at each other, odd occurrences and questionable events from past association with Jerry began to fall into place. Remembering that first year at Drummond when he invited speakers from Berkeley's Gay Alliance to his classes; we thought his choice of speakers not wise for the school. But since Jerry was a friend we both decided to accept his invitation and bring our classes to hear the speakers. In dress and expression the speakers were bold, graphic and a little much for conservative suburban Drummond High School. Reactions to descriptions of sexual orifices used were met by a shocked pin drop silence. The following student discussions after we returned to our classrooms were unsympathetically harsh. Our students now wondered about him but still, it never crossed our minds that Jerry was gay. On another occasion Jerry invited a girlfriend, Temnee along on one of our travel club trips. I happened to see her/him flat chested wearing a lop sided wig near the women's bathroom one morning and thought; "She sure looks like a dude."Regardless, we were pleased to see that Jerry, Thomas and sister Maddy were all happy and good friends; more power to them.

So before the events happening at Jerry and Thomas's new house Barbara and I were all set. Spending much time together and liking it, we decided to share her apartment on Capitol street downtown Drummond.

Unmarried, at the time it was pretty revolutionary; especially for two teachers, one black and the other white working at the same school. Needless to say blacks were still being lynched in the south for even speaking to white women. This was especially shocking to Barbara's parents. They immediately sold their Drummond house moved away and refused to speak to Barbara for the next twelve years. Her father was apoplectic and just couldn't understand why his one child would choose to bring such embarrassment to his family. Barbara was also a few months pregnant and beginning to show, about to add a child to her daddy's racist drama. A son due in December, in November we decided to slip off to nearby Reno and tie the knot. But first I had to divorce my first wife, also named Barbara who I had been separated from for more than three years. Three hundred dollars to a local law firm and it was done, I was a free man, for a minute. We drove to Reno one Saturday morning got married and was back home the same afternoon. Expecting a child and married to a Black man, luckily Barbara wasn't completely isolated from her family; her Aunt Jelsie, Uncle Frank and many cousins filled the void left by her fleeing parents. The following year, with the wife, a child just learning to walk and a family friend from Rhode Island; we decided to drive to the east coast during summer vacation. The plan was to travel from California to Oregon, Washington and into Canada at British Columbia. From there we drove across the continent from west to east on Canadian Highway 1. Reentering the USA near Niagara Falls we planned to hang with friends in New Jersey for a while. On our return trip we would travel east to west within the United States on Highway 80. Finished with our teaching activities by the end of May we packed the red Toyota Land Cruiser's roof racks and gas cans with all the traveling and camping necessities. Very stoked and looking forward, so began our first great family adventure.

The Final Carry: Driving and camping through Northern California, Oregon and Washington we covered much of the same territory and used some of the same camp sites used during the days of The Travel Club. Excitedly rolling slowly towards the Canadian border crossing, we were up for some serious driving on Canadian Highway 1. The border guard asked the usual questions regarding fruits and vegetables and whether we were carrying firearms. "Yes I carry a small pistol in the glove compartment when I travel." I responded. The fellow suddenly got crazy. Pressing a button on his booth intercom he was quickly joined by other border guards as he yelled, "Get out of the vehicle!" Looking at him s if he was nuts I said, "Relax buddy I am getting out." Weapon in hand, "Open the glove box!" was his next command. Standing at my left shoulder; close enough for me to feel the spittle, he yelled, "Step back!" as I unlocked the glove compartment. Reholstering his weapon, with my small pistol in hand; leaving the wife son and Julie in the vehicle, I was escorted to an inner office and asked the usual questions.

Big Red

Following the interrogation the fellow calmed down and was helpful. He directed me to a gun shop on the US side of the border where for a small fee I could mail the pistol to our home address. Mailing done, the border guards welcomed us to Canada and wished us a safe trip. Traveling across the continent on Canadian Highway 1 and interacting with Canadians was an enlightening experience. Overall they seemed comfortable with the idea of Black folk. One Canadian service station attendant in the town of Moose Jaw, what a fantastic name; it sounds so pioneering and roughhouse western. So the attendant, unasked clarified the racial situation in Canada for us. "Black people are OK but those dam Indians are a real problem." Not pausing or asking for an explanation, I gassed up and drove. Later we discussed whether the guy meant Native Americans or South Asians when he spoke of Indians. If I had happened to have been Native American or South Asian, would he have told me that Native Americans or South Asians are OK but it's those dam Black people he can't stand? Regardless of meaning or group intended, I suppose it is still racism. Moving on to the Canadian campground just off Highway 1 we couldn't help but notice the seriousness of the signs warning about bears. You couldn't miss the note just below the "Beware" part of the sign saying, "Yes there really are bears and they are dangerous!" Weaponless after the border stop we were believers and that night the four of us crowded inside and slept in Big Red.

Rolling from **British Columbia** through towns in neighboring **Alberta** Barbara and Julie talked me out of driving a few miles north and searching for the stadium headquarters of my favorite Canadian Football League team, The Edmonton Eskimos. With few differences we found that travel across Canada was much like travel across the United States. There were few border markers, and wandering from Canada to the US and US to Canada was completely unregulated. Many of the border residents never seemed to have considered which side they lived on But on the Canadian side with the unusual town names, a very Wild West kind of feeling prevailed, even in the major cities. Regina, the capital of **Saskatchewan** was our next stop as we continued rolling east. The intertwined histories of both Canada and the United States came to mind as we traveled; seeing the names of cities change from English to French and Native American. The French and Indian Wars, The United States War of Independence; final stops on the Underground Railroad and all of those shared histories were reflected in the names and faces of the people we met in those Canadian towns and cities. From Saskatchewan the sun was still high so we kept on rolling through the city of Winnipeg in neighboring **Manitoba** province. Routinely driving from morning until night with short stops for lunch, using the daylight; we kept on to **Ontario**. As we drove into Ontario province there was a town sitting high atop Lake Superior with a name so impressive we had to stop.

Canada oh Canada

Moose Jaw

Thunder Bay: Truly seemed the perfect enhancement of the true look and feel of Canada. Pulling into the campsite while the sun was still very high in the sky, we wondered why there were no people about and the other camper tents and vehicles were tightly closed. Strange; even the campsite store was closed, all seemed to have gone to bed. Finally spotting a fellow standing outside of his trailer taking a smoke I asked, "Where is everyone?" "Asleep, it's past 11 PM you know." I didn't know, and then it hit me, that was why the place looked like a ghost town. Having never been so far north we couldn't imagine bright sunshine at eleven o'clock at night. Sleep time had always been a part of darkness. We had never slept while the sun was so high in the sky before that Thunder Bay experience. In the morning sunshine we continued our trek eastward. From earliest memory, having listened to stories and myths, and seen numerous pictures of them we now headed for Niagara Falls. Finally, after rolling in Big Red for more than 3500 miles from Drummond and across a continent, we paused for pictures on the Canadian side of Niagara Falls before reentry at New York. Dropping Julie off at the train station for her trip home to Rhode Island; we found Jean Long's apartment. Jean had been one of the younger teachers starting with us during our first year at Drummond. Her husband applied and was admitted to graduate school at Columbia so they moved to New Jersey where she was now substituting.

East Coast B-Ball: During the week or so we were there, husband Sean took me to the basketball courts. Listening to Sean's warnings about East Coast basketball being so much better; I found it Interesting but not so different. Yeah, east coast basketball seemed pretty much like basketball any other place; you had to score to win. Playing several games on New Jersey and New York basketball courts I noticed there wasn't much inside play, most seemed to rely on their outside shots. Usually if my game was on; when I couldn't score inside popping from outside was OK with me. Work or play most of us just do what we do without much self consideration or notice. But sometimes you can't help seeing others giving you 'that look'. Looks like, "That fellow doesn't miss…Did he really shoot from that distance?" Sean was surprised and impressed to have me on his team as was his friends, we won. We also spent time with the wives visiting the Statue of Liberty, Harlem, Times Square, Central Park and the Museum of Modern Art. Being a tourist was almost as exhausting as basketball. It was interesting seeing Jean; a California girl and Sean; a New York boy, comfortable in their routines and adjusted to their new surrounding in the "Big East' New York City. Although Sean reminded me often that he was not a child of New York City but a Jersey boy. All the same to me neither was a Cali man☺ It was our first long trip and vacation as a family and we enjoyed out time on the east coast. Too soon it was time to prepare for the return trip home to Cali.

Taking Sean and Jean out for a celebratory dinner on our last night we thanked them for their hospitality and began planning the long return trip.

80 West: Although still feeling a bit uncomfortable without a weapon I decided the Canadian Border stop was the end of my weapon carrying days. Yes it was time to stop carrying guns or any other weapon on my person or in my vehicles. A respectable husband and father no longer living in Los Angeles and hanging with those gun toting LA road dogs; finally I should seek a simpler safer life. Easily thought and said, but learning not to carry was a hard, hard task. Traveling more than 6,000 miles across the continent and back with a wife and child was a scary thing. In Canada, the northernmost Underground Railroad stop for those blacks escaping from slavery in the United States I felt I could relax more in that country. But having to make the return trip inside my homeland, the good old USA; the country Blacks were running from at the time of the Underground Railroad caused some concern; especially riding with my child and not one but two white women. Camping and passing through the various states on the return trip along Highway 80 West we hardly noticed reactions because we only stopped during the daylight hours for gas and to change drivers. Leaving New Jersey; compared to the west coast, the states seemed so much closer together. New Jersey, Pennsylvania, Ohio, Indiana, Illinois, and through the farmlands of Iowa and Nebraska; was a blur of humming tires on long tractor trailer truck filled highways. The gas stations were truck stops so there too we were jockeying for position to fill up the tank just like on Highway 80. Crossing into Wyoming brought that certain USA western feel that we missed while on the east coast. California and home was in striking distance. Utah and the Great Salt Lake soon passed and we entered Nevada. Nevada in the AM surely meant home by the PM. Sure enough by early evening we pulled into the driveway at home on Hermosa Street. Amazing summer adventures but thank God it was over and we were home in Cali, home sweet! There had been no incidents, because Highway 80 runs north of the southern states. It also helped that we drove practically non-stop on the return. Traveling for weeks without a weapon with a family to protect was hard on a brotha , but we adapted. Finding an old tire wrench I kept it close at hand, although it was not a reasonable substitute for the 32 automatic. Following such an amazing continental excursion we were happy to be home, but as the beginning of the new school year approached we thought that maybe our east coast Canadian adventure ended much too soon. That being neither here nor there; Drummond was ready for the new school year.

Coaching: One of the major Drummond teaching job attractions was the addition of the Drummond High Varsity Basketball coaching position. Before signing the teaching contract the superintendent promised me that the coach was retiring and the coaching job was mine.

Niagara Falls

Taking him at his word I signed the contract; but to my surprise at the start of basketball season coach Fred Farson did not retire. Four years later when I moved to a teaching position in another district Fred Farson was still coaching with no intention of retiring. So to make up for the superintendents lie I was assigned several other coaching positions including; Junior Varsity Basketball Coach, Assistant Track Coach and Cross Country Coach.

A sprinter and miler when in high school and still running distance and playing semi-professional basketball, coaching was just another workout and fun; besides the extra pay was kinda nice too. Most interesting was the differences in the kids I coached. Typically at Drummond like most high schools at the time and today (2017); AP (Advance Placement) and college prep classes were small with mostly white teachers and students. Black kids were scattered throughout the school in lower level and special education classes. My Cross Country team was all white AP kids with one Latino and my JV Basketball team was all Black. I did training runs with the cross country team during practices and training runs with the basketball team as well. Of course I also played basketball with the junior varsity basketball team during practices. Finishing ahead of most of the basketball team runners during practices was acceptable because I was a runner, but coming in ahead of most of the runners on my cross country team was not acceptable, to me. Not necessarily that bright but somehow all members of the cross country team were enrolled in AP classes. And they weren't the least embarrassed letting and older fellow like me beat them, even when I yelled at them for their lack of effort. Speaking for the slackers, Everett who was most often the last runner in said; "Ah coach it ain't no big deal." Most of the other runners agreed with Everett. No one responded or even listened when I asked; "How the hell can you win if you don't mind losing, aren't you embarrassed?" Six losses into the season Ruthie, one of the cheerleaders called me aside and filled me in. She said cross country was one of those sports where students were only on the team to get an easy varsity letter. Wearing that varsity letterman's jacket looks good in the yearbook, she said. Working with the black basketball team, no pun intended, was like night and day. Their competiveness, work ethic and caring for their sport was reflected in hard practices and an undefeated season. In a scrimmage with the varsity team my JV's lost by one point. That loss was questionable since the scorekeeper was a varsity cheerleader. Those kids were the real deal, completely opposite in attitude and play when compared to my cross country team. After another loss to neighboring Morris High School, I said to the team; "You guys are so bad my JV Basketball team could beat you any day at your own sport on your own course!" All upper classmen, mostly seniors; I thought that might get a rise out of them since all the JV Basketball players were lowly freshmen with a couple of sophomores.

In the disinterested silence I told them that I was going to set up a joint practice. The basketball players were going to run against the cross country team. Was this going to be a black white thing? Well, yeah; the basketball players were all black and the cross country runners with the exception of Fortunato were all white. But in my mind, although the black kids noticed, color was insignificant, this was about athletic competition. "Coach we'll kick those slow ass white boys asses." Ronnie Pratt said loud enough for the cross country runners to hear. Soon I was to learn that neither color nor athletic competition was important to my cross country runners. A look at the cross country team faces showed the same boredom, except for Fortunato's, he was ready to win. The ten JV basketball players were poised at the start of the race as if they were doing wind sprints in the gym instead of a 2 ½ mile cross country course. Wearing Converse low topped sneakers instead of running shoes, at the sound of my starters' gun they bolted down the trail. Harshly competitive, already they were elbowing and crowding each other at the forest entrance near the bottom of the hill. The cross country runners followed. The next time I saw the group they were coming out of the trees at the top of the hill, about a mile into the course. The captain of the basketball team, Trayvon Jones was leading the pack. Step for step right on his heels in a ragged line came eight other members of the basketball team. Fortunato, from the cross country team was in the 10th spot followed closely by Ronnie Pratt from the basketball team. More than a minute behind I watched the rest of the cross country team come slogging up the hill. Already they were beaten; those basketball players led by Trayvon were setting a blistering pace. Again coming out of the forest at the bottom of the hill with an unquestionable lead as he approached the end of the race one couldn't help but notice Trayvon's long loping stride. First to cross the finish line, he was barely sweating.

Although showing the strain on their faces, right on Trayvon's heels was the rest of the basketball team. They placed 2nd through 9 following Trayvon with Fortunato of the cross country team finishing 10th. Ronnie Pratt finishing 11th did "...Kick those slow ass white boys asses." Trayvon not only finished first but also set a new cross country course record time. Fortunato and I were pretty 113am impressed! "Coach can we get those guys to join the cross country team?" he asked. Later as we stood around waiting for the cross country team; "Is practice over coach?" Everett asked. Looking at those cross country faces, I canceled my closing speech, thanked the basketball players for their participation in my little experiment and sent everyone home. Cross country and basketball were both winter sports but I was certainly hoping to see those JV basketball players running distance for me during track season in the spring. Ronnie Pratt a sprinter had already told me he would be coming out for track in the spring.

Ronnie Pratt: Ronnie joined the track team in the spring as promised and was one of our quickest sprinters. He ran the 100m and 200m dash very fast. He had the speed, but there were a few minor glitches. Ronnie had been mainstreamed into regular classes from the Special Education Program. Ronnie was never a problem and unlike many of the students in his regular classes he did the work. However outside of the classroom special allowances and assistance was sometimes necessary, especially during track practice and meets. Surprised we noticed at the end of his 100 and 200 yard sprints Ronnie kept on running until someone caught up to him and told him to stop. That was difficult because Ronnie was so fast and few people could catch up to him. Consequently a faster sprinter had to be stationed at the end of Ronnie's events to catch him and tell him to stop if he wasn't flagged down at the end of the races. He finished first in most races, so few sprinters in the county were fast enough to catch him. Soon we found a simpler solution, by placing a team manager at the end of his races at home and away to stop him. The team manager was also used during track practice; problem solved☺ A couple of hours before track practice on a beautiful blue and gold sunlit afternoon; I was thinking of the great season we were having as I walked across Marcelino's map in the quad toward the main building. Just before reaching the tall steps surrounded by high bushes, I heard whimpering cries from the left side of the building. Odd at the time because all students were supposed to be in class; and even when changing classes the sides of the buildings were off limits. Stepping past the high bushes toward the noise; first I saw Annabelle. She was smart, athletic, vivacious and the more popular of the two black cheerleaders on the squad. Back pressed against the wall of the building, short cheerleader skirt above her navel, underwear down below her socks; Annabelle was crying as Ronnie pushed his body against her. Pants below his knees with a 45 pistol in his right hand, Ronnie was frantically humping Annabelle. Unarmed, foolishly I approached and said; "Ronnie what the hell are you doing?" Immediately stepping back, gun in one hand and grabbing at his pants with the other; "I'm sorry Mr. Williams, I'm sorry." Ronnie kept saying. Eyes on his right hand as I stepped closer and the crying Annabelle moving away from the wall pulling up her panties and straightening her clothes I said to Ronnie; "Give me that gun!" Raising his gun hand, the barrel was pointed at my stomach, I watched Ronnie's finger still on the trigger as he handed me the heavy weapon. Gun in hand; we attracted lots of attention walking past the open classroom doors to the main office. Annabelle stood quietly crying while I banged on the office door yelling for the school nurse. Standing on my opposite side in the hallway Ronnie waited while I explained to the nervous school nurse, who kept glancing at the 45 in my right hand; that we had an emergency and Annabelle needed to talk to her. Ronnie and I continued down the hall to the principals' office where I left him and the 45 to wait for the police. Discussing the situation with the wife, she told me what I already suspected.

She said that even though I knew him; it was foolish to approach Ronnie or any other student holding a loaded gun. That incident turned out to be just one of several leading to life altering decisions. Suddenly we were seeing the city of Drummond in a new light. Heretofore ignored, we were now discussing the community fights and drunken sailors prowling the streets on weekends. No longer the single adventurer who just a couple of years before had gleefully chosen this town, I was now a husband and father; suddenly seeing the city in a new light. Balancing work in the schools while considering the schools themselves as a place for our child in the future was now a serious consideration. We decided Drummond was not where we wanted to live and raise our child. Just like that, decision made; summer was a time for action on the decision.

Move, Not Easy: As parents most often do, we began looking at our entire lifestyle differently. Not only anticipating educational futures for our child, but practicalities such as no more drunken parties ending with several southern California friends passed out on the floor. Only two my son asked; "Pop, why are Guzzie and Frank asleep and smelling funny?" Further, Drummond was a military town with a large naval repair base and one couldn't miss seeing that' 'devil may care' attitude on the faces of servicemen downtown on Friday evenings. It was easy to recognize because just a few years earlier I had been in the Air Force and wherever stationed had that very same devil may care attitude. Yep, it was time to move. Barbara had family to the north in the town of Fieldsburg, so we both started looking for jobs in and around that city. I was the first to find a job at Renton Jr high in the town Fieldsburg. As the beginning of the new school year approached it looked as if Barbara would still be working at Drummond and I would be working in Fieldsburg. To shorten her commute we thought it wise to buy a house halfway between the two jobs. Both working full time with a house to sell, we were not poor, and assumed with no money issues; buying a house wouldn't be a problem. Summer vacation was upon us and it was time for some serious house hunting. The town of Sonoma sat halfway between Drummond and Fieldsburg . Hot, sweaty Sonoma during the summer was irritating and tiring but was the perfect location. We were in for a rude awakening. After visiting all of the five realty offices in town, every one found reason NOT to show us a house for sale. Saturdays and Sundays, their busiest days; white customers were in and out of the offices buying houses while we sat waiting. We had over $200,000 in cash from the house we had just sold plus other assets; but not one house was we shown. The next weekend we tried another town between the two cities, Petaluma with the same result. There again realtors found reasons not to show us houses for sale. The general comments were; I'm so sorry, we don't have anything." "We just sold that one."

This was being said as their co-workers unashamedly, practically trampling us; rushed white customers past and out the office door to look at and buy houses. Undaunted, we thought that areas around the nearby university Sonoma State might be different and more accepting of people of color. So we headed for the neighboring cities of Cotati and Rohnert Park. Well there the realtors were different; several wore tie-dye tops and head bands; but the language and the results were the same."We just don't have anything." We were told, even after we had driven around the neighborhoods and found for sale signs on several properties. Their stock response was. "Oh that house is in escrow, we just haven't had time to take down the for sale sign."Summer was ending and our house in Drummond had been sold and we were renting it from the new owners until we found a place. We realized that we might not find a house at all. The clock was ticking and not only did we have to find housing but also childcare for our two year old. Resigned to the fact that Barbara would have a long commute we started looking in Fieldsburg, where I would be working. Here again we drove the neighborhoods in areas that we liked and found houses listed for sale before going to see the listing realtors. Results were the same with a slight twist; in Fieldsburg there was a poor black community with run down houses, a ghetto. Sure, you may read about them and friends may remind you that there are anti discrimination laws and federal agencies where violations of those laws are reported. That's all well and good, but on the front lines are the realtors; the people selling houses who could care less. They know that most folk don't have the time and/or patience to deal with such an unfeeling government bureaucracy monitoring housing discrimination. The reporting process and adjudication could take years, meanwhile we, like most needed a house soon. After the fourth Fieldsburg realtor took us to that very same poor black community with cheap run down houses to show us a "…better…" neighborhood than the ones we had chosen I kind of lost it and told him, "Sir, we have money, we are not poor, and are sick and tired of you red neck racist realtors showing us the same shacks in that dam ghetto!" Reckon I took it out on him but deservedly so, after all the racist bullshit we were getting just trying to buy a house. White people are so twisted; refusing to hire, rent or sell to blacks in their comfortable suburban neighborhoods. Do they really believe blacks prefer living in ghettos? Lacking or diminished services, poor schools and unsafe streets; whites seem to assume that blacks want and love such communities. A word to the white unwise and others; blacks live in those neighborhoods because whites directly and indirectly force them to live there. Silently fuming with those thoughts and many more, the wife led me towards the door and out of that realtor's office before I really lost it. Later that very same day Barbara told her uncle and aunt about our growing housing crisis. It turned out that her uncle, an insurance salesman, happened to have a friend who was a realtor.

In no time at all Rosemarie found a great house in a neighborhood under construction just a few blocks form k-12 schools and Annadell State Park. Ours was the first house built and occupied in the neighborhood. Consequently, I gleefully stood out front watering our new lawn as prospective white buyers with looks of surprise and shock drove past checking out the remaining lots and new houses. It was all coming together; finding a babysitter for our young son was the final piece of the puzzle. A fellow teacher at my new school Renton Jr. High recommended Mrs. Ingalls who had babysat her kids when they were younger. A storehouse of community knowledge, Mrs. Ingalls our new babysitter also suggested a family doctor. September and the start of the new school year was suddenly upon us; luckily with the help of family and friends we were settled in our new home and ready. I was starting my new job at Renton Jr. High in Fieldsburg while still at Drummond; Barbara would be commuting in our other summer purchase, her new Porsche. After such a frantic summer things fell into place in our new town and I was now teaching at Renton Jr. High School. Major changes, but no real changes at all, teaching school was still teaching school.

Sitting in front of the principal's gigantic redwood desk, I listened as he went through the interview process. A process I'd gone through with his boss the district superintendent who had already hired me and assigned me to his school. But all powers must be assuaged. Principal Bardini discussed the physical aspects of the school as well as the teachers, other administrators and students. Like the superintendent he reiterated that this was "…a tough school…" Bardini was unaware of my prior briefing about him and other faculty and administrators at the school by one who wasn't introduced during orientation. On my earlier unofficial visit to the school I had called the one brother working there aside and introduced myself. Wise and watchful, Jim pleased to see me; first mentioned he and I would be the only black adults at the school. He also verified what I had suspected all along that "…tough school…" was simply white code meaning black kids attended the school. Thankful for Jim's information my meeting with the principal ended with a final handshake; and so began the new adventure. Regardless of color or economic circumstance; I say again, teaching school is teaching school. In new situations good teachers make the necessary adjustments on the fly, providing extra materials such as paper, pencils, books, food, clothing and other things on the QT; whatever is needed for student success. Those routine adjustments made, much like during the years of my college and university attendance, I made that other adjustment as well; to being the only black and person of color teaching at the school. Of course most humans never really notice their color unless someone else makes a point of directly or indirectly identifying imagined stereotypical differences; and acting on those perceptions.

To the students without differentiation; I was just another teacher with common teacher expectations. Renton was a country school, located on the side of town near farms and dairies. Sometimes students and visiting parents rode horses to school. Fresh from bay area cities I just thought so is life in the country, and rolled with it. What did I know, just the other day (2017) I saw a couple on horseback ride past my apartment. Students and parents at Renton were used to older teachers who had been at Renton for many years. Most would remain at Renton until death or retirement. Enrollment figures were constant so new teachers were a rarity; and as in most of California then and now (2017), a black one was/is a rarity indeed. Several of the middle aged teachers were former basketball players; so we played pickup games after school a couple of days a week. Those were the teachers I associated with during lunch and break times. Although a small school I couldn't help but notice several Renton teachers who unspeaking, habitually walked past looking straight ahead. Never a good morning, good afternoon or hello, but I was cool with that. Who wanted to associate with unfriendly folk, not I. Although rarely done by teachers; during that time spanking was allowed in California schools. Students were usually sent to the office for discipline. Two of the older teachers in the classroom next door and across the hall were heavy spankers. Several times a day they were out in the hallway beating students with four inch wide two foot long plywood boards. Spending so much time in the hallway, I wondered when they took time to do what they were paid to do, teach.

Mr. Twichell & Mr. Hornbeck : Twichell and Hornbeck were two mean faced men who seemed to really enjoy hurting certain students. They were a disruptive distraction for mine and other neighboring classrooms; we soon learned to close our doors. Even with our doors closed, the beatings could still be heard by our students and everyone else in the area. Glancing out into the hallway at varying times on different days I couldn't help but notice each time I looked out the student being beaten was black. It was merely a confirmation of the warning I had been given by Jim the black custodian and several of the black students and parents. They also said both Twichell and Hornbeck called the black kids "niggers" inside their classrooms. Standing about 6'4 at around 250 pounds, salt and pepper gray hair combed straight back with the heavy under the eye bags of an alcoholic; a retired marine; Mr. Hornbeck seemed to especially enjoy beating the kids. With a big smile bragging to other teachers; he laughingly called the stick he used for the beatings "The Board of Education" During breaks and lunch Hornbeck discussed by name the kids he beat in the hallway each day. Most often sharing a table with his best friend Mr. Twichell and other older white men; Hornbeck talked about how hard he hit, how loud the kids yelled and how high they jumped when he beat them. Failing to see the humor in his loud comments as did most teachers in the lounge,

Renton Jr. High School

I avoided Twichell and Hornbeck along with the bizarre jokes they were also telling about the black and Latino kids being beaten daily.He and Twichell said the beatings were "necessary student discipline."Unskilled at disguising or hiding my feelings; the sidelong glances and comments made by Twichell and Hornbeck let me know that they were aware of and disliked my daily unsmiling hard looks of disapproval. Generally, most of their comments were not heard beyond the tables near them in the Teachers Lounge. But on this day with the smiling encouragement of his friend Hornbeck, Twichell made sure that I and everyone else in the lounge heard his extra loud comment; "If I didn't know better I'd say you was calling Williams a nigger too." Black and a new teacher, reckon they assumed I would fearfyully put up with their racist bullshit. In shock and awe; our fellow teachers couldn't avoid seeing me react in a most unteacher like manner. Three quick steps brought me to their table where I put my face close enough to see my spittle drops glance off Twichells' nose and said; "Go ahead, I'm right here, call me a nigger motherfucker!" Suddenly sweating profusely Twichell glanced quickly at his buddy Hornbeck as did I. Showing obvious surprise and discomfort; Hornbeck sat blocked in his chair with walls at his back and on both sides. Ignoring Twichell and leaning toward Hornbeck I fronted him in his corner. In the quiet of the loud silence, I waited several counts for Hornbeck; Twichell's guide and mentor to make his move, or not. In such absolute stillness; we seemed to be the only people in the crowded lounge as I said to Hornbeck; "I didn't think so!" Broke eye contact turned and walked from the room.

Maybe I was missing something and just couldn't understand why Twichell and Hornbeck, after their racist actions in the teachers lounge acted as if they were afraid of me. I never said a word to them following the incident. Mentally and physically I had moved on, but when they saw me in the hallways they immediately turned away. The same in the faculty lounge when I entered they'd ease out the other exit. Replaying the incident in my head I thought surely there must be something I don't understand about white folk. That day in the lounge they were the aggressors, speaking loud enough for me to hear, they wanted me to hear. Twichell even raised his voice so that I would hear his nigger comment. I heard it as did every teacher in the lounge and the secretaries in the neighboring offices. Did they think I would pretend I didn't hear it or just laugh if off? What world were they living in? Twichell eventually stopped coming to the faculty lounge. One day I saw him in the hallway outside of his classroom and he immediately rushed inside and slammed the door. Twichell retired at the end of the year and moved to parts unknown. Abandoned, by his number one ace and running dog; Hornbeck became a quieter person and stopped beating kids with his "Board of education. Most students knew nothing of my conflict with Hornbeck and Twichell. But Jim the custodian and a few parents were aware.

Jim even told me of several run-ins he had with Hornbeck for beating his step son before he got him out of Hornbeck's class. On another note; Renton Jr. High being my first junior high school teaching experience other than teacher training; I'd forgotten how tiring the job could be. Maybe it is the age but junior high school kids are hyper and flat out crazy. On yard duty during breaks and lunch; daily I'd stop a group of 'stoner' kids having the time of their lives, absolutely enjoying themselves throwing rocks and killing sea gulls on the athletic field. Then too much like the high schools there were the fights between the various groups. Blacks against stoners, Latinos against Blacks, jocks against Blacks and Latinos, girls against boys and other combinations were common. Interestingly enough in junior high many of the girls were bigger and stronger than the boys and managed to embarrass and kick a little male ass. The fights got even more interesting when parents showed up during the fights. Having started my full time teaching career at the high school level, junior high was a hard adaptation. It required much more energy wasted on details having little or nothing to do with subjects taught. At least fifty percent of the school day was spent on moving kids from hallways and other areas to classrooms. Once inside the classrooms assigning and moving seats, trips to the bathrooms, lunchrooms, offices was a constant distraction. Then too there was classroom bully control, student bullies rather than teacher bullies. During those very long and tiring junior high school days I kept a lookout for openings at the local high schools. After three years of hell my prayers were answered. That summer I heard of a fall opening at Renton High School for a History/English teacher. Maybe their need for a token black outweighed the token black needs of the junior high. Just like that, I was hired! It was so nice to be back to a high school teaching position, yeah it felt good. Suddenly my students were all juniors and seniors preparing for college and the full time adult world instead of borderline insane 7th and 8th graders, hallelujah! Things were really going well when lo and behold I discovered another black teacher in the PE Department. Two black teachers at the same school indeed that was a crowd for some, especially when we were in the same room during faculty meetings; but all was good for the two of us. The white jungle was easier to take when not alone☺ A few months into the new job just as I was getting a feel for the new school the teachers union called a strike. My wife having finally ended the long commute to Drummond, now too was working for the Renton School District at the local continuation high school. Pregnant with our 2nd child and now on strike; we were both reporting to picket lines daily instead of our classrooms.

Strike: So there we were participating in the first strike of our lives with house payments, car payments and other related responsibilities. Without monthly paychecks, yes the future was looking shaky. But union assistance during the strike was enough to keep us going.

Not allowed on campus during the strike, our day began in the parking lot in front of Renton High School, strike headquarters. The union provided coffee and donuts while dividing us into groups with picket captains and sending us to other schools in the district. Walking back and forth in front of the schools where we worked, carrying signs and chanting during the school day while someone else sat at our desks inside our classrooms felt strange. Nice support but even stranger was seeing our students coming out to the picket lines during lunch and breaks to tell us what was happening in our classrooms and to point out the cars of the strikebreakers (Scabs) in the parking lot. SCABS the strikebreakers were derisively called when crossing our picket lines each morning.

The first week, was a new experience for us all; hanging out with friends during what would normally be a workday. Yelling at SCABS and bumping their cars as they drove past was a union sanctioned chance to be naughty and it was kind of fun. But by the end of the 2nd week there came a different feel to the strikers, there was anger. Suddenly roofing nails and tacks were discovered in the driveways leading to and from the schools. At one of our end of the day meetings a picket captain told of an incident where a SCAB was cornered and threatened at a lunch counter across the street from the high school by several striking teachers. Ironically a student was present to shame the teachers into breaking up the pushing and shoving melee. There were those who claimed that I was an active participant in that melee, possibly. Yep things were getting tighter and harsher as the strike lengthened. Although teachers had been specifically told NOT to talk to school administrators, several were spotted leaning on their picket signs as they kissed ass; smiling and yukking it up with administrators. Few were surprised when those ass kissers abandoned their fellow striking teachers and returned to the classrooms; joining the scabs before the strike ended. Weak rationalizations and excuses were leaked back to those of us still on the lines. "I have kids and bills to pay." Was the most common excuse, as if the rest of us out there on the lines didn't have "...kids and bills to pay." Those teachers still on the lines who made excuses for those who went in were looked upon with well deserved suspicion. "You just don't understand his/her situation." was a common refrain from that group. They too were often seen kissing up to administrators. None were surprised when soon after the strike ended; those very same ass kissers and sellouts were promoted to administrative positions themselves.

Picket Squad: Things got even more critical and paranoid on the lines when it was discovered that those ass kissers were also sharing union and strike information with administrators as they suddenly disappeared from the picket lines. Roving picket squads were formed to add extra punch to our strike and to discourage SCABS and sellouts.

Renton High School

Not assigned to a particular school as were other pickets; we roamed from site to site and responded to crisis calls from picket captains. Roving pickets also took the strike to the homes of principals, superintendents and other administrators. Not welcome and an embarrassment; we marched back and forth in front of the homes of administrators in well to do neighborhoods after dark no less. The administrators never failed to step outside and take a good look at the strikers in front of their homes; those pickets were in for some surprises following the strike. Mean people have longer memories. Roving pickets we were on scene at most of the schools and the district office administration buildings. Roving cynics as well; we began to notice an uncomfortable camaraderie and friendship developing between our teacher strike leaders and the school district administrators. We were unpaid for weeks and pissed off, but our leaders were smiling and having lunches and dinners with the enemy. Possibly we were tired and unreasonable after so many weeks on the line; but it seemed that strike management and school management were in bed together. Adding to our suspicions was the agreement soon to follow our observations. Strike management suggested that we accept a small percentage raise that no way covered the money lost during the time we were out on strike. Not having to pay salaries for hundreds of teachers during the months we were on strike the school district made money. With such a pittance of a raise they came out way ahead of the game, no thanks to our teacher strike management team.

Strike over and back in our classrooms, we were told that we had won. "We really showed those dam administrators." So said our union president; at our first meeting following the strike. All in the audience had discovered that she had somehow managed to get a plum teaching assignment after the strike. The new lessons learned from the strike intruded, pushing boldly into our lives. We assumed we knew our strike leaders, their motivation and integrity. It turns out we didn't know those people at all. Not knowing her personally, I had been told our union president, an ex nun married to an ex priest absolutely could be trusted. If you can't trust ex nuns who can you trust? Maybe we all should have picked up on the warning signs; EX-NUN married to an EX-Priest hmmmmmmmm? The EX may have been the most important part of their pasts to consider. Anyway, Alice the ex nun and union president unapologetically took the new money from the raise in pay on her new job following the strike and continued talking union bullshit. We all like to think we know what is going on in our worlds, thinking we can easily read and anticipate people. But we are often surprised to discover we knew nothing at all about folk we're supposed to have read and understood. So ended my dealing with Alice and the union; but I couldn't stop paying dues taken directly from my check. Thereto began my healthy distrust of any and all union management.

That distrust was reinforced in spades with administrative strike revenge a year or so later.

Payback: Although there was noticeable tension at the schools between administrators and teachers who left the strikers on the picket lines and those teachers who stayed out for the entire strike, the wife and I were happy to be back in our classrooms. But soon I was to learn a frighteningly harsh lesson; not forgetting my very active strike participation; administrators have long, long memories. After three years for most the strike was a distant and unpleasant memory. The school day started much like any other with my first period US History class and at the bell in came my 2nd period World History Class. Still standing at the lectern beside my desk I had just finished taking roll for 2nd period, when the head secretary from the main office walked into the room. Odd, I had never seen her out of the downstairs office in the three years working at the school. Standing in the doorway obviously uncomfortable she said; "Mr. Williams you're wanted down in the principals' office. I'll be here with your class." Very curious, I had never been called to the principals' office in all my years of teaching. Trying to imagine what the principal could want with me that couldn't wait until after class I walked the long down ramp to the first floor and the open door of the principals' outer office. Moving past and behind the counter fronting the inner office I also noticed the nervousness of the office clerk. Door open, wordlessly the principal waved me into his inner office. Once inside, he stepped past and closed the office door behind me. Now I could see the two men who'd been sitting behind the open door with their right hands on their heavy black belts. Both crouched leaning forward in their chairs, they had guns. "I'm officer Yellen and this is office Newell. We had a report of a crime committed. Without handcuffs, we're going to walk you to our car out front and drive you down to the station." Both now standing poised as if waiting (hoping) for some physical reaction from me; paused before moving to the side door. One in the lead the other following; I was taken to a Black Crown Victoria sitting at the curb in the red no parking zone in front of the school steps. When all of your life has been in different circumstances and routine; when it suddenly becomes extremely dangerous for you and your loved ones; how does one react? Going where I had never been before, I sat in the back of the police cruiser with tinted windows and no inside doorknobs as it rolled from Renton High School to the police station. At the station I was taken to a room, much like the ones seen on TV with a table two chairs and a large mirror. Sitting across the table from me officer Newell asked; "Is there anything you want to tell me?" Thinking what the hell I would want to tell this dude, maybe they should be telling me something! Of course I said. "No." "Do you want to call a lawyer?" Uh yeaahhhhh. Looking through the yellow pages I found the name of the lawyer who had represented the teachers union years before during the teachers strike, Robert Y. Fell.

His secretary told me not to say anything to the police and that she would get back to me in a couple of hours.

Detained: Meanwhile I was subjected to several memorable experiences. My mug shot was taken; I was fingerprinted and then moved to a cell where I remained for hours. The silence, and the isolation in the cell with a camera mounted in the upper right corner of the room; I assumed was some kind of police psych game. Hopefully my attitude toward the conditions spoiled it for them as I snuggled onto the jailhouse bunk and took a nap. Eventually I was taken from the cell at the police station and transferred to the county jail. Still no handcuffs, I was put in the back of another police cruiser and driven the three miles across town to the jail. During the drive the pot bellied balding cop said in a friendly tone; "You know we all make mistakes in our lives." Getting no response, he continued; "You must have really pissed someone off, who was it?" A few blocks of my silence finally quieted him. Arriving at the county jail, the prisoners in the hallways, noticing my dress began discussing my guilt or innocence and guessing at my possible crime. One mentioned bank embezzlement, and his companion said, "Do you think he did it?" "Naaw, not the type was the response." That was the last I heard before being led into a room for my 2nd processing of the day with prints and pictures. Finished, I was ushered into a cell with seven other folk. Finding a spot near the front of the cell, I stood alone until a skinny, scruffy looking white fellow approached. "What did you do?" Ignoring him I walked to the other side of the cell. A few minutes slipped past and then the other black guy in the cell approached; "What's happening brother?" "Not much." I said and walked to the other side of the cell. Following me the brother said; "What's whitey trying to stick you with brother?" Walking away for the 2nd time I think the brother and the other jailhouse snitches finally got the hint; I had nothing to say to them. Reckon the jailers watching on camera decided I wasn't going to confess to some dastardly crime so after about an hour they moved me to a single cell. As I was being moved I saw the wife sitting in the waiting room with our youngest child on her lap. Helpless with no control over the situation and with mixed emotions; I was proud and ashamed at the same time. Proud that I had her stand by me in those awful circumstances yet ashamed that she had to sit in a county jail waiting room with our child. My attorney Robert Y. Fell had been busy and may have had something to do with me being moved to a single cell, I assume a pre-release procedure. Yes I was about to be released on my own recognizance for the time being. Whatever get me out! Meeting in the waiting room, gratefully I hugged the wife and baby. In custody since early morning, it was now late afternoon, about 4:00 PM as we drove to Renton High School. Filled with sadness, I wondered what my fellow teachers and students thought about my sudden absence for the day as the wife dropped me off to pick up my truck.

Now the lone vehicle in the parking lot, I approached the well worn Gray Mazda pick up, still under the large eucalyptus tree where I had parked at the beginning of what I thoughtlessly assumed would be just another routine day. Overwhelmed by the surreal poignancy of the moment; I watched the fading early evening sunlight filtered through the limbs and shade of the tree lined parking lot. Never to be the same again, things could and did worsen. Home that very evening I received a hand delivered letter from the Renton School District advising me that I had been placed on administrative leave from my job until further notice. More to come; "High school basketball coach suspended for having sex with students!" was the front page headline in the following morning's paper. No need to name names, there was only one high school girl's basketball coach and there I was sitting at home while a substitute teacher was in my classroom, obviously I was 'the one'. The wife also a teacher in the school district where both sons attended schools; with horror I couldn't imagine what they must have been going through, especially the kids. Even when helpless and unable to control the situation or circumstances; as a parent that responsibility, that instinctive obligation to protect family from all harm, be it physical or psychological came to mind. Standing underneath the open garage door, with no comment from the wife and kids; for the first time in our lives, I watched them go through our daily morning routine and head for school without my participation. On administrative leave, not since early childhood in Arkansas had I not worked on weekdays. Suppose I should have been pleased that my leave was with pay, but it still felt really strange being home.

Robert Y. Fell: What to do, I called Robert Y. Fell who needed a $10,000 retainer to start work with $200 an hour charges to follow. For what; I had committed no crime; although guilt or innocence didn't seem to matter. Fell's major concern was insuring his fee; from me and my union as well. Not hiding the fact that he had automatically assumed I was guilty as the newspaper headlines proclaimed, Robert Y. Fell sounded disappointed when he finally asked after some research into my past; "Who the hell are you Mr. Clean?" Was I supposed to apologize for not having a criminal record? Observing Robert Y. Fell's antics confirmed my very first observations; he only cared about the money and circumstances justifying his fees, so I paid. My defense attorney continued being surly, pouty and disappointed after further inquiries still found no criminal history. I did wonder whether his anger was because I didn't fit his black stereotypes. Or maybe he was angry because he could have charged a higher fee if I had a criminal history, who knows. Lawyers, like doctors without the caring pretense are strange inhuman creatures. After months of being in limbo and $30,000 in legal fees out of my pocket and whatever the teachers union kicked in for my defense.

We finally had our day in court to discover that no charges were ever filed by anyone. The main accuser, who had been well coached by school administrators and the police department changed her mind and decided not to stand by the lie that she had told. Naturally her retraction, printed in a small space deep in the interior of the newspaper came long after several other front page news stories about my alleged criminal activities with underage girls. So what was that whole thing about, simply to make me a jobless man? Was it simply payback for my strike activities? With lawyers and investigators they put a lot of taxpayer time and money into a project to get me fired. My basketball players and students told me about police and school personnel coming to their homes and interviewing them and their parents. Did the school administrators really believe the bullshit about underage students? Although I returned to my teaching position the adverse publicity and continuing manipulations of the school district administration and the police department made any semblance of normalcy impossible. Daily a van sat in the parking lot across the street from the school with a telescope looking object protruding from its roof pointing towards my 2nd floor classroom. So were they trying to see me having sex with students in my classroom? What utter police stupidity, unfortunately they haven't changed over the years; except nowadays they'd just kill me. My white co-workers treated me as if I had the plague, I wasn't surprised. Later I received a letter from the chief of police, in which he said that I had been questioned and never arrested. The chief's letter was supposed to insure that I would not have a police record. Meanwhile police followed me to and from work daily. I even found one lurking in the creek behind my house peering through the boards on my back yard fence.

DOJ Files: Regarding police records, later I was to learn that typically the police chief was lying; he sent the record of my supposedly "non arrest" to the United States Department of Justice (DOJ) where it remains to this day on file for police departments all over the country and world to view, forever. Years later when I checked to see how to get it removed I was told that such police action was common practice and that I would need a lawyer and a fee for removal. So it is, guess here I could rant about having to pay for the removal of false information in a file created by racist police but so is life. Afterwards when applying for jobs in other school districts I couldn't help but notice the change in attitude of the human resources folk after running my name through their local police departments. Feeling somewhat overwhelmed by negative events in education I thought it might be time for a life change. Having observed the school administrators and their lawyers deftly exacting revenge for my overactive strike activity with magically created charges backed by career destroying publicity, I wondered; "How can they do that?" Also listening to union management and their lawyers I concluded that as a group lawyers spoke a language which I did not understand. That bothered me. For the safety of my family I decided I must learn that language, I was going to law school. The wife didn't think it was a good idea. Was this definitive; is this the way of life? Somehow having survived the strike, jail and serious attempts to destroy my family and my career, what more could be done do to me? Maybe law school would be a means to prepare for other unknown horrors; to anticipate future actions against my family; so I believed.

Law School: So how does one go from more than a decade and a half in the public school classroom to law school? First comes the LSAT, the law school admission test. Upon completion, much like the GRE, the graduate record exam for admission to graduate school; one waits for a score and then applies to the school of choice. Supposedly the higher scores broadened ones choices; pardon my cynicism, but like the GRE and graduate schools; law schools too tended to go with the money. More Benjamin's equals more choices. A few months after the LSAT several law schools held an open house at San Francisco State University, in The City. A rare sunny day out in the avenues found tables set up in the quad with representatives from several law schools. With many memories of my brief sojourn at San Francisco State during my Teacher Corps years I walked past several booths and tables picking up flyers from the various schools. Most of the school representatives were formally dressed in suits and ties, dresses and heels; proper courtroom attire. All 'properly' dressed except for the one table I spotted in a far corner. At that table the law school recruiters were wearing fatigue jackets and tie dyed shirts and blouses. As a survivor with fond memories of that era of tie dye and all the accompanying life styles, I couldn't resist. Following a brief conversation with those folk I was sold on New College of California's School of Law at 50 Fell Street in San Francisco. Located just around the corner from City Hall and the courts the New College location was ideal. The courts nearby, courtroom observation and clerking opportunities would be available. The American Civil Liberties Union (ACLU) was also in walking distance. I was ready for law school.

Another Orientation: Another beginning, with classroom schedules in hand I had mentally prepared for the daily four hour round trip bus commutes from Fieldsburg to San Francisco. College days back at Pepperdine many years before was my last bus commute, so I was all eyes and ears into the new experience. Of course back in those Pepperdine days; Los Angeles Rapid Transit District Buses catered to a very different clientele. High school students, end of the line riding homeless folk, and factory workers was an interesting contrast to the suit and tied, heels and Chase handbag Golden Gate Transit crowd. Relearning public transit with that Northern California twist was also a part of my orientation. Fieldsburg was the end of the line for Golden Gate Transit where I was one of 6 regular commuters.

However, with major pickups in Petaluma and San Rafael by the time we reached The City all the seats were full. Reckon I was quite the country hick; my very first day looking out the window as we pulled up to my stop in front of the courthouse in San Francisco I couldn't help but notice the variety of people being dropped off. Suddenly, doing a double take; face glued to the window I saw several men kissing men and women kissing women goodbye as they were being dropped off for work. Some were routinely boarding other buses. Wow, too much! Looking around me I realized it all was ho hum to the other commuters and I was the only one reacting with shock and surprise. After a while gays in The City along with other new sights became routine to me as well. Still there were other interesting occurrences on the bus during my two hour rides. Although the seats were deep comfortable and private on the large Greyhound like vehicles, we were still sitting in an open bus. One morning just after our stop in San Rafael I heard a female voice, it sounded like she may have been seated to my front left. I couldn't hear the man or her partner; but clearly she was making recognizable sexual intercourse sounds. I suppose it could be done on an open seated public transit vehicle if folk covered themselves with coats or jackets or something, but who would have sex on the bus? By now everyone on the bus must have heard as she neared her climax the sounds grew more frantic and louder. Reaching her climax the unknown sexual sensitivity assailant began winding down with quieter and quieter moans of pleasure. But looking at the faces of my neighboring passengers and fellow riders I saw no reactions. They acted as if morning sex on the bus was just a part of the commute. Checking the passenger faces as we got off at the end of the line I saw nothing to indicate the guilty sex party or parties. Straight faced the bus driver; he had to have heard the loud moans; said to each of the passengers his routine, "Have a nice day." Another happening was chalked up to law school experience. An imposing multi storied building just around the corner from Market Street and Van Ness Avenue New College looked impressive. An oddity I noticed on the very first day and every day thereafter was the flag. Unusually shaped and multi colored; flying high on the flagpole in the center of campus it was neither the United States Flag nor the California State Flag. Outside of class New College was pretty relaxed, so I just assumed someone was trying to be funny and had placed a colorful rag on the flagpole. It was San Francisco, The City, and not conservative Fieldsburg where I called home. In new situations oftentimes I miss the obvious; it must have been my third and final year before I figured out that flag and other related occurrences at New College. But, meanwhile that first law school gathering found nearly two hundred students crowded into a first floor classroom. Most of that first day, with a short break for lunch, instructors for Criminal Law, Contracts, Civil Procedure and other classes gave little introductory pep talks and answered questions. Listening to student questions and discussions was intimidating.

All were first year students as was I but most of them seemed to have prior knowledge and experience in the areas of the courses offered at the school. Thoroughly frightened, with a backpack stuffed with several hundred dollars worth of newly purchased books I dragged myself home at the end of the day. Explaining to the wife and kids that law school would be all consuming and that I wouldn't be around very much for the next three years was done over an extended period of time; not all in one sitting. But they couldn't help but notice the desk I built in a corner of the garage stacked with law books where I sat for hours day and night. With a BA from Pepperdine and two Master's degrees since; yet law school was the hardest thing I had ever done. No one told me that studying law was very different from studying in undergrad and graduate school. I reckon no one told me because only law school survivors understand. Law school was buy the books, brief the cases, and ready or not class starts; and you WILL be prepared when called upon. Just to survive, to keep my head above water, I spent every waking hour studying. I stopped to go to the bathroom, eat and sometimes sleep. Holidays, birthdays, Christmases, New Years I spent at that makeshift garage desk. Additionally fearsome were the growing number of empty desks of first year student dropouts. They were painfully visible reminders of the possibility of failure at the start of classes each Monday morning. All of those most talkative folk from that first day of orientation were gone. The San Francisco Labor Organizers and street demonstrators from that first day with so many words left cold empty seats. It turned out that the most talkative guy from orientation, rumor said he couldn't read or write. The guy was illiterate and starting law school, go figure. How the hell he got into law school only the New College Registrar knew. And I in my first day silent orientation jitters thought such talkers would be the last to fail or drop out. Even the empty Monday morning seats had to be pointed out to me; head down deep into studies 24/7 I missed things at home and at school. Missing things other than law school around me and in my life did what I had to do and by hard as work and the grace of God I survived 1st year Law School. It is said that if you survive first year the rest is a "piece of cake." Understanding the routine and having learned how to study law made things clearer but there was no cake.

Late 2nd year of the three year program, Mildred the registrar, and the only black face on the New College staff started dropping hints about how things were done at New College Law School. "Were you at the party this weekend at Stan's house? Most of the students and faculty attended." Giving me a look saying much she didn't respond when I said I didn't know about the party. On another occasion she asked, "Did you get the preview study sheet for Cilla's Torts Test?" She had me print out copies and all the other students came by and picked up one. Didn't she tell you?" Of course Mildred knew before I said no and thanked her for a copy.

New College of California School of Law

Without her help and secretly looking out for me there is no way I could have survived New College. Law school was hard enough, but Mildred put her job on the line to make sure I got the same opportunities as did other students. I thought Mildred told me that I probably wouldn't enjoy the parties so that I wouldn't feel bad and left out, but it turned out that wasn't the reason. First she mentioned what I had noticed my very first day at the school; that multicolored flag, OK. "Well it's called a rainbow flag and represents gay people." In response to my; "Oh", she claimed that more than 90% of the law school faculty and student body were gay. Well finally some clarity which helped to explain a number of events and reactions at the school. Thanks Mildred. God bless that sista, having no other friends at that school; walking onto the stage for my Juris Doctor after a long three years would have been impossible without her. Hope I didn't cause any problems for Mildred by announcing on stage at graduation that I wouldn't have made it without her wise counsel; but back to year 2. Of course learning how to study law and studying law took much time and effort, but so did learning how to deal with the preconceived notions and racial stereotypes of the New College teachers and other school officials. Most of the students at the school were on financial aid, and looked it; I was not. One would think that the finance officer would be pleased with my monthly tuition payments, he wasn't and showed it. He didn't even try to hide his displeasure when reluctantly accepting my checks. Yes, it irked me that the asshole was pissed off because I was not poor and on financial aid! As I parked my new mini van in the school parking lot, I couldn't help but notice him from his 2nd floor office window; hands on hips staring at the vehicle and giving me a hard look. Mildred had already warned me to watch him closely. Weird shit! Several students in my study group mentioned, without specifics; deals they had worked out with the finance officer to take care of "...tuition payments at a later time." It could have been BS but I knew they had little or no money yet they were still in law school, and attending faculty parties.

Two of those questionable characters were sitting on stage with me to receive their Juris Doctor. A four year college degree is a perquisite for the Juris Doctor upon completion of law school; but for Andre and Ricardo being friends with the finance officer and partying with the 'right' people seemed to have paid off. Sitting on stage with their family and friends in the audience, having barely completed two years at City College; they received their JD along with the rest of us. During law school working for other lawyers in offices, courthouses and other legal institutions are a fundamental part of the educational process. The 'right connections'; meeting and knowing the right people while clerking may lead to an excellent job upon completion of school. New College being a public interest law school clerking for organizations that worked for the public interest fitted perfectly into the ideals and goals of New College.

ACLU Clerking: My first law clerking job was for the American Civil Liberties Union (ACLU) at the start of my 2nd year of law school. By 2nd year it is assumed that law students; having survived first year, have learned enough of the basics to work in a law office. Whatever the legal issues being litigated clerks do the research; finding supportive cases and doing the writing for practicing lawyers who argue the cases in court. Clerking is a time for lessons of close observation and analysis. For starters getting to the ACLU offices was a chore in itself. It was just down the street from the law school but upon arrival at the fortress like building off Mission Street one had to buzz the intercom to be let into the building. Once inside a special code was needed to open the elevator, the only access to the 2nd floor offices of the ACLU. On the 2nd floor another code was necessary to enter the door to the offices themselves. At first I thought such security ridiculously overdone, but after a few weeks of looking over our cases and clients I decided that such security was truly necessary. There are people out there who really hate the ACLU. Such reality was driven home one morning when reporting to work I found the attorneys and clerks in the lead attorney's office. He was working on a corruption case involving the San Francisco Police Department. Standing at the back of the assembled group I noticed a lone 9 millimeter bullet, centered on his desk atop a bulging legal folder. "Whoa, what's up with that?" I thought listening to his explanation. The first in the office that morning he said; "The police file was taken from the drawer and placed on my desk, with the bullet sometime last night." All knowing that there was no way the average Joe could bypass ACLU security we weren't surprised at his conclusion which matched our own. "Clearly this is a serious threat and warning from the San Francisco Police Department." Listening to other statements and mumblings attorneys and clerks; all were left with serious thoughts about the danger. There were other clerking jobs but none matched the exciting issues, attitudes, and yes; latent danger of working for the ACLU. But soon after that incident, then came that very special time; the aforementioned graduation. Overwhelmed with guilt for the three years of hell I'd put them through, it was finally done; I sat with the family at graduation from New College School of Law. Looking at the faces of my fellow graduates that first day of orientation again came to mind; and the voices of all those talkers who seemed so much more knowledgeable than me. Not one was present for graduation. Of the more than two hundred students from that first day's orientation more than three years ago just thirty five of us sat on stage for graduation. So ended the pomp and circumstance and now began the exploration of the profession.

Having put up with my virtual absence for three years the wife was ready for me to make tons of money as all lawyers do, or so she believed.

Enjoying the perspective; new knowledge and a different way of looking at societal interactions I never really considered the financial possibilities. The major reason I attended law school was the discomfort I felt because of my lack of legal knowledge. But on the other hand the wife thought studying law simply to acquire legal knowledge was ridiculous. "When are you taking the bar? When do you start making real money like other lawyers?" Those and similar questions she kept asking as early as completion of my first year of law school. Hoping she would listen I told her, "I need time to see how this stuff actually works." Now back home in Fieldsburg her expectations were especially high. Clerking at home was by no means the "big money" the wife expected me to make, but working in the town where she still worked and my kids attended school s was an interestingly unique experience.

Fieldsburg Public Defenders Office: Working in Fieldsburg was also special because of teaching there; it was nice to be back. More and more, dealing with lawyers, already I was beginning to miss education, students and teaching.In teaching right and wrong weren't nebulous concepts or ideas, they were real and people made consequential life choices based on one or the other so I believed. In law one soon learned that right and wrong are minor aspects and most times irrelevant. Such lessons were immediately evident in the public defender's office. There, it was not uncommon to be given several cases to prepare on the very day; just hours before our clients were due in court. With luck, you'd have time to review the charges and interview the client, but time to prepare a defense would indeed be gravy. Public defender clients means poor clients; justice and the law has little sympathy or time for folk with no money.On my 4th day working for the Fieldsburg Public Defenders' Office I was given a stack of cases, twelve, and sent down to the main jail for interviews with our clients. Before getting to our clients of course I had to deal with police prison mentality. Even with proper identification the jailers didn't believe I had a law degree and was working for the public defenders office. What's new, huh? After a couple of phone calls, and mumbled 'racist pig' comments the metal barrier was moved aside and I was admitted to a small hallway with open fronted cells on both sides. Walking down that metallic hallway and trying to read the names and cell numbers on the case files, I was startled by the sound of inmates yelling; "Hi Mr. Williams." Completely taken aback, recovering, I saw several of my former students from my teaching days at Renton Jr. High and High Schools. Seeing those faces brought back many pleasant memories. Although I didn't say it; I wasn't surprised at all to see a couple of those faces in jail cells. We had a nice reunion as I moved between the cells preparing their cases for court. Unlike me, all were familiar with the "justice system" and had no great expectations. Guilt or innocence rarely mentioned seemed ALWAYS a minor consideration.

At such young ages, sadly they had already learned those 'justice' lessons that I would later come to thoroughly understand. Straightforward, lacking ambiguity" Money wins..." was a hard, hard, lesson to learn. Legal research writing and case preparation was oftentimes discouraging. Then there were times when our clients were clearly innocent of all crimes, but clumsily set up for undefined reasons by the local police. Unfortunately the system always seemed to side with the District Attorneys office and the police. Palmer's was a typical case. He was driving his cousin's car when stopped for no apparent reason by the Fieldsburg Police. They claimed he did a rolling stop and ran a stop sign. Guns drawn two cops approached the vehicle and told Palmer, one of my former students, "Get out of the car with those black hands where we can see them!" During the search of the vehicle the police found a baggie of marijuana under the back seat. Preparing the case the first issue that came to mind was the police stop. Palmer said that there were traffic lights and no stop signs at that intersection. Checking the intersection where the incident occurred we did find that there was no "...stop sign..." there. As Palmer said, there were traffic lights at that intersection; and had been for years. Taking pictures of the intersection we added them to Palmers case file. If the stop was illegal so was the search. Yes if there had been no stop there would have been no search. Secondly, without a warrant the police had no right or cause to search the illegally stopped vehicle. Even after the illegal stop and search of the vehicle we didn't mention the possibility that the police put the marijuana in the car. Furthermore, the license and registrations showed that Palmer was not the registered owner of the vehicle in which the marijuana was found. With a lecture from the bench for the DA and local police the judge freed Palmer who had spent three days in jail. We won one out of twelve; and I was told that wasn't bad for a first batch of cases. Really, after three years of law school; one out of twelve a good job, was not what I wanted to hear. When I told the wife about the one out of twelve she put away the papers she was grading and reminded me that law was what I said I wanted to do. "I wanted to know it, not necessarily do it!" I said again. But she was right as often was the case, I'd put all that time and money into the law project, maybe I should at least give it a chance. Maybe just a constant whiner, forever seeking change but I couldn't explain to her or anyone outside the business; but I had discovered the hardest part of law was the people with whom I had to work and associate. And I don't mean the criminals; I am talking about the lawyers. They are even worse than the police, at least with the police the emotion, racism, and hatred are visible and expected; but lawyers are skilled at showing nothing. Some folks believe they show nothing because nothing is there. With a straight face above all else the goal is to get the money; to win is preferable but to lose isn't so bad getting the money is what matters. Looking back, five years; three of law school and two of clerking was the measure of how long I had been out of the classroom, away from teaching.

Fieldsburg Public Defenders Office

My credentials were still good, maybe it was time I started looking around for education opportunities. I found an unusual school that piqued my interest in the field of computer assisted instruction as well as school administration. With a couple of interesting twists there was a means to ease on back into education.

Jail Time: So, driving in for the first time and taking a look at the imposing penal edifice; I thought it looked better than some apartment buildings I'd lived in except for the fences and men with guns in the surrounding towers. Education in a county jail setting was unusual, odd, possibly but who needs it more than jail inmates? Besides it felt so good returning to the classroom in any place in any form. Meeting with the captain of the guard and watching her stiff formality, I was reminded of my military days in the US Air Force. I listened as she and the director of education explained the educational program at San Francisco County Jail #7. Having recently purchased 34 new Dell Computers with educational software, I was hired to set up and run a school for jail inmates in a vacant buildings sitting next to the jail facility. Breathing a sigh of relief, I thought at least I won't have to work inside the jail. Momentarily pleased, I was quite surprised to read the form offered for my signature by captain of the guard Sandra Holtzman. Sensing my reluctance as I sat staring at the paper she said that if I wanted the job I had to sign the form. After moments of serious thought about two young sons and a wife at home, I signed the damm form; which Sandra quickly snatched from my shaky hand. That pretty much settled it and I prepared to be working with criminals and guards; thank God for uniforms, the only way to tell the difference between the two. Furthermore I had just signed a form stating that if taken hostage by those very same criminals, "...there are no hostage rescue plans..." and if the hostage takers decide to kill me, "...under no circumstance or condition are the city and county of San Francisco or their employees liable."A little something, something to think about; but bottom line, I needed the job. Taking a few days to set up the workstations and test the software, to soon; not knowing what to expect, I had students. The first couple of sessions I administered math and reading placement tests then placed the students in individualized programs from elementary to college level. Several of the students were struggling to learn their A, B, C's and how to read. Others worked on a variety of elementary and secondary school subjects including GED preparation. The men were brought over in the morning and the women followed in the afternoon. Most were courteous, respectful, and seemingly very pleased to participate in the program. Relaxing, I thought; "These jail folk are pretty much like students on the outside." Even though school attendance was a reward for good behaving inmates, later I was to learn that that wasn't necessarily true. After bringing the inmates over for class the guard often stepped outside for a smoke or waited in my office.

San Francisco County Jail #7, San Bruno

Much like students in any environment they had issues totally unrelated to learning which surfaced during class time. Just as when working on the outside one tries to stick to the subject matter and ignore those unrelated things; still they may ooze into the classroom. Moving from desk to desk checking student progress, I paused behind Chuck who sat staring at his blank computer screen. "What's up"? I asked leaning closer to listen as he responded in a voice barely above a whisper. "You know doc, I had both hands around his neck, and I kept squeezing and squeezing. At first he was moving his legs and arms, but I kept squeezing until he stopped." Listening to the emotionless flat monotone, I did wonder whether I misunderstood what Chuck was telling me. Finally realizing that I did indeed understand what he was saying, although shocked to the core, teacher mode kicked in. Pretending to be unaffected by what I had just heard I said, "So Chuck are you going to finish that reading assignment you started yesterday?" Hearing his "Sure doc."; and needing a moment, I turned and immediately left the room. In the office I found Rene, the guard, feet on my desk reading the morning newspaper. Nonchalantly responding to my question about Chuck she said, "Yeah he killed his brother a couple of years ago. He's on his way to San Quentin's Death Row." OOOOOOKKKKKK, again reminding myself as I returned to the classroom, "gotta remain aloof from inmate personals."The men's class ended and I took a short break while Rene walked them back over to the dorms and returned with the women. As stated earlier the inmates attending classes were the best behaved and intellectually the 'cream' of the jail crop. Of course that cream was pulled from a population where more than 90% of the inmates are high school dropouts with reading and math scores below 4th grade level. Staggering information when added to the knowledge that compulsory education is the means used by governments, including our own; to indoctrinate and prepare responsible citizens. School is where the rudiments of cultural homogeneity necessary for nation building is first learned. From an early age with their first school experience one is taught directly and indirectly love of country and belief in 'the system'. Unfortunately, many of those folk who don't finish, or are unsuccessful in school, are on the outer edges of society. Lacking those societal preparatory tools only learned in schools; not surprisingly; we find they are not responsible citizens. Jails, addictions, half-way houses, mental institutions, recovery programs, welfare and unemployment are common. Better educated with a 50% dropout rate, the women are subject to the same and other conditions. Oops, sorry; the soapbox again ☺

Consequently, I would be lying if I said I didn't prefer the women's classes. Beyond the educational factors what man in his right mind wouldn't? Even if I had horns, being the only free man they'd seen in ages, those women still would have appreciated me. Besides, although wearing those ugly orange jail uniforms, several of those criminal ladies were knock down fine.

Keesha was all of that. Sitting at a corner computer station on the left side of the room, she was working hard on her assignment with just one hand with the other resting comfortably on her lap. One of the first lessons taught in introductory keyboarding classes is hand and finger placement; **a, s, d, f** for the left hand placement and **;, l, k, j** for the right. Walking over to her work station I asked, "Keesha, what about that other hand?" Stepping back as she raised her right hand, I couldn't help noticing the deep scar across the first two fingers and her palm, ending about two inches along the upper wrist. "Damm!" I thought as I listened to her response to my stare. "My man was shaving with his straight razor when I came back from the store; I bought bread and some milk for the baby instead of his Colt 45 beer. He swung at my head and I blocked the razor with my hand, but it still bounced off and hit my neck." Noticing her neckline for the first time I could see just inside the collarless orange top a thick scar closely hugging the carotid artery. "Ok Keesh you keep working with the left and use the right when possible." Easing past her I quietly mumbled, "And stay away from razor toting men." I wasn't quiet as I thought, she heard me. "Doc, he's my husband, home with the kids." She said. So what did I know about love and marriage, reckon not very much? Those life lessons learned from sista Keesha were nothing compared to the lessons learned from brotha Andy. HIV Positive: Andy in the men's class was also the keeper of the buffalo. Yep, real live buffalo, American Bison. The county sheriff kept a large open pasture in front of the county jail where buffalo lived. Andy's job was to feed the buffalo every afternoon and check their water supply. This was a plum job because it meant lots of relatively free time outside of the main jail. He was a student in the men's class but the buffalo feeding job gave Andy even more time to wander. During that free time in the afternoon after classes Andy would drop by the office. Classically 'jailhouse buffed' standing about 5'10 dark complected with a tidy afro Andy was looking forward to getting out of jail in the coming weeks. In one of our conversations Andy mentioned that he had been HIV positive for years. Don't know what I expected but he didn't seem sick or anything, he looked and acted like anyone else. Andy couldn't wait to get out and join his lady friend who he had met inside the jail. She found an apartment for the two of them on the outside. Having gotten out of jail weeks earlier Lilac was back in San Francisco waiting. Listening daily to Andy's past and future planned sexual activities when he got back to San Francisco, I had to ask' Does Lilac know that you are HIV positive?" Hearing his no answer I asked, "Are you going to tell her?" That question too was followed with a no answer. Hearing those no's any reasonable man would have to continue with the questions. "So of course you use condoms, right?" with an irritated tone Andy said, "I hate those things, I've never used one!" So I was listening to a man denounce the use of condoms who had been HIV positive for decades.

Andy was in jail for petty theft and drugs but here he freely confessed to an even greater crime. Horrible fears and sadness crossed my mind as I wondered how many people had Andy infected with the AIDS virus. It doesn't stop with one especially if the folk don't know that they have been infected. Knowingly passed on by Andy but unknowingly those partners could pass AIDS on to a different partner who may pass it on to others and so on. AIDS kills people. How many people had Andy killed? I had to say it, "Over the years do you realize or even consider the number of people you may have infected and even killed?" With a big smile, "Doc you putting way to much on it." Andy said. After that conversation I managed NOT to find time to talk to Andy. I heard that he got out soon thereafter, and by the time he returned; unfortunately most did, I was long gone. More than any words, jail is an indescribably odd place. It is unusual on so many levels but within a very controlled environment, yet one is never sure who or what to expect.

Another day in class I approached the desk of a noticeably older woman,   Most of the county jail inmates were in their twenties or early thirties but this woman seemed to be in her early to mid fifties. She looked familiar so I asked that unforgivable jail question, "Don't I know you?" Andy had schooled me earlier on inmate jailhouse rules and protocol. One major rule was if you see a friend acquaintance or even a relative pretend you don't know them. He never explained the why, of that rule, but I had just broken it. The woman sure looked like someone I knew. Turning away at my question she answered, "No." Later as the inmates were being lined up for the march back to the dorms she hung back to the end of the line and whispered to me, "In here they call me Margo, but yeah I'm Matttie, we used to teach together at Havenscourt Junior High School in Oakland." I knew it, Mattie Robinson; I'd been to parties at her house high in the Oakland hills. She had nice kids and a husband who worked for the city of Oakland. During the following months in bits and pieces Mattie told me her story. It seems her husband Ronaldo was killed in a car accident on the bay bridge. A horrible blow to her and the kids, she didn't handle it well. Finding herself alone for the first time in more than twenty years Mattie started a relationship with one of her former students who introduced her to crack cocaine. Doing the unthinkable for a teacher she started missing work without calling in for a substitute or any other pre absence preparations. On more than one occasion, the school principal, a family friend, walked down the hall to check on her noisy classroom to find no Mattie. Without notice she would disappear for days. She not only lost her job and teaching credentials but also that beautiful house in the hills. Her boyfriend Buster cleaned out her bank account and disappeared with her new Mercedes. Homeless, suddenly a 'working girl' on the streets of The City calling herself Margo; one day she found herself in San Francisco County Jail #7

SF County Jail #7 Buffalo

That first jail experience was three years past. Since that time she had been in and out of jails and drug treatment centers in San Francisco, Oakland and Richmond across the bay. Sadly, those three beautiful children, all under the age of 18 were now in foster care. Mattie too certainly brought home that John Bradford statement, "There but for the grace of God go I…"

Gee Whiz: Looking back, it sounds like a corny title today, but Gee Whiz was the title of a favorite song from my high school days sung by Carla Thomas. Carla was not only a beauty but the sista had voice, she could sing. When Erna brushed past me as students lined up to return to the jail dorms; I couldn't help but notice the firm breasts rubbing across my arm. Looking at her back as she continued past, Erna turned and smiled. So the titty brush was intentional. The following days Erna found reason to talk to me during and briefly after class. I never asked those important questions but Erna told me that Carla Thomas the singer of Gee Whiz was her mother which may or may not have been true, Interesting for maybe a heartbeat, but not really. There was a slight resemblance but Carla Thomas was from Tennessee, so I did wonder how her daughter ended up in San Francisco., and in San Francisco County Jail. But parentage wasn't the issue; I wondered what I should do about her touching me with her body daily. Erna obviously wanted me to do the nasty with her. If I reported Erna she would get in serious trouble and I would be labeled a 'snitch'. Such a label would destroy any trust I had built up among the inmates and possibly destroy the educational program. New to the jail environment, even if I wanted to participate with Erna I didn't know how sex could be squeezed into just minutes of privacy. Minutes at what cost, loss of job, jail time, loss of family, loss of credentials, I could go on. I stalled as Erna managed to be the last person to leave the building at the end of class. She also used my office bathroom several times during class. One day without preamble or notice she just kissed me, pressing her body against mine with a hard sexual grinding. Crazy woman, the guard was just outside the door lining up the other inmates. Having never happened to me before, what should I do? Should a man yell for help in such a situation or enjoy it? Disregarding my reluctance the 2nd time she kissed me Erna grabbed my hand and put it inside her pants. Wearing no underwear; I could feel her tight curly pubic hairs. We could have had a' quickie' then and there, Erna was more than ready, but still I was overcome by caution. I also had to consider those married man feelings of guilt as well as feelings of guilt, even though she was a determined aggressor, about taking advantage of her being trapped in the jail situation. Even a fool who went along with Erna would have to consider the possibility of AIDS, remember Andy. What if Erna was a plant a setup? How would one explain the inexplicable, staff and inmate relations? Frustrated and angry Erna finally realized I wasn't going to do anything.

So following one class she told me she had hooked up with "Johnny Boy' one of the guards during the night. Whew, there is a God, I was thankful. One morning soon after the Erna incident, Pamela the education director informed me that the power was out in the classrooms so the women's classes were cancelled, but I would be teaching the men's class in the dorms. Hmmmmmmmm, The jail dorms was real jail with all the inmates not just the students in my classes. Jailhouse dorms were not where I wanted to be. My cautions and suspicions kicked in, I had noticed a cooling strain in my relationship with Pamela and other jail administrators since I had been having lunch with the female acupuncturist daily. She being only one of two staff members I knew not in a same sex relationship; the other being "Doc" a blind teacher at the jail who I also spent time with. I had also discovered that Pamela too was a graduate of New College School of Law which she didn't mention during my interview for the job. Pamela a fellow New College Alumni who had hired me; I began to wonder, other than work qualification and experience, what additional assumptions went into my hiring? Suddenly finding information about the jail administrators without specifics, I also discovered that the head administrator, as a young man had killed his father and served time in San Quentin, His partner also worked at the jail. It turned out that the captain of the guard was Pamela's partner, and Rene spent much of her time in my office talking to her girlfriend who worked for a local computer company. Daily in the lunchroom I listened to the same topic of proud discussion from the other tables about 12 step programs and days of sobriety. Not gay and having no personals to add to their discussions, heaven forbid, I was not fitting in; which didn't bother me at all. Fool that I was I just wanted to work and go home..

"Blowing In the Wind" Observing the lunchroom faces daily I noticed looks of surprise turn to outright hostility as they observed my talks with the acupuncturist. Clearly we weren't talking about 12 step programs or our number of sober days; it was also well known that neither of us were drinkers or meat eaters. I kinda figured that their lives; who they lived with, who they slept with, what they ate, or drank was very personal and had nothing to do with me, I didn't care! But I expected, no demanded the same courtesy, that's how people live together and get along in a society. But typically it had to be the hard road. Epiphany, suddenly it all made sense as I remembered the rainbow flag back at New College school of law and its' majority of gay students and faculty. The question wasn't on the application for the job at County Jail # 7 but having graduated from New College I could see how Pamela and the other interviewers could happily conclude that I too was gay. Regardless, it seemed to me that even if I had been gay, being gay and or having been addicted were my business and not something one bragged about.

So, that said; was the teaching assignment inside the jail dorms my punishment for having deceived Pamela and the gay multitudes running San Francisco County Jail #7? Was I being sent to work in the dorms because there really was a loss of power? No one had come over to check the classrooms or building. My office was in the same building and the lights and power worked just fine. Yes I wondered. A major reason I preferred not working in the dorms, other than it being inside the jailhouse; was I had to deal with the guards. Driving into the facility and parking in front of my classroom building next door to the jailhouse was about as close as I wanted to get to that irritatingly hostile, slow witted police mentality. Periodically the inmates filled me in on the activities of the guards in the jail dorms. There was Renfro the enforcer, a perfect example of 'little man's disease'. Renfro a former boxer standing about 5'8 on his tippy toes, who with the unstated blessing of the jail administration escorted disagreeable inmates to a room down the hall on the first floor of the jail and beat the shit out of them. Then too there was "Johnny Boy" who took nighttime liberties with both male and female inmates. He even managed to impregnate two inmates during the short time that I worked there. Both had been in county jail for more than a year and a half, so there were quiet chuckles when it was argued that the women were pregnant before they came to jail.

The Dorms: So it was what it was, with arms full of notebooks, pencils, paper and a dubious lesson plan I headed for the jail dorms. Being buzzed through the various doors automatically locking behind me I remembered the hostage form I signed and knew that I was truly in jail. Once inside the dorms, immediately noticeable was the segregation, the separate living areas for the various groups of inmates. Comfortably accepted by the guards and inmates; the blacks occupied the beds and two large tables on the right side of the very large room. Not sure whether it meant anything but the basketball courts were just outside the door from the black area of the dorms. The setup, without the inmate enforced segregation, reminded me of the dorms I lived in when in the Air Force. Other tables were near the entrance and beds were also in the back of the room. Opposite the blacks at the front left side of the room were the Surenos, the sworn enemies of the Nortenos Mexican gang. The Nortenos were seated at the far end of the room near the beds in the back. Another group of Latinos sat at a center table near the door underneath a poorly drawn flag. I was told that the flag was of the Dominican Republic and that they were Dominicans guarding their turf. My students came to the tables I set up in the neutral center front area of the room. There, we were far enough from the various territories including the white area in the back of the dorm. When working in the classroom, several non reading black inmates had shown flashes of anger when I corrected them or gave verbal instructions.

They took it personally as if I was trying to embarrass them or make them look bad. Tony T. was a pretty big fellow. I am 6'3 but when standing next to Tony I had to look up to see his face. Looking into the yard through the fence outside my classroom I watched the inmate basketball games where no one dared call a foul; Tony. T. dominated the court, he was a star. He also seemed to be the leader of the black inmates. Unfortunately that stardom didn't translate into the classroom where even though the computer programs were individualized; others could see the screens and hear my instructions. Consequently, to his absolute embarrassment and loss of face, it became known that Tony T. could not read or write. Just doing my job, I was trying to teach him for starters his A, B, C's; but Tony blamed me for exposing his illiteracy. So on this my first day in the jail dorms, at the start of class I found Tony T. sitting on top of one of the tables. Handing out the writing assignment and treading softly around Tony T. on his home turf, I suggested that the students could work on the assignment alone or in groups of two. The work seemed to be going well with all students participating; even Tony T. joined in the discussion of the questions by pointing out how they related to life outside the jail. Collecting papers and gathering my materials at the end of class, I prepared to leave. When I turned toward the door I saw Tony T. and two other non readers blocking the aisle near the exit. Keeping a steady pace; pretending nonchalance, I also saw the three other blacks not in my class; come from the bed area and sit on the tables blocking the other aisle. One look at the faces and the physical arrangement, any fool could see that it was a set up for a so called 'accidental tripping' followed by an ass kicking, my own. Turning right and disrupting the obvious plan, I walked through the Dominican area to the door and buzzed the guard. Jailhouse mentality in full bloom, the white guards thought it funny to make the "uppity nigger teacher" wait. The longer I stood there at the locked door waiting and watching for Tony. T's group to make their move toward me, the more I considered the possibility of collusion between the guards and Tony T. Several buzzes later the exit door was finally opened, but the jailhouse drama did not end there. Hearing the locks clang behind me I turned left and started down the hallway. A very loud authoritarian "Stop!" came from the speakers just above my head. "Turn around and take the corridor to your right!" Was the command given in a very loud voice. Later Andy told me why I was not allowed to use the same hallway I had used to enter the dorm room. The jail guard Renfro the boxer also known as 'The Enforcer' was working over an inmate in the special punishment room down the left hallway. Just learning the rules as I moved down the 'correct' right hallway, I found quite a surprise, lo and behold there was a familiar face from my not so distant past approaching.

Angela: Back in the late 60's, I drove over to UCLA to attend Angela's afternoon class.

Upon arrival there always was a long line of mostly non UCLA students outside the building, waiting to crash Angela's class. Of course I was there because I had heard rumors and listened to several stories about the numerous fine ladies inside and outside of her classroom just dying to associate with and talk to black men. Any way there with me in the hallway to the right at San Francisco County Jail # 7 was none other than Angela Davis. A little thicker and grayer, she looked pretty much the same. Pleasantly surprised, I stopped, "Hello Ms. Davis, it is an absolute honor to meet you." I said. Ignoring my outstretched hand and looking straight ahead Angela Davis soundlessly walked past as if I wasn't there. Later talking to Lance, a Native American activist who taught at the jail, he said Angela was one of several former activists teaching at the jail. Her full time teaching job was just down the road at San Francisco State. Having only met her in my reading, Angela Davis was nothing like I imagined. What a rude arrogant bitch. So much for past heroes, who should remain in the past.

San Francisco State University: The following Monday power was restored and classes resumed in the building alongside the main jail. Three of the students in the classes had completed most of their high school level programs and were deep into advanced math and science college courses. They would be out of county jail by early spring, so I came up with what I thought was a great idea. Two of them already had high school diplomas and the third inmate had finished his GED while in my class at the county jail making them eligible for college. Crazy idea, why not? I set up a meeting with the three young men and told them about the plan. With my help they were going to apply for fall admission to San Francisco State University. Yeah, that was a bit much for them and it took a while for them to wrap their heads around the idea, but finally they reluctantly agreed. During the following months Freddie Lee, Ted and Leo, still in jail couldn't attend the required campus orientation interviews. So after work each day, in their stead I visited the various offices and orientations they had missed advocating for my students. During the coming months Freddie Lee, Leo and Ted were the envy of their fellow inmates who called them "The College boys". Needless to say San Francisco State administrators and staff weren't pleased with the idea of county jail inmates attending their school. I pointed out that my students like many of us had made petty youthful mistakes; small time drug charges in this case; and that the hard work done in my classes was clear evidence of Freddie Lee, Leo and Ted's rehabilitation. Listening to my daily pleas, San Francisco State administrators finally agreed to admit them on a trial basis for the fall semester. I was overjoyed, high fives all around. Of course the warning from the school administrators I also passed onto the boys. I was told that at the first indications or hint of any problems, Eddie Lee, Leo and Ted would be immediately dropped from the school.

Angela/Before

Admission to San Francisco State intact, a few weeks before the start of school in September the three were outside back in San Francisco. Once or twice a week I called to see how things were going with questions like, "Have you been down to the school? Have you signed up for your classes?" Flat out no's to all inquiries did cause a bit of worry on my part but I didn't know what else I could do. Things quickly came to a head on the first day of school when only Ted showed up for a required freshman orientation. Ms. Huddleston, head of admissions who I had argued with a number of times to get those guys admitted was running the orientation class. In an irritating I told you so voice she said to me, "Ted was the only one of your convicts who showed up and he was drunk." Guess it couldn't be said that I didn't see it coming. In my conversations with the three of them, sensing their fear I thought maybe hope and great expectations might overcome minor obstacles. But obstacles sometimes too are point of view kind of judgments. Their culture of fear was much bigger than I anticipated. How does feelings of overwhelming hopelessness and low expectations and assumptions of failure develop? Where do those feelings of inferiority and that, "I absolutely cannot do it." belief about the simplest tasks develop? I have been told that disappointment often follows great pride; although Freddie Lee, Leo and Ted didn't seem at all proud or disappointed about the San Francisco State debacle. On the contrary they were greatly relieved. Neither of them ever made it to a class before being dropped from the school. That pride and disappointment was more mine than theirs. I was the one proudly bragging to jail administrators, teachers and other students about getting them into San Francisco State. Foolishly ignoring past history and negative habits I anticipated this great turnaround in their lives with great futures ahead of them I, I, I, I, Me, the jail, San Francisco State was far less than the tiniest blip in their lives. Ms. Huddleston summed it up by saying, "Dr. Williams you put your heart and soul into getting those young men into school. Unfortunately, they put nothing into the process. Let it go, shake if off, and enjoy your life." Well that was a mouthful coming from that woman who I had referred to as that arrogant hussy several times. So with new lessons learned, I was back to the reality of the day to day jail time.

Caged: Guards, administrators, inmates and teachers; all were engaged, caught up in the 'normalcy' of that abnormal jail environment. I suppose it is only human, wherever we happen to be or in whatever circumstance; after a while we convince ourselves that it is 'normal', just routine. It bothered me daily the thought of, and the participation in a process that kept poor people and mostly men and women of color caged. Maybe the failure of my San Francisco State project was the catalyst but afterwards I realized I wasn't helping to alleviate the problems but simply adding comfort to an unchanging situation.

One couldn't help but notice, when being processed out, in their outdated clothing with faces to match, the inmates really didn't want to leave. Guards laughingly told stories of inmates who had been outside only a few days before breaking a store window downtown or doing some other act of vandalism to get arrested and returned to jail. Those humans didn't want to leave their cages, their shelter. Speaking to numerous aspects of our society such knowledge was scary in its profundity.Still, on the other hand, I saw those very same sad faces pressed against the metal fence when walking to my car on Fridays preparing for that long drive home. In my rearview mirror I could still see the tearful conflicted faces wishing for the outside as I drove freely past the armed guard at the main gate. All were wishing for the outside, although knowing they were afraid of having to leave. Outside dreams were the one story, but the other story reflected the sadness seen in the eyes of animals locked in cages at the zoo. Animals, including humans should not be caged. To cage an animal is merely a means to confine sadness for visual display. At the zoo folks are paying to see such a display, while pretending the caged animals are happy and content. Those very same folk pay taxes and finance a system of police, laws and courts which cages the mentally ill, chronically poor and people of color. But in the jails there is no pretense of contentment; the one goal is to keep those human animals locked away from the majority population. The various caretakers and others are well paid to isolate and guarantee that the caged humans are NOT seen or heard. Yes much like their fellow zoo animals they are caged and confined but rarely on display because their cages are in isolated and unseen places. How do we positively change the situation for both caged animals? Maybe education and training could be salvation for the animals in the jails, and we could bring salvation to those in the zoos by returning them to their natural habitats. To reiterate, teaching is a major aspect of that societal fix, that is what schools do; prepare citizens to participate in the governmental process. Starting at Pre School it's all about making productive conforming citizens. Unfortunately, if not tuned in at an early age to successful cooperative participation in schools (government), it is practically impossible to find success later in life. Much like other animals, we are indeed creatures of habit, and those positive habits of reading, writing and arithmetic in all variations, MUST be started as early as or before one year of age and continued throughout one's life. The earlier the better, middle school may be too late. Just imagine the chances of success if by their early 20's our young citizens in training habitually find themselves in jail. With that indisputable 20/20 hindsight it should not have come as such a surprise that the three inmates admitted to San Francisco State were no shows. Just the thought of their past and present obstacles that had to be suddenly overcome is humbling.The multifaceted complex fix for theirs and similar situations starts long before the application to San Francisco State or any other college.

Yes, pre school for ALL children with food, clothing, housing and safety a surety for ALL. Of course that would take lots of Benjamins and a relaxation of the racism and overall bigotry of our 77% white privileged majority population. It would also necessitate and end to US polices that pay trillions of dollars to groups and countries that hate us. We pay just to try to make them like us. Sounds simplistic and stupid, well any fool can see the stupidity except those morons in Washington. We might also stop attacking and destroying the governments of countries we dislike. That 'become a democracy' or we are going to kill you' attitude is outdated, imperialistic, senseless and dumb. If we break away all the political vested interests and other bullshit, salvation is simple. Remember the schoolyard kids who pay off other kids to like them are disrespected and called punks and wussies. Those who force others to think and do as they do are called bullies. Yes, all that ass kissing and bully billions of taxpayer monies paid to other countries by self interested Washington politicians could be spent here at home to insure the preparation and well being of ALL our children which in turn would guarantee the future well being of our country. I could rave on about the fixes forever, but who's listening? No one; politicians spend years making a great living by avoiding talking about those fixes while thinking about and doing what their billionaire backers suggest.

But drag me from the soap box and let me get back to teaching at San Francisco County Jail #&7. County Jail #7 was where I had been teaching for two years. Two years is a very long to be confined, in jail. Not a criminal, officially; other than the criminality assumed to go with skin color by that police mentality, wherever encountered; yet my weekdays were spent in jail. Working in a jail the guards, towers, gates, locks and guns becomes a major part of your weekly, monthly, yearly life. Slowly those visuals, presumptions and attitudes of the job in a jail steals away the hope and joy of teaching. In jail I was facing daily the end game; that is dealing with the results of the untaught. The untaught prisoners in jails includes both locked inside; the guards and the inmates. And, 'quiet as it is kept' both groups seem quite comfortable in their respective positions of ignorance. Observing their comfort and that of a growing system supporting them; merely added to my discomfort and need to get the hell away from there immediately. I learned a lot at County Jail #7, much of which I didn't want to know. I saw things I didn't want to see and heard much that I didn't want to hear; but then education and teaching is also a learning process.I took the job at the jail to get back into education, I was back and the job had served its purpose and it was time to start job hunting again. Looking at the openings in the inner cities I didn't think finding a new job would be a problem. Fortunately and unfortunately; there weren't very many black males lounging about with proper licenses, credentials and a doctorate. Consequently I figured the search would be a 'piece of cake'.

But I also had a wife and two kids and bills at home as added incentive and a teensy bit of worry. Yes, the most important part of life was/is always the home front.

The Home Front: Many of us get so wrapped up in our work and other things outside the home, supposedly to make home a better place we ignore that which is central to everything we do; the place itself and the people we love. With the wife also working full time as a teacher and two sons in 1st and 7th grades at Fieldsburg Elementary and junior high schools we were learning how to build and maintain a family. What's it like being a husband, wife, mother, father, a child; who remembers? There are no manuals, all the training is on-the-job. But so many things; a part of the experience; good and bad are unforgettable. The miracle of the birth of YOUR child is a mind altering lifetime happening as is the death; and all the occurrences and events that preceded and follows. Birthdays, schools, teams, friends, pets, toys, travel, and reading, "The Night Before Christmas" yearly with the rapt attention of both listeners from early childhood and into their early teens are also memorable. Most fathers I try to shield the family from all potentially dangerous and scary situations. Agreeably parenting is a full time job, as is being a husband, but I do suspect that raising two black sons was much harder; not that being a husband was easy. We all want our kids, our families to live in safe neighborhoods with excellent schools. Unfortunately such neighborhoods and schools most often are located in white communities. White people like most are comfortable living in the cleanest, safest and beautiful cities and neighborhoods. But many feel anxious and get angry if blacks dare seek that same comfort, cleanliness, safety and beauty for their families. While the wife and I were jumping through those aforementioned racist hoops to find and maintain that comfort, beauty, cleanliness, and neighborhood safety; our kids too faced unique obstacles. From grades K-12 our sons were the only black kids in their classes and at times the only black kids attending their schools. Although maintaining a constant watchfulness, still there were issues and many things we couldn't control. During the work week we all came together after school for homework and during dinner. At such time the four of us sat at the table where we shared comments, questions and the day's activities. How was school today? How did you do on that test were typical dinnertime queries. Also on this day sitting at the table curiosity was running amok as we wondered why green peas were on the floor underneath Sulo's chair. When asked why Neemie said, "Pop those are Sulo's peas!" Smiling we listened as Neemie blamed his older brother Sulo who sat on the opposite side of the table for the floor peas. A very tolerant older brother, Sulo accepted most of his little brother's nonsense. And of course we all knew how much Neemie hated veggies.

Sulo: Other than the day to day routine the home; the first major crisis came when our oldest moved from elementary to junior high school. Suo from an early age was fairly closed and rarely talked about his experiences outside the home. Our first child and for most of his life until his brother was born he was the only black kid in the neighborhood and at his school. So I always suspected that things happened that he didn't mention to the family. Whatever he might be going through we had to pry it out of him, partly because he wasn't quite sure how his Pop would react. Sulo's greatest fear was the thought of me storming down to his school and going off. Sulo having just started junior high I asked, "Are any of the kids from elementary school in your junior high classes?" "Nope, I have only one class and we're in the same room all day."Sulo said. Both knowing how schools work; he wife and I looked at each other. Unspoken rule, from the look in her eye I knew it was one of those things fathers take care of. After the kids were put to bed we agreed that I would take off from work the following Wednesday and see what was up at the junior high school.

Fieldsburg Junior High School: Reporting to the principals office I found Faith Massey who I had worked with when she was a teacher at Renton High School. Unchanged, cherubically overweight dark roots still showed in her short blond hair. Faith had been one of the first teachers to go in and join the SCABS during our teachers strike. Maybe it was strike memories but she wouldn't look me in the eye in her office or the hallway. Sitting off to one side, Sulo greeted me with a wink when we walked into his classroom. He was one of twelve students, all black in the class. I never realized that there were twelve blacks in the whole town let alone one junior high school classroom. Were they recruited? A quick look around at the various work stations and the hands on materials one could easily see that it was a Special Education Class. After meeting and chatting with the teacher, we headed back to Faith's office. My very first tactless question was, "What the fuck is my son doing in a special education class?" Faith stammered, "As you well know student placement in the class is dependent on their test scores in reading and math." "Have you seen Sulo's test scores Faith?" I asked. She got up from her desk and closed her office door; reckon I was getting a little loud. "Well no, but I am sure the counselors have."Her racist bullshit didn't surprise me; black kids regardless of scores, without a parent or other advocates to this day are routinely placed in low level and special education classes. We had been working with both our kids daily since birth; the wife even read and sang to them when they were in the womb. We knew their strengths, weaknesses, and their test scores. Sulo had tested above 10th grade level in both reading and math when he was in the 6th grade. Regardless, when moving from elementary to junior high school; test scores be dammed; he had been placed in a special education class simply because he was black. So for more than a month Sulo had been sitting in that classroom twiddling his thumbs all day. I was pissed.

"Tomorrow, Thursday my son will be out of that class and in the regular college prep academic program or we will talk to a judge in a court of law!" I didn't slam the door but when walking out I saw serious concern on the faces of the secretaries and students on the benches. Sulo was all smiles at dinner Thursday evening when he told us about his new classes. Those new classes was the easy part, there were more complex child raising issues. Sulo and his mother were especially close, although when he was much younger we spent time together. I worried about him often. One day driving along on the freeway, Sulo must have been two or three. Sitting on the passenger side in the truck he was holding a balloon which accidentally blew out of the window. Sulo suddenly stood crouching to jump out of the window at 60 miles an hour to grab his balloon. Horrified, grabbing his chest and pushing him down into the seat I pulled off to the side of the freeway. Sweating scared out of my mind I tried to explain the danger and that it was only a balloon. "Can we go now pop?" Sulo asked. Surviving that scare I wrote it off as just a frightful child raising incident, until the next one.

When he was about six years old Sulo and I often traveled to our land located near Middletown in Lake County. Highway 29, a two lane road over the mountain past streams, waterfalls, boulders bigger than houses, deer and other animals; was a beautiful drive. After heavy overnight rains, on this day I decided to stop and take pictures of a fast running waterfall, ferociously dragging giant boulders and large trees down the mountain. Clambering upon a gigantic rock, awestruck we watched the fury of the powerful water rushing down the mountainside. While taking pictures, I happened to glance to my left at Sulo standing beside me. With a far off look in his eyes he was beginning to lean forward on our high rock perch. Before he completed his plunge into the foaming, bubbling, downhill rushing water; I grabbed him and carried him to our waiting truck. "What the hell is wrong with you? You were going to fall into that creek! Are you nuts?" Frightened, pissed, what to do, I was at a loss. Driving home, fruitlessly I tried to have a conversation about life and death, about living and dying but I am sure it meant nothing to a child. Home, I didn't tell his mother what happened because I didn't know what to say. "Our six year old son tried to commit suicide today." Are six year olds even aware of the concepts of life and death, the idea of suicide? It's certainly not a common topic among parents, maybe at certain younger ages it is just the craziness of childhood. My eight year old nephew I caught sitting quietly behind the wheel of his fathers car as he was about to back out of the garage. I snatched him out of the way in time and gave him a good spanking; still such childhood actions are inexplicable. Perhaps they are routine, but neither as a child or an adult did suicidal craziness ever cross my mind. Unable to forget the look in Sulo's eyes on that rock above the rushing water I put him on a special watch list following that incident.

Middletown, California

Maybe just the common occurrences of child raising but soon thereafter followed another frightful event. Living in a small neighborhood complex at the end of a dead end street, we knew all the neighbors well enough to say hello when passing. One day during the morning rush to get the kids ready for school and the babysitter we suddenly noticed that Sulo was not in his room or any other part of the house. Hurriedly preparing for the workday and one of your kids is missing, what do you do? This was no movie; it was real life happening to us! Getting 'the look' from the wife I knew whatever action taken was the responsibility of the father, me. Leaving Barbara and Neemie on the couch in the living room I told her I would start by going door to door in the neighborhood asking if they had seen our missing child. It was very early, 6:00 AM on a weekday morning when I knocked first on the door of the neighbor to our immediate left. He hadn't seen our son or anyone else other than me that morning, so on to the next house. Brad, a beefy 6'4 construction worker with a wife and two kids in high school was the next house. Not necessarily a friendly family but they hadn't shown hostility the two years they'd lived in the neighborhood. Such neutrality was a win for me and the family as far as I was concerned. After Brad opened the door I peered around him and saw Sulo sitting at their breakfast table with his wife and two kids having a bowl of cereal. What the hell! I couldn't imagine how a family could let a kid from down the street into their home without any communication or permission from their parents. When I called his name Sulo got up from the table and without a word we walked home. Overwhelmed with happiness at finding our lost son safe, I don't remember the words within the family, but I do remember being pissed at Brad for a long time. You would think they would have asked Sulo, "Do your parents know you are here?" To soon there was another frightening occurrence.

On another occasion we were visiting a friend in Mendocino with young Charles Patterson Junior, about 11 or 12 at the time. We left baby Neemie with our friend Julie while the four of us decided to go wading in the river. Flowing at a fast pace, our steps in the river was slow and wavering. Standing together and looking to our front we saw Sulo about five feet away floating past underwater with a big smile. Panicked, both the wife and I running against the current, we knew we couldn't reach him before he was swept away and drowned. Of course seven year old Sulo couldn't swim a lick. Glancing from my son to his mother, I saw our shared look of helpless horror. Charles Junior standing much closer reached out a hand grabbed Sulo's arm and snatched him still smiling to the surface. Floating past underwater and unknowingly scaring the hell out of his parents Sulo was having a great time. With a puzzled look on his face, he didn't understand the joyful hugs and the unending thank you's, for junior as we dragged him to shore. Yeah we were still learning that child rearing was stressful and more.

The Neptunes: Upon our return home from the near disastrous Mendocino trip Barbara started looking around for swimming lessons for Sulo. He spent the summer taking lessons in the city pool to become a beginning swimmer. One of the summer coaches also coached the city's youth swimming club, The Neptunes. The Neptunes swim team enlisted kids from ages 5-18 for swim training and competition against other city teams in mostly Northern California and sometimes Southern California cities. The two hour practices were usually after school but at times before school as well. It was a welcome relief when Sulo learned to drive; now he could drive them both to practice each day. Both Sulo and Neemie grew up with the Neptunes and the Neptune families. Camping out in motels during weekend meets in various towns and cities we became a part of a swimming fraternity of kids and families. Vallejo, Benicia, Petaluma, Sonoma, Healdsburg, Berkeley, Palo Alto, Cloverdale, San Jose, Eureka, Ukiah, Concord, Walnut Creek, are just a few of the cities that comes to mind. Most starting out as toddlers it was amazing watching the kids and Neptune families grow together. As they aged, many of those very same kids competed with and against their fellow Neptunes on high school swimming and water polo teams. A good thing because many of the same families who were used to watching out for the kids during Neptune meets; with a bit more subtly continued to do during the high school years. Having grown up with the Neptunes by the time Sulo reached high school he was a very good freestyle sprinter. Forever etched in my memory are the many times sitting in the bleachers watching him; poised on the starting blocks for his specialty the 50 yard freestyle. Barely 5'6 and always the only black, one couldn't help but notice how the white sprinters rarely less than 6'4; towered over Sulo. Parents in the stands and the kids competing against him wondered, who is that little guy wearing a superman t-shirt? Habitually finishing first with a 50 free time in the low 20's; after a while all knew that the kid in the superman shirt was Sulo. During those hot summer days crowded around pools throughout Northern California, coaches and families provided a safe nurturing environment for kids. With music lessons for both added to swim activities, their days were pretty full. Especially when things are going so well, we do imagine, hope that the next day, week, month, year, will be the same. As you may well know, there really are unimaginable things that happen, not just in stories told, books read or just to strangers, but to people we know and love, and to us as well. Unfortunately, herein I must tell such stories. Comfortable at our jobs, the kids were active and well monitored, things were going very well. But there were other child raising surprises. God is good.

Life: After a major, most frightening surprise, very close to a parent's worse nightmare; our relationship with our son Sulo changed dramatically. That change and the additional awareness will remain with us for the rest of our lives.

Sulo and Neemie

Neemie

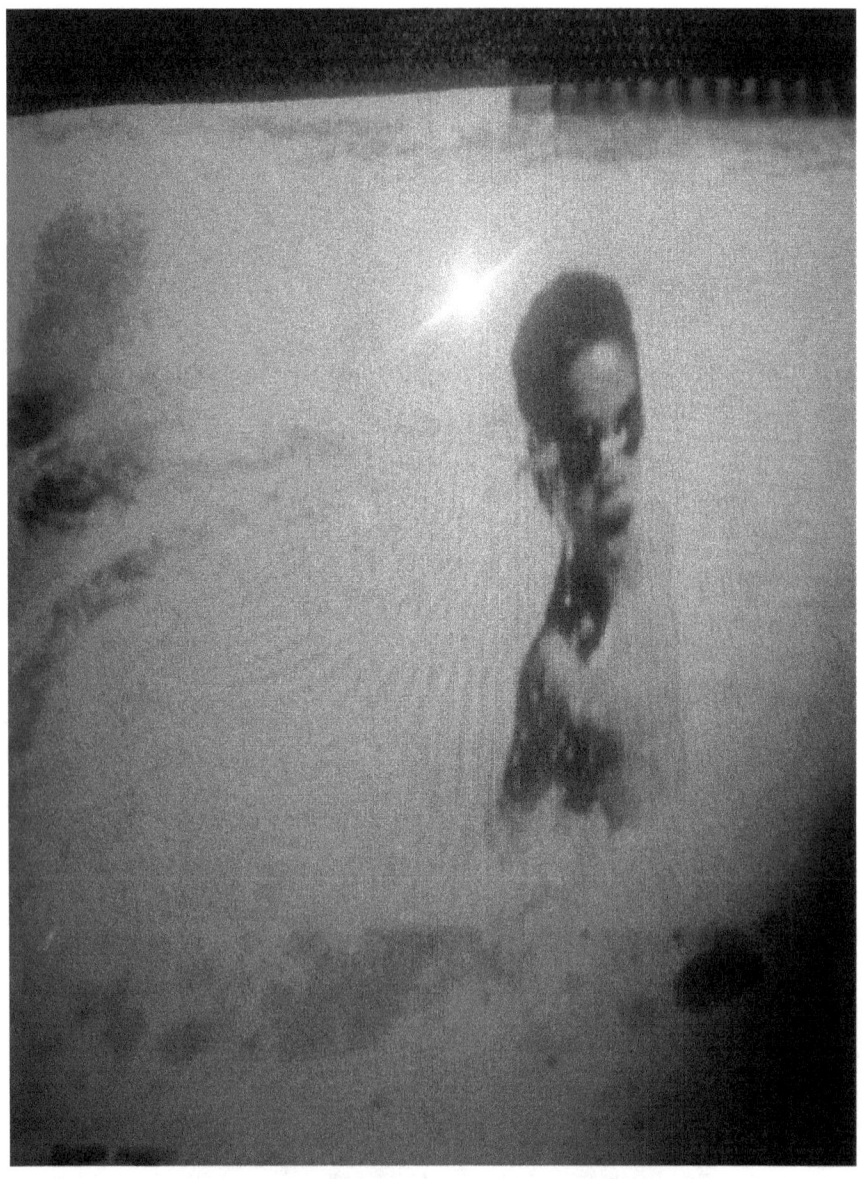

On this day; Sulo was 14 or 15 years old; we all came home from school and went about our normal routines. As mentioned earlier the most important part of our after school routine was the meeting at the dinner table, where unlike the morning rush it was a slower family time. With all present we would share our day's activities. Seeing Sulo's empty chair I asked Neemie, "Where is your brother?" Unconcerned, continuing to eat his dinner Neemie said, "He's lying on his bed, he doesn't feel good."Having never happened before, early evening skipping dinner and in bed was odd. With growing concern, we shared the 'parent' look. Still learning fatherhood and parenting, and knowing that if I made a wrong decision I would hurt the only people on the planet I absolutely unquestionably loved; I couldn't help but feel a sudden fear and discomfort. Rising from the table and turning left walking down the hallway towards Sulo's room I felt all those things and more. Yeah I was scared. Reaching the corner and turning right through the open doorway I saw Sulo lying on his unmade bed in a fetal position holding his stomach. "Why aren't you having dinner?" "Pop my stomach hurts." I asked, "Is it something you ate?" "No I took some pills." He said in a tired monotone. Not one pill but"…I took SOME pills." He said to me. What to do, all my emergency alarms went off, I had never been so afraid. Forcing myself to stay calm I asked, "How many pills?" Pointing to the discarded topless Tylenol bottle on the floor he said, "All of them." "Get up!" Pulling Sulo from his bed, leaning on my shoulder we wobbled down the hallway. His mother and younger brother Neemie looked on in wild eyed horror at the droopy stumbling Sulo. Meeting at the garage door I told Barbara what happened. Putting Sulo in the passenger side of the truck; "Call the emergency room at the hospital and tell them we are on our way" Slamming my drivers side door as Barbara opened the garage, I quickly backed out and started the longest trip of my life. Driving mostly with my left hand I ignored speed limits and the color of traffic lights. Early evening in that small town where many families after a long day were comfortably sitting down to dinner with their children; but not my family today. On the drive luckily I didn't see one other vehicle on the road. Shaking, poking and slapping with my right hand to keep Sulo awake, until after forever; we finally arrived at the hospital emergency room. Jumping from the vehicle, engine still running; I dashed inside carrying a dozing Sulo. "Right this way"; said the young dark haired nurse wearing surgical greens. Now limp in my arms, I was directed to place Sulo on the shiny metallic treatment table in the small room. After listening to my additional explanation, Barbara had already called and told them what had happened; Dr.Moriarty suggested that I could wait outside. But I didn't move, not wanting my son to be alone in the crisis, whatever was to happen I stood rooted beside the table. Feeling that overwhelming need to monitor, to watch and see what they did to my son, with great reluctance I finally left the room. Filling out the hospital forms only took a few minutes, and then the wait began.

Before the age of cell phones, sitting on the bench near the treatment room doors for hours, I had no way of contacting Barbara. Sure there was a pay phone outside but I wasn't leaving that seat by the door of that room for any reason. Three hours later, Dr. Moriarty came out and explained that they had pumped out Sulo's stomach. He said the thought they got everything out in time and hopefully there would be no permanent damage to internal organs. Meanwhile Sulo had been moved to a room on the hospital ward for observation. Eerie is the word that comes to mind as I remember standing beside the hospital bed staring at my sleeping oldest child. Somewhat relieved, I was still left wondering how such a thing could happen to my family. A very long night but at least two of the four family members slept well that night; the oldest with a hospital drug induced sleep and Neemie the youngest enjoyed the sleep of youthful innocence. With a mental picture of her sitting at the kitchen table drinking cup after cup of coffee, I finally called Barbara about 3:00 AM and told her that I would be staying the night at Sulo's bedside and that we would be home when he was discharged later that morning. Overwhelmed as was she by the circumstances and the sadness in her voice; I listened as Barbara agreed that staying with a sleeping Sulo was a good idea. Arriving home with Sulo early Saturday morning we found Barbara still sitting at the kitchen table with the stack of papers she had graded during the night. Maybe he was uncomfortable with the staring questioning eyes from the three of us, but Sulo didn't have much to say during breakfast which he finished quickly and went to his room. Yes alone in his room for the moment but Sulo would be observed with caution by his family and whenever possible, monitored by the three of us for the rest of that day and the rest of his life. At the time we did wonder whether such craziness would affect his younger brother, but maybe it was the 6 year age difference, not at all.

1st **Suicide Attempt; What Now?** Like most folk the thought of suicide never crossed our minds; it was some bizarre thing that you read about in books and newspapers which a few unfortunate others must contend with. Now, uninvited suddenly suicide was a part of our lives. Even when your loved one survives the attempt there remains that feeling of confronting death. After an unsuccessful one you can't shake off the possibility, the consequence of a successful attempt. What do we do about the unspoken anger there amidst the love and joy; how dare Sulo bring such disruptive fear and drama to the family! Then too there are the intrusive reminders as hospitals and related agencies, heeding the call of the Benjamins try to step into the heretofore closed family circle. Without our permission or consultation the hospital scheduled appointments for the family with sociologist, psychologists and other uninvited helpers who we had to avoid keeping any sense of family normalcy. Pardon my cynicism but hospitals comfortably collect their exorbitant fees, whatever the insurance carriers will bear, plus what extra they can squeeze out of their patients. And then they freely suggest and make those unrequested appointments with other related medical hustlers waiting in the wings. A week after our emergency room visit we got a telephone call at home telling us of a scheduled appointment with a Dr. Arby Vicuna. Walking into the psychologist's office the first thing I noticed was his size, or lack thereof. Sitting in the chair at his desk, I saw his fwwt dangling at least 14 inches from the floor. After chatting for a few minutes and asking very personal questions, such as; "Are you happy in your marriage? Does an interracial marriage create problems for the children?"Dr. Vicuna then suggested that each family member, including Sulo and Neemie set up individual appointments to see him in the coming weeks. Knowing the first appointment, at a cost of $100 an hour was covered by insurance; I didn't cuss him out. Of course it helped that Barbara, anticipating my reaction; surreptitiously elbowed me in the side before I could say what I wanted to say to that moron. As we were walking out of his office, without setting up family appointments; Dr. Vicuna obviously irritated, gave us the name and phone number of the sociologist assigned to 'our case". Humph, it felt so good not getting mired in that psycho-socio hustle. Avoiding the bullshit we took all our recent drama back home with the family. It was now well past that time for the conversation we had been avoiding for weeks as we, worried and watched Sulo 24/7. Yes, the suicide conversation, that most unenviable task fell to me, it was the fathers job I was told. Like Barbara and younger brother Neemie I too tried the impossible; to keep an eye on Sulo at all times. But what about when he was at school or walking to and from school? How could Barbara and I continue working, dropping off and picking up the youngest, plus attend meetings and other activities and watch a suicidal child 24/7? Impossible, something had to give, so came that one sided conversation that I had been putting off. But first, why did he even contemplate and attempt suicide? We heard from one of his friends at school that Sulo had asked a girl to the movies. She told him that she asked her father for permission and he told her she couldn't go out with a "...damm nigger!" I got that information from one of Sulo's friends before my suicide speech, not that it would have changed anything. "You are our son and brother and we all love you. Having no idea why you would choose death rather than life, now we are constantly watching, afraid that you will try to kill yourself again. But I have come to realize that at your age, or any age, it is your life. Although it would bring unimaginable pain to all of the family; if you choose to end your life there is nothing I or anyone else can do about it." Not one to show lots of emotion, after the longest speech I had ever given for him; I hugged Sulo; "We love you son," and walked from his room. At the time I had no idea that I would have cause to remember that speech, no parent would. We survived that attempt and proudly watched Sulo 'kick ass' academically and athletically the following years.

Princeton

Straight A's through junior high and high school, upon graduation he was accepted every place where he applied. After acceptances at Stanford, Cal, Harvard, Princeton, and Yale we stopped applying, application fees add up. Majoring in English with a Theatre minor Sulo is proud to be a Princeton Alumnus. At the time of Sulo's junior high suicide crisis Neemie my youngest was dealing with his own issues at the school Sulo had just left, Fieldsburg Elementary. Of course Neemie was so young; I don't think he realized they were issues. Maybe the rewards, and the joys of accomplishment are greater yada, yada, yada; but again raising kids is no joke, especially when color is added to the mix. Yes, "Black is beautiful" and too "Black Lives Matter" but its hard ass work. Not only must you like other parents, try to shield your kids from the normal pitfalls of growing up, but you must also protect them from the many racists and the racism that permeates all aspects of society. Other parents, students, neighbors, police, teachers; all must be monitored when interacting with your child. Generally most adults will go out of their way NOT to harm children, but unfortunately; that's all out the window when the child is black or brown. Much too soon Neemie's unspoken idol, brother and protector was at the junior high school. .

Fieldsburg Elementary School: Literally from birth, Neemie was in the spotlight.Barbara, his Italian-American mom had been to the hospital several times for checkups during the pregnancy. My first visit to the hospital came immediately following Neemie's birth. Looking around the wife's room I of course asked, "Where is our son?" Her calm response scared me, "He's in ICU." What the hell, just born and he was in the intensive care unit, and she didn't know why. Arriving in a panic at the ICU I asked the duty nurse; "Why is my son here?", "His name?" Upon hearing Neemie Williams, the tall thin white nurse, face reddened with embarrassment, just looked at me and said, "Oh!" Neemiewas immediately moved from the ICU and into the room with his mother. Much later we got a chuckle or two out of the absurdity as the story was told to us by the wife's gynecologist, Dr. Woodson. Having never seen me the black father, hospital staff saw baby Neemie, born of a white mother and immediately thought his skin was dark due to oxygen deprivation; although there were no other noticeable breathing problems. Other symptoms be dammed, dark color alone meant oxygen deprivation, so they rushed him to ICU. Hey, 'better safe than sorry'. Neemie was probably the first black baby they had ever seen. That ICU baby was soon in elementary school; oh the wonders of medicine. Overall Neemie the 2nd son's time spent at Fieldsburg Elementary was much easier than his older brothers. Neemie was a much more relaxed, maybe it's that 2nd child syndrome. By the time Neemie got to Fieldsburg Elementary School we had spent many hours volunteering at every opportunity looking out for Sulo.

Faculty and staff knew that Neemie was Sulo's brother; the child of parents who if there was any hint of mistreatment or unfairness, would immediately come down to the school. Tom Minton the new Fieldsburg Elementary Principal was a friend and distance runner as were we. We often saw Tom at local races. He was also a fellow student in my graduate classes at nearby Sonoma State University. Relaxed and well spoken, Tom liked Neemie, also a young 5k and 10k runner; who he had first met at running events. So things were going as they should have gone; exceptionally well for Neemie at Fieldsburg Elementary. So it came as quite a surprise when Neemie in his relaxed comfortable manner dropped a bombshell at the dinner table. He asked, "Pop what's a nigger?" "Where did you hear that word?" Barbara gave me a look; it seems my sudden intensity was frightening the kids. With maximum concentration willing myself to calm down and listen, we heard Neemie's story. He said the class was noisy right after recess and his teacher, Mr. Gehring yelled at him; "Neemie, sit down you little nigger!" Neemie said he later asked several students, "What is a nigger?" and no one knew what the word meant. After explaining the mean history of the word beginning with the Niger River in Africa in the past, and its current use by racists and haters today, I listened as the kids talked about other aspects of their school day. Kids, how easily they move on, I didn't. The following morning, taking a day off from the job, I walked the three blocks to school with Neemie. We arrived before the morning bell, so Neemie put his backpack in the classroom and joined his friends on the playground. Entering the room, I saw Mr. Gehring, who we met at back to school night, sitting alone at his desk. Hearing my approach the 5'8 twenty something, weighing in at possibly 130 pounds soaking wet; Mr. Gehring stood and asked; "May I help you?" Wordlessly stepping behind his desk and grabbing his shirt front and shoving him hard against the chalkboard I asked; "Are you the redneck son of a bitch who called my son a nigger?" Mr. Gehring couldn't have answered if he wanted to; my left arm was tightly against the little hater's throat. Hard at my task, I didn't hear the bell sound or kids entering the room. Shocked to find the teacher pinned against the chalkboard, one ran down to the office to get the principal. "What!" Letting go the shirt I turned ready to strike; when I noticed it was Tom standing behind me with a worried look on his face. "Mr. Williams if there is a problem we can step down to my office." Glancing around the classroom; picking up on the drama I noticed my son Neemie and the other frightened little kids, all crowded around the doorway staring wide eyed. Embarrassed, unhanding that asshole Gehring, I sheepishly followed Tom from the room. Walking past the other classrooms and teachers I felt like a naughty kid being taken to the office to see the principal. Comfortably seated in his office Tom asked; "What the hell was that all about?" He listened as I told of the family discussion at the dinner table the night before. In the following silence I saw surprise, bewilderment, and other emotions flitting across Tom's face as he sat quietly.

No Mistake; the Neighborhood

I couldn't shake that old elementary school days feeling of "being in trouble in the principal's office." Sitting there also gave time to consider the possible negative consequences for my rash actions witnessed by so many, including the principal. Assault and battery on Mr. Gehring for starters, not to mention possible emotional distress inadvertently inflicted on the children who witnessed the minor altercation. Finally I listened with patience and understanding as Tom outlined the steps I should have taken before confronting Mr. Gehring. Yes, I should have called Tom or dropped by his office and told him what had happened the day before in Gehring's classroom. No, I shouldn't have laid hands on Mr. Gehring. Tiring of my looks of staged contrition, Tom stood, offered his hand and said, "I'll take care of it." And that was the last I heard of "…it…"but the very next day a new teacher was in Neemie's classroom and we never saw Mr. Gehring again. Neemie's remaining years at Fieldsburg Elementary were uneventful, other than teacher expectations. Brother Sulo was a hard act to follow. Neemie was expected to perform academically just as well or better than had his older brother. Easily as bright or brighter Neemie showed little or no interest in school work. Friends, social activities, and play were much more fun. Tracking down missed homework was frustrating; we knew the work was done because we helped with and checked his homework daily. But upon completion of the work Neemie often lost it or forgot to turn it in. We found missing class assignments behind his bed, on the floor or underneath the bookshelf in his cluttered room. Six years younger than his older brother, the people aspects of life were much more interesting to him than academics. In many ways the boys were so much alike yet very different. Sulo always showed more interest in his Italian-American roots and spent time hanging around his Italian-American relatives. Whereas Neemie leaned more toward his African American roots and wanted to hang with his African American family members. It was all good with us as parents; but helping Neemie discover his African American roots led to several memorable occasions in Compton, CA., Gould, Arkansas, and other places during family gatherings.

Roots Weekend: Living in the town of Fieldsburg, I was far away from Los Angeles and Compton, where I lived while attending college during my early California years. I worked very hard so thankfully my wife, Sulo and Neemie could avoid that inner city experience. But suddenly Neemie, living in the practically all white world of Fieldssburg, wanted to experience "Black things." So I called my brother CW, giving him a great laugh as I explained that Neemie was having some kind of identity crisis and wanted to taste ham hocks and chitlins. Having listened to my Compton and LA stories, and now listening to Compton rappers Neemie insisted on visiting Compton and hanging out with his Black relatives. Fine with us, we hadn't seen the LA folk in a while.

But first I had to explain the LA rules. Never look at others on the freeways or streets, keep car doors and windows locked at all times, and other precautions. But in the excitement of arrival I remembered that I had forgotten a few LA rules. Just like back home in Fieldsburg, Neemie decided to kick the soccer ball on the sidewalk in front of the house on Cressey Street in Compton. Quickly his uncle CW explained to him that was a No! No! "Never play in the street, on sidewalks or in the front yard. Drive bys happen all the time and those fools don't care who or what they hit." So if kids play at home in Compton, they play in their fenced back yards. There were other surprises. Sitting in a soul food restaurant for Neemie to have his first taste of chitlins and ham hocks; there was a loud bang out front on Rosecrans Ave. We all ducked underneath the tables, except for Neemie who asked; "What ya'll doing?" Luckily it was just a car backfiring. By the end of dinner, leaving most of his ham hocks and chitlins with a side order of collard greens uneaten; Neemie decided he wasn't especially fond of soul food. For our rare visit, the following day brother CW had a celebratory barbecue and invited the neighbors and other friends. Neemie always observant, always listening, rarely missed much. Pulling me aside he asked about a conversation he'd overheard between Cousin Keith and one of his friends. With wonder and awe in his voice Neemie asked, "Pop was Ted joking?" "Joking, joking about what?" "Ted told Keith that he wasn't still mad at him for shooting him in the chin." South Central and Compton memories, I was already nervous because we were standing in the front yard with a large crowd at a house in Compton; ripe for a drive-by. So what do I say to my 13 year old son? "Uhhhhhhh Neemie no, Ted wasn't joking." "So that's why Ted's chin looks so funny." Neemie responded. Yeah, Neeemie had much to talk about on the drive home. I listened as he started working on his mom prepping her for his next adventure. He suggested that it was now time us to visit grandma in the town where I grew up, Gould Arkansas. After all he had never met grandma and the Arkansas relatives. Over the years he had talked to grandma on the phone but he wanted to see Grandma Tang in person.

'Arkansas Tis a Name Dear' from earliest memory growing up in Arkansas I always wanted to leave. On the other hand Mama Tang wanted to keep her kids nearby as long as possible. Mama Tang was pleased that three of her children stayed in the town where they grew up and raised her grandkids just a few doors down from the family home. But the other four of us chose California, as far away as possible from that racist town where we grew up, but we all have mothers. Even with major stops in many other places; home is always wherever mom may happen to be. After the Compton, South Central Los Angeles visit Neemie started pushing even harder for the Arkansas trip. Nearing the end of summer vacation, I realized it had been more than three years since I had been home; so it was past time for me to check in.

Having grown up in the South, I knew of the dangers and worried about my family of naïve Californians. In California I could shield them from the hateful stares and hard looks with looks of my own. Also in California, unlike in the South, I knew things would rarely go beyond the looks. Barbara and the kids never noticed the threatening interplay between me and local racists as we went about the business of living in California. I was proud of their ignorance and naiveté; but in the South, a white woman and black man with kids visually represented what thousands of white southerners had died in a treasonous war against the USA, their own country, to prevent. A historian, I was also aware that thousands of black men, some even in the 1970's, were lynched and killed to prevent the creation of families like ours. Now here we were, traveling to the former Confederate State of Arkansas; into "…the belly of the beast." Driving south from Fieldsburg and across the Golden Gate Bridge, Neemie excitedly watched the planes taking off and landing as we approached San Francisco International Airport. Leaving the car at long term parking, in no time at all we were boarding our flight to Arkansas. In 'The City', San Francisco and at SFX our non traditional family was hardly noticed. Riding with a planeload of Californians, the three hour flight to Dallas, where we would change planes for the flight to Little Rock, was very comfortable. Off loading in Dallas, a stewardess who befriended Neemie yelled; "Have a nice time at Grandma's Neemie!" as we entered the chute for the walk to the terminal. With brother Sulo away attending college at Princeton it was just the three of us popping out of the chute in Dallas. Listening to Neemie's excited chatter we were several feet inside the terminal before we noticed the silence. Silence, keep in mind that Dallas is one of the busiest airports in the world, also noteworthy is the fact that most folk traveling by air then and now are white. The workers at the counters, passengers between planes, workers in the shops; all stopped and stared at my white wife, me and our child as we entered the main terminal. They didn't know they were staring until I said to my karate trained wife, "Get ready." Not knowing what was coming, our son between us, we were alert and waiting for the first fool to act. Grudgingly, with backward glances 'normal activities resumed. Hurrying down the long corridors and ignoring the 'Southern' looks we arrived at our gate for the short connecting flight to Little Rock, Arkansas. Observing the pilots, stewardesses and passengers, obviously this was not the same type crowd as was on our morning flight from San Francisco. Yep, we were in the South, and the looks and attitudes of those folk were southern. Consequently, after the terminal entrance crisis, the wife and son started to relax and didn't notice the continuing threat, but it was my job, so I did. In about an hour we landed at Little Rock International Airport (Bill & Hilllary Clinton National Airport) Entering the terminal we saw a few other black travelers and all of the workers at the ticket counters, housekeeping and car rental agencies were also black "Mixed" family, they didn't blink.

On the contrary, knowing we were from California they went out of their way to facilitate our Southern experience. So my protective burden was eased somewhat by the warmth of the brothers and sisters at the airport. I smiled seeing that my loving family never noticed the unspoken back and forth between me and the airport workers as we prepared for the drive home. Concerned and very aware I knew we still had to go through 60 miles of white racist countryside before reaching the safety of home. Timing, being after nightfall was in our favor. I was doing the driving and there were no stoplights on the interstate. No one could see inside the vehicle, so unless we were followed from the airport, checking the rearview mirrors, we were not, so we traveled non-stop to the safety of home. Arriving in the city limits a little after 10PM and making that left turn off highway 65 onto the oh so familiar "Red Pike" road I was flooded with so many memories. Driving past First Baptist Church, Tuckers Store, The Dales, Gooleys, and Murrys; houses and families I had known as a child, we soon pulled into the front yard of Route #2 Box 581, Gould, Arkansas and home. Neemie, first out of the car, ran to the front door and rang the doorbell. While waiting for Mama Tang to answer the door I said to Neeemie; "After hugging grandma, take a peek at her right hand." Sure enough after giving Mama Tang a big hello and hug, Neemie poked his head around the right side of her housecoat; "Grandma you got a gun!" Not commenting on Neemie's observation, very pleased to see us, smiling she greeted the rest of the family. The family and all the neighbors knew that Mama Tang answered her door with a 38 in her hand. The 38 was inherited from her father Walter Davis, our grandfather who we called Poppa'. This was the very same gun Poppa had left in his open trunk, which he normally locked on that fateful day. That was the day Poppa told Mama Tang that the trunk was open and if her boyfriend Floyd came by to beat her as he often did when Poppa left the house; get the 38 from the trunk and use it. She did and killed Floyd. On most days not wanting to face Poppa and his guns; Mr. Floyd would wait until Poppa left on his daily walk downtown before dropping by the house to beat Mama Tang. Presently, the following morning, our first day, Neemie and Grandma Tang were in the kitchen chatting and having breakfast when we got up. Neemie was going over the list of places he thought we should visit with Mama Tang. Over the years he had listened to the stories I told about growing up in the South; and now he was looking forward to seeing those places and people from his Pop's past. Our first stop was at my Brother Lee Willis's house whose baby boy was Neemie's age. Also in the visitation mix was my old high school and the gym; where I taught many visiting teams how to lose when playing the Gould Colored High School Panthers. He also wanted to see the fields where we chopped and picked cotton for $3 dollars a day "...from sunup to sundown."And too he wanted to see the hanging tree, located in the fields behind the family home. Yep, my grandfather told us that was where whites actually lynched blacks.

Gould, Arkansas

Each morning before setting out on our visits around town, just like back in California; the wife and I started the day with a five mile run. When growing up in Arkansas our house was the last house on the street called the "Red Pike", the last house within the city limits of Gould on that road. Looking pretty much the same, we ran alongside the 'red pike' road, past the cotton fields and soybean crops adding more fuel to the kindling of my Gould memories. About a mile into our run I saw a large black 4by 4 pickup truck speeding toward us on the unpaved gravel road. Closer it came with very dark tinted windows making it impossible to see inside the vehicle. Suddenly a harsh mustachioed white face appeared leaning out the rolled down passenger side window with an object in his hand. Grabbing Barbara's arm, I pulled her aside as the coke bottle thrown from the truck whizzed past within inches of her head. Thrown to my left side the bottle was clearly intended for Barbara, a white woman who would dare be with a nigger in Arkansas. A direct hit would have sent her to the hospital or much worse. We shook it off and continued our run, but the incident served as a reminder to me that much like 'back in the day' venturing from the old neighborhood should be done with caution. During the remaining time in Arkansas I spent a part of each day in the Chevy rental car cruising the streets and back roads of Gould, with Mama Tang's 38 on the seat beside me looking for that Black 4X4. Slipping the 38 under her pillow on the right side of the bed where she had kept it since my childhood days before nightfall, Mama Tang never knew I had borrowed the gun. In retrospect, I was a crazy man, and in the South no less; thank God I never found that truck or the guy who threw the bottle.

Much too soon for the two of them; Neemie and Grandma Tang;, it was time to head home. They had hit it off quite well as did the cousins, uncles and friends with Neemie. He was that kind of kid open, caring, always a positive attitude and a smile, even for strangers; folks couldn't help but love him. An aside; in later years there were certain friendships that raised a few eyebrows, especially ours. One evening now a teen –ager Neemie and friends were throwing rocks at an abandoned building in Petaluma. The cops came and decided to ticket only one of the nine rock throwing kids, the black one, Neemie, A few weeks later we were sitting in the courtroom with Neemie waiting his turn before the judge handling his case. While waiting we couldn't help but notice ten or twelve young men brought into the courtroom by sheriff deputies wearing orange jail outfits, chains, leg irons and handcuffs. Not one or two but several of those jail guys raised their handcuffed arms and gave Neemie a smile and a wave. Neemie not only returned the smiles and waves with a "What up?" greeting but named names, Neemie personally knew those kids! The judge, staring down from her lofty podium even took notice. Knowing it would be fruitless to ask Neemie how he knew those criminal kids, the wife and I just shook our heads thinking; "Yep, that's our boy."

Mama Tang

But back to the end of our Arkansas trip. Saying our goodbyes to the family gathered at Mama Tang's was a moving experience. Knowing Mama Tang was well into her years, we considered the possibility but hoped this wouldn't be the first and only meeting with Mama Tang for Neemie and Barbara. Unfortunately it was. A few years later Sulo would give Mama Tang a very pleasant surprise by stopping by to see her on his drive from Princeton to California. Loaded into the rental car we headed for highway 65 turning right for the drive to Little Rock International Airport (Bill & Hillary Clinton National) which was without consequence, as was the flight from Little Rock International to Dallas. It helped that most of the passengers departing Arkansas were from the North and West. Ignoring the shocked quello rojos at Dallas, soon we were on a flight with laid back Californians headed for San Francisco and home. Home in time to get Neemie ready for the new school year and to make our own preparations as well. For me the new school year meant another school and a new teaching experience, bring it on! Although it served a necessary purpose at the time; getting me back into education and teaching; I was finally moving on from that depressing assignment at San Francisco County Jail #7. Praise God!

West Contra Costa Unified School District: Having spent most of my teaching career working in schools where I was not one of two or there but most often the only person of color; West Contra Costa was a welcome difference. Finally, a job where I didn't have to deal with racist presumptions, assumptions and stereotypes was kinda comfy. Yep, it was very nice finding a job in a mostly black school district in a predominantly black city, Richmond, California. After the interviews and hiring, a few weeks before the start of the school year; I was assigned to a rarity in Richmond, mostly white El Cerrito High School. I started preparing my classroom at El Cerrito High School for the year; but two days before the start of school I was reassigned to Gompers Continuation High School. Last minute, the change did seem odd, but being the new man, who was I to complain; a job was a job wherever in the school district. **Gompers Continuation High School:** Counting law school, I had been away from public school education for more than five years and soon was to learn that schools are oftentimes the first to reflect changes and current trends in their respective communities. Gompers was in the heart of central Richmond, located well within the so-called "Iron Triangle." It was so called because railroad tracks delineated the triangular boundaries of the downtown area. Most of the downtown stores, restaurants and other businesses are surrounded by tracks and located within that 'iron triangle' formed by the railroad tracks. Gompers was very close to downtown, in walking distance for lunch. Arriving at Gompers and noticing the steel entry doors, reinforced windows and metal detectors, I began to suspect that my last minute transfer to Gompers was not for my impressive academics,

Sylvester Greenwood Academy, formerly Gompers Continuation High School

but rather for my experience at County Jail #7 in San Francisco. So following my County Jail #7 experience, reckon they figured I wouldn't be afraid, they needed muscle in the classroom. The faculty parking area, easily viewed from office and classroom windows sat snugly against the main building, teachers wanted to see that their cars were safe during the work day.

A little under 6 feet wearing a blue Levi jacket a black top, matching jeans and black flats she introduced herself as Ms. Smith. The very dark, high cheek boned, aquiline nosed, willowy Ms. Smith was a product of local schools and had gone above and beyond dues paying in the 'iron triangle'. Her one child, a son had lost his life to gangs and gun violence. That story was told to me by others. Even after we became friends Ms. Smith never mentioned her son or his young daughter who had been with her since his death. During the interview she explained she wanted me to teach History and English using computer assisted instruction. Two periods a day I was to work in the new computer lab teaching basic beginning computers and computer assisted instruction in History and English. Reckon she actually read my resume. It was also nice NOT hearing the usual rhetoric born of racial fears when more than half a dozen kids of color were attending; "…this is a tough school" I heard over and over again from white principals Tough, such a statement would have been comparatively recognized as just another white absurdity at Gompers. Here not 10 or 12 but ALL of the students were black and as did I they listened to the pop pop sound of nearby gunshots throughout the school day. Additionally, the iron entry doors, barred windows, and metal detectors spoke volumes without inherent stereotypes and the use of meaningless words like "tough". Yeah, Gompers was deep in the hood and I felt right at home. Before our first faculty meeting Ms. Smith called a pre meeting in her office with me, the counselor Mrs. Williams; also a product of and still living in the triangle, and Harold Greer. Mrs. Williams was noteworthy for the actions of her husband, also named Harold. Retired, Harold would sit in his car in the school parking lot during the day mostly watching Greer and I. Insanely jealous, at every meeting or conversation with Mrs. Williams Harold gave us hard; "Stay away from my woman!" warning looks. Greer, who knows how they found him, was a retired prison warden newly hired as school security. Sitting in her office we listened to the principals description of each faculty member; it was not complimentary. She said they all were poorly performing rejects just waiting for retirement working alongside teachers without proper credentials. Such a mix was typically common to alternative education. It seems we were the team within the team and Ms. Smith's main backup. Our first faculty meeting introduced me to that aforementioned mix of teachers common to alternative education. In the coming weeks they noticeably fitted the mold. Surviving from payday to payday, regardless of subject when the bell sounded they closed their doors and little or no work was done by them or their students. All had systems to appease the students for that hour of class time. Ms. Bindson, the token white at the school, was the frumpy overweight art teacher who wore mismatched clothing and socks daily. She allowed her students to leave the classroom without a pass anytime they felt the need to be outside. Consequently, they were often found in the parking lot or walking the halls interrupting other classes. Greer, the head of security spent most of his workday herding her students back to class. The ceramics teacher; Cleevie, who insisted that her students call her by her first name; was teaching in a space that had once been the Home Economics classroom, and unfortunately the ovens still worked. She and her students baked cookies and cakes; and played cards and dominoes daily. On the same floor was Ms. Taylor an English teacher who weighed well over 350 pounds and was sexually aggressive. Greer nicknamed her "the blimp" She had been working at Gompers for five years on an emergency teaching credential, In an emergency, that is when school districts claim they can't find qualified teachers they are allowed to hire folk who haven't put in the extra time and coursework to earn a credential. Ms. Taylor's classroom was at the far end of the hallway from my own and I happened to notice on several occasions Greer in intimate conversation; bodies close enough to touch with the woman he had nicknamed "the blimp". Was Greer tapping that, I wouldn't put it past him. Across the hall from Ms. Taylor was Mr. King who taught General Math and Calculus. Ms. Smith nicknamed Mr. King "Jeri Curl" pointing out his greasy collar from his processed hair and hanging 'jeri curls". With so many nicknames, I never found out the one I had been given. Mr. King kept his red Corvette convertible parked just outside of his classroom. He was rumored to have weekend parties at his sumptuous home in the Berkeley Hills with his male students. Ms. Smith described one of those parties which she happened to attend. She said she was the only female present and that Mr. King was in drag. He seemed to be an excellent teacher, his classroom was well organized with various levels of student work on display; but at every opportunity he voiced his dislike for Ms. Smith. Maybe Mr. King so disliked her because she made jokes and laughed at his jeri curls, but I suspected it was a little deeper than the curls. Daily as Ms. Smith walked past his room or encountered him in the hallway Mr. King silently turned his back on her. Although they seemed to dislike each other so much I couldn't understand why Ms. Smith was invited and why she would attend one of Mr. Kings' parties. None of the rest of us working at Gompers was invited to that party. Was this a 'gay' party, is that why Ms. Smith was the only one of us invited? Not our business but maybe there was something Ms. Smith wasn't telling us. If you're going to tell part of the story maybe you should tell it all☺

I spent a year teaching at Gompers as a member of the "In Crowd." Ms. Smith, Greer, Mrs. Williams and I met each morning before school in her office where we shared the latest gossip, donuts and coffee. Following my work at County Jail #7 the laughter and camaraderie made it a great year. I must have passed the first test in the school district because I was offered a summer school teaching job at Richmond High School. With lots of copy machine use and pre-planned lessons the summer went pretty fast. Always observant, purely by accident I had discovered a harder student element there at Richmond High. Walking through the open area in the center of the main building daily to and from the office I noticed a side door leading to an outside area. Like the other doors leading outside it automatically locked when closed allowing no re entry. Periodically I had seen students exiting the doorway but never adults or teachers. I asked a student about the door and he said, "Teachers don't go out there." Places in the school off limits to teachers, now the old curiosity was really piqued; I thought how absurd. At the end of my classes the next day I took a little detour on my way to the office and opened 'the door'. Standing in the doorway I saw a grassless area of brown dirt surrounded by a high fence. Inside the enclosure several young Latino men were leaning casually about smoking. Smoking was not allowed on the school grounds. Upon my entrance there were no furtive attempts to extinguish or hide the cigarettes. Amid the hostile stares a young fellow with measuring, hard unblinking black eyes said; "Teachers don't come out here" and looked quickly away. With one foot on the brown dirt lawn and my left hand holding open the self locking door, weighing the possible consequences I made a quick decision and backed into the building; pulling the self locking door closed.

A few weeks following the end of summer school I was asked to interview for an administrative job, a Dean's position at Pinole Valley High School. The possibility of an administrative position was another advantage that came with working in a predominantly black school district. Living far north of the Golden Gate and working in those very white communities where I was barely tolerated as a teacher; although I had had my administrative credential (License) for more than ten years; administrative jobs were out of the question. Over that ten year period after submitting hundreds of applications I didn't get one call back for an interview. Whereas after teaching in West Contra Costa Unified School District for a little over a year and sending out no applications; they were seeking me out for administrative positions. It seems that the rumor circulating for years among the few black educators in Northern California was true; if you wanted an administrative or any other job in education you had to go where the black folk live, the bay area. Another day, another job, another interview: Ms. Anderson, graying hair and eyes was in her late fifties early sixties, very close to retirement.

Pinole Valley High School:

Conservatively dressed in a light gray suit with a knee length skirt and charcoal blouse, a nice lady, she was the principal of Pinole Valley High School. Andy Bocci, a short chunky forty something Italian-American was the vice principal who rarely left his office; and seemed to handle all of the administrative details of school operations. Jerry Cooper, standing about 6'5 was the other high school dean at Pinole Valley High School. Following a relaxing interview; a few days later the faculty and administrators met for orientation at a local junior high school gymnasium. Following the introductions and the orientation meetings we all moved the chairs and cleared the gym floor. Cooper, who just happened to have a basketball in his car challenged me to a game of 1on 1 half court basketball. Sure of himself, taller by 3 or 4 inches with fair skills; it showed in his eyes that he was one of those white fellows who got a special thrill out of beating black guys at basketball. Cooper was easy to read, and so arrogant and impatient that he didn't take time to notice or read me. Reckon such prejudgments too are an integral part of racism. It was slightly irritating that some guy not knowing me from Adam was absolutely certain he was going to beat me at basketball. What arrogance, he even gave me first outs. Later, after I had put a merciless whipping on him three games in a row, we sat around drinking sodas. Then I told him that I had played high school basketball where I earned two college scholarships, in the military, college and semi professional basketball. No way was I going to let him beat me.

Although he would have been shocked to know that I considered the possibility that he was a racist, Jerry Cooper was routinely typical in his soft prejudgments. After working together for most of the year he invited me to the gym where he played basketball on Saturday afternoons, The Jewish Community Center in San Rafael, CA. About and hour's drive from my home Cooper told me he would meet me there at the front desk at 12:00. Arriving a little before 12:00 the front desk clerk told me that non members of the club had to be invited by a member for access to the club. I told her that Cooper had invited me so she let me inside the gym where I stood around waiting and watching others play 3 on 3 games for more than an hour before Cooper came slinking in. No hello or other indication of recognition, we played several 3 on 3 games and Cooper never once acknowledged me in front of his Jewish friends. Outside when we were leaving he suggested that we stop for sodas at the nearby 7/11. Not wanting to spend any more time with such a bumbling incompetent racist I declined the 7/11 invite. Although he had invited me to the gym he had waited until past the time we were supposed to meet to see how I was received. Cooper didn't want his Jewish friends to know that he had invited the black guy, me. But, hey, I still had to work with this guy every day, so sociability was required. Further, he was the guy I was supposed to observe to learn the ropes, how to be an effective dean.

During my observations I did notice that Cooper rarely suspended a student, regardless of the offense. Fights, thefts, cheating, lying; all got the same 'punishment', a day or two hanging out in Coopers office chatting. Unhesitant about suspending for fights and threats, I may have been a little more serious about the job. But then too I wasn't a patronizing racist trying at all costs to kiss up to the black kids. Being a school administrator was very enjoyable. It was nice not having to deal with 35 students per hour in a classroom. As an administrator, Dean of students; more than three students in my office during the week was indeed a rarity. A suburban school, Pinole Valley had few discipline problems. After so many years of crowded classrooms and questionable conditions this was 'easy money'. Being a successful administrator was much the same as being a successful teacher. Using those skills learned assigning, judging and monitoring thousands of students over the years; it wasn't hard reading those few dealt with as an administrator. An administrator and a "boss" meant judging and grading teachers was also a part of the job. But having been a teacher for so many years, judging was just a 'been there done that' kind of thing, A quick glance inside a classroom reading the body language of the teacher and the students told the story of educational progress, or not. Classroom color, design, teacher and student location; their activity and attitudes within the room are all judgment relevant. The hardest part of the job was getting used to walking campus patrol on the three mile campus four or five times a day. Some of the discipline problems were unusual and part of the learning curve for me the new dean. The girl fights seemed senseless and downright strange. Handling my first girl fight; once the combatants Kelly and Ranece were in my office I asked Kelly why they jumped Lesette in the hallway. She said they jumped her because "…she is pretty." What the hell, and the kid wasn't joking. "We tore that face up!" Ranece bragged. Feeling out of touch I wondered, since when is good looks or "…being pretty." a bad thing? The girls were upset because boys were attracted to Lesette, more importantly their boyfriends. Sounded like crazy shit to me so suspension with psychological counseling before returning to school seemed necessary. That was the most school punishment I could dish out, although I felt that they both should have been locked up someplace. There were more pleasant duties, like the homecoming parade.

During the homecoming parade the whole town turned out alongside the downtown streets to watch the Pinole Valley High School Marching Band, decorated cars and floats, horses, cowboys and cowgirls tossing candy to kids along the parade route; all made for a very special day. The parade ended at the football field where the homecoming game was played the following evening. During the game we walked along the bleachers inside the stadium and just outside looking for illegal alcohol and rowdies.

The crowds inside the stadium were mostly families supporting their kids, rarely were there problems. Outside the stadium was another story; there we would find former students, homeless people and other drifters. On this night we had been told to go check on a noisy gathering outside the football stadium. Walking along the unlighted sidewalk in front of the school, suddenly I was on South Central LA and Compton alert. But Cooper, my white privileged San Rafael Marin County co worker walking about five feet in front of me was so relaxed I thought he might be on something. Clipboard in hand suddenly we heard grunts and scuffling coming from the alley ahead. Watching from a few steps behind, Cooper reacted; I saw that fool do the unthinkable; he immediately rushed into the dust clouded darkened alley. "Break it up! Break it up!" I listened to Cooper yelling at the fighters. A momentary pause as I approached and thought, it would be pretty dam nutty to go into a dark alley not knowing how many fighters you was facing or whether they were armed. But that crazy ass Cooper had gone in so I had to back his play. Wordlessly, following his lead into the dust filled alley I started snatching fighters and pulling them out onto the sidewalk. Luckily they were unarmed, most being former jocks and students were fairly respectful under the circumstances. Without police involvement and no major injuries we sent the fighters home. All known to Cooper; the fighters were a mix of preppies, blacks, Latinos and stoners. I'd come to know many of the stoners who I would see hanging out underneath the bridge a few blocks from the school where they cut class, smoked, and did a little dealing during breaks and lunch. A closed campus meant students were not allowed to leave campus during the school day. Periodically we'd stroll down to the bridge hangout to apprehend the rule breakers, but they'd see us coming and scatter. One day while standing blocking the usual getaway path to the neighboring street I confronted Warren before he could disappear down the creek with his pot smoking buddies. "Uh, Warren I see you and know who you are, you can come with me now or I'll simply pick you up in class today or tomorrow, your choice." Back in the office I asked what would be the best time to schedule a meeting with his parents. "I live with my grandpa who is fucking my mom, he doesn't work." Warren said. Whoa! Much too much information: I didn't need or want to know that "…grandpa was …fucking mom." This was going to be an interesting parent conference. The very next day the meeting with gramps and mom was held in Principal Anderson's office. She sat behind her desk while Cooper and I sat in front and off to one side of the desk. Principal Anderson was in the dark, that is she didn't know what to expect, but Cooper did; and he had gotten quite a laugh when I told him about the unusual parenting relationship. Straight faced with caring parent looks; Mr. Teatley, the grandfather, and Mrs. Teatley, the mother sat in chairs alongside Principal Anderson's desk facing me and Cooper. Starting the meeting Principal Anderson mentioned that Warren had been suspended several times for smoking and being off our closed campus during the school day. Mr. Teatley said; "You must have the wrong child, our Warren doesn't even smoke. And I can't imagine him leaving the school grounds without permission." "Sir, suspension notices are sent to the address listed on the student records, I guess Warren intercepted them. Need I remind you that we are sitting in this meeting because I found Warren off campus under the bridge smoking?" Responding in a loud voice Mr. Teatley said; "You're a liar, Warren said he never left campus, and wasn't smoking!" Measuring I looked at the little old balding man, standing about 5'5 and weighing maybe a hundred thirty pounds at most. "Did Warren say that I was lying, well you should hear the things he said about you?" Suddenly, it seemed that old man and I were the only two people in that room.

Maintaining eye contact I said; "Unasked your grandson said to me "...My grandpa is fucking my mom..." Springing from his chair fists balled, Grandpa Teatley took two steps towards me. Quickly out of my seat and facing him I waited. Principal Anderson was cool, "Both of you sit down!" Still waiting, continuing to stand, I heard her but my eyes never left Teatley. Looking hard at me the old man slowly returned to his seat, and then I sat. Afterwards following the near action initiated by that old man, things went smoothly. Thanking the parents for coming Principal Anderson informed the Teatleys that Warren was suspended for three days. Pausing in the doorway, before leaving Principal Anderson's office; old Teatley turned and gave me a long look. I yawned. In retrospect, staying with West Contra Costa Unified School District would have been great for my career, but I had been moving all my life and saw no reason not to continue looking for those 'greener pastures' always just over the next hill, Why leave the job at Pinole Valley and West Contra Costa when things were going so well, one major excuse used was 'mo money'. Checking on educational job sites I noticed several higher paying jobs in neighboring Pittsburg Unified School District located in the town of Pittsburg, CA. Living north of the Golden Gate those areas with interesting and unique aspects were all new to me. Driving out for an interview one couldn't help but notice the isolated long highway stretching for miles out into the seeming nothingness of the California Delta. Although not quite as dry, it matched the forlorn looks of loneliness seen on a similar highway toward California City, CA near the old bauxite mines in the California desert. Pittsburg Unified School District offices were easy to find, located just off the main drag on Railroad Avenue in the city of Pittsburg.

Pittsburg Unified School District: Driving that lonely highway #4 out into the California Delta I was surprised to find a fairly large community of black people in the city of Pittsburg. Too soon I saw those classic railroad tracks separating black from white communities all over the country there too in Pittsburg. Antioch, CA is the 99% white city sitting across the tracks from 99% black Pittsburg.

Yes, Antioch is the city where just a few middle class blacks live and where the few remaining whites still living in Pittsburg dream of living. High end stores and the major shopping center plus the movie theatres are all located in neighboring Antioch. So I was pleasantly shocked and surprised to be interviewed by a black man, Dr. Landon, who was Superintendent of Schools for the more than 60,000 student Pittsburg Unified School District. Well all right, with minimum fanfare I was hired. At the first administrators meeting of the school year I met seven other newly hired black administrators, more than I had seen in one district in all my years of teaching and administering. Strutting and preening, we were so proud of ourselves. Certainly a California and maybe a national rarity at the time as eight black administrators were added to the four already working in the school district, making for that amazing total of twelve black administrators in Pittsburg Unified School District. I Wondered, is this Black Superintendent Landon a crazy man, surely he must know he is pissing off every white in the district and in the surrounding areas.

Principal of Alternative Education: My new title was impressive, as Principal of Alternative Education I was in charge of not one but several schools and programs in the district. Riverside Continuation High School, Riverside Community Day School, Riverside Elementary Community Day School, and The Pittsburg Home School Program; all were within my administrative bailiwick. This was a big deal, and a major promotion. In a little over two years I had moved from working with inmates doing hard time in San Francisco County Jail #7 to a classroom teacher job then to Dean at one school, and suddenly I was an administrator in charge of several schools. With no Coopers thankfully, around to coach me on this one I was on my own. Also with no other deans, vice principals or principals to assist me, clearly it was easy to see that being 'the man' was very different from being just one of several administrators. There was no one to run interference or to handle administrative details; and that famous Harry Truman "…buck stops…" quote was frighteningly applicable.

Riverside Continuation High School: From my main office at Riverside Continuation High School I worked closest with that faculty of ten. Newly hired I found myself facing a teacher's strike, where the lines between teachers and administrators were clearly drawn. When I was a teacher the line was unquestionably obvious but as an administrator I didn't see the need for the line at all; was it administrative indoctrination, who knows? The nine whites and one female black teacher looked at me with caution and mistrust. That was hard to take, walking into a room and seeing dislike and fear in the eyes of people you've never offended, people you didn't even know, supposedly your co-workers was daunting. Yes it was a bit much for me the new man in the district; I was left wondering how I could be so disliked.

Principal of Alternative Education

It seemed that the hostility against administrators was a union tactic; now in the middle of negotiations with the district, they were preparing teachers for the upcoming strike. For most of my life I had been and still was a dues paying member of CTA, The California Teachers Association, the major teachers union in the state. In the past I had also been an active teacher participant in a bitter strike; but now on the other side, seemingly there was no possibility for reasonable dialogue. Alternative education teachers very much like their students, rarely fitting the common mold; they too have their unique views and perceptions of reality. At every opportunity I tried to remind them of that special connectivity between alternative education students and their teachers. Finally, following several very intense faculty meetings, we agreed that our alternative education students had special needs above and beyond the strike.

Consequently, although it pissed off the union; not one of my alternative education teachers struck. Not participating in the strike the union rep took personally. The students, was a different story, a few stayed home but most knowing that alternative education was their last chance to get a diploma came to school. Besides school was fun! With a more than 99% African American student body; the language of basketball transcended all barriers, even illiteracy. Still able to play a better than average game, using basketball diplomacy we managed to open a few doors and establish positive relationships with students. As I had done in other schools, male and female captains were chosen from each class and organized teams were formed. Games and tournaments were played during lunchtime and after school. Trophies, ribbons and notice in the school newspaper were all rewards for success on the basketball court and in the classroom. More than 90% of the students in alternative education are there because they refused to attend school, so we figured if we had a program to at least get them on campus 90% of our battle to educate was won. After the basketball program was established we witnessed a 60% improvement in attendance. Visiting the classrooms, it was amazing to see students who hadn't opened a book or picked up pencil and paper in years asking questions and struggling to complete assignments. School attendance and passing grades in all classes were requirements for participation in the basketball program. Maybe the success of the basketball program and improving attendance had something to do with our teachers ignoring being called "scabs" as they reported for work each morning during the strike.

The Home School Program: In the past having observed home schools from a distance, they were always interesting an informative, so I tried to visit each of the alternative education school sites at least once a week. The Home School building located across the parking lot had three teachers with one also acting as part-time administrator as well.

Home school, generally meant that students working at home came in periodically to turn in completed assignments and to pick up new ones. Rarely did students spend more than a couple of hours per week on campus; they did their schoolwork at home. Home school teachers graded the assignments and awarded high school credits for work done, fulfilling high school graduation requirements. Blake, a tall thin balding white fellow in his mid forties was the on site part time administrator/teacher. He was the classic go along with the program and make no waves kind of guy. Silently watching at district meetings, clearly Blake was a survivor. Tyler was shorter, maybe 5'8 and the other white fellow working at the home school building. His small hard blue eyes showed his dislike with his "What you doing with this job nigger?" looks. I gave it right back to him and waited for him to make a mistake so I could get rid of his ass. During his rare moments of clarity Tyler realized I was his boss and that made him obsequiously nervous. Natalie, the black female in the building, I couldn't help but notice. All business and good at her job; she got maximum effort from her students and constantly found ways to facilitate their high school graduation. An attractive face and body, the first time I saw her I complimented her on her beautiful cornrows; with a blushing "Thank you." Natalie walked away. Later I was to learn that those boundaries between administrators and teachers are firmly established and never crossed.

Riverside Community Day School: The community day school was located across Railroad Avenue in a building with two teachers and about 25 students in grades 9-12. Working on individualized programs the female students worked with Ms. Trainer in one classroom while the male student worked with Mr. Cannon in the other classroom. Ms. Trainer, an awful teacher, reckon I'm not holding back on this one; found it hard not to show her dislike for the students. Meeting her mom would have been interesting, especially after meeting her white father, a man with hate filled eyes who she adored. I began to suspect that she generally disliked black people. During my classroom observations, I told her to stop making derogatory comments like, "That's stupid; don't be such a dummy!" to her students. So much for my suspicions, but students, especially alternative education students are very adept at reading people and they too felt her blatant and patronizing dislike and acted on those feelings. I spent too much time in her classroom trying to smooth over her racist edges. It was strange dealing with a black person who hated blacks. One who stupidly called herself "mixed" as if that made her kinky hair straight and thick lips thin. Ms. Trainer was certain that she was white. In a meeting with her and Mr. Cannon I mentioned how important it was to have two black teachers at the school when she said that she was "mixed." It really pissed her off when I said that "mixed" was a meaningless label used by folk trying to hide from their blackness, all humans are mixed Mr. Cannon didn't comment but smiled at my statement on race. He was a product of city schools, rumored to have some jail time in his past; that was an excellent teacher andgot maximum effort from his students. Community day school students were about the same age as continuation high school students and they too struggled with school attendance, but there were differences. Community day were the students who had been expelled from regular school and were on probation and/or parole but I didn't notice much of a difference in the students. Maybe they were a bit more "thuggy" to quote Mr. Bunting one of our substitute teachers, but they seemed to know that thuggy might work in the streets but not in school. Not following school rules usually meant a quick return to jail (juvenile hall) and jail rules. Once a week after my classroom visits I enjoyed thrashing all comers on the basketball courts. Those Riverside Community Day kids seemed to get a special kick out of trying to beat the "old man" on the basketball court. After Riverside Community Day it was time to drop by for a visit with the kids at Riverside Elementary Community day school

Riverside Elementary Community Day: Elementary community day was located in a building adjacent to the home school across the parking lot from the main office and the continuation high school. Kids in grades four through six who had been expelled from elementary school for fighting and other offenses found themselves at Riverside Elementary Community Day. It took a while for me to believe such tiny kids could be so bad. Fighting, bullying, extortion, drugs the list goes on; reading their files was an eye opener. Mr. Kelly ran the elementary community day program with 9 students enrolled in a computer assisted program. All seemed to be educationally engaged when I happened to visit the classroom. Mr. Kelly, a 60ish salt-n-pepper gray haired fellow with a slight paunch put lots of positive effort into his program. Unforgettable was the day Mr. Kelly brought a cussing; flailing arms and legs, nine year old to my office. Students and teachers in the other classrooms were leaning out of doorways watching the drama. Physically restraining young Kinsey in the chair in my office, Mr. Kelly explained. At the beginning of class when told to take a seat, the nine year old Kinsey told Mr. Kelly, "I'll whip your old ass…" and ran toward Me. Kelly throwing punches and kicking. Telling his class to continue work on their assignments, Mr. Kelly put Kinsey under his right arm and brought him to the office. Very independent, I was surprised Mr. Kelly didn't handle the problem himself; maybe it was a test for the new administrator. My secretary called moms to come pick up Kinsey. She had to take off from work and the look on her face when she entered the office immediately changed Kinsey's demeanor. Beyond the routine administrative tasks during that first year as Principal of Alternative Education there were staff changes, another first for me, I actually hired some folk.

New Hires: Hiring folk for the Alternative education program was a major priority during my 2nd year in the district. The first year went well with increased attendance and many new students joined our program. We needed additional teachers. The superintendent suggested I attend a job fair at a nearby university and hire a couple of teachers. Ms. Rhinehorn, looking all of her years in her early to mid fifties, clearly was the oldest job seeker in the building. Most of the others were young folk fresh out of college teacher training programs. Moving with a visible reluctance Ms. Rhinehorn was slow to approach district representatives. Shocked that I chose to interview her Ms. Rhinehorn explained that she was an experienced credentialed teacher but new to the area. Knowing that an experienced teacher would be perfect for alternative education she was again surprised when I hired her on the spot. After hiring Ms. Rhinehorn for Riverside Continuation I still needed a teacher for the community school. Talking to the one black male applicant at the job fair was impossible; he was surrounded by folk wanting to hire him. Turns out Isaiah lived in Pittsburg and he jumped at the chance to work close to home. Two new hires I was ready for year number two.

Ms. Rhinehorn taught English but also a very special business class. Daily I was monitoring students slipping off our closed campus during breaks and lunch for trips to the local grocery to buy candy and other snacks. Hopefully, to cut down on the detentions and suspensions I suggested to our new teacher the possibility of a student store to sell on campus those things they were leaving campus to buy. So for academic credit in her business class Ms. Rhinehorn's students sold snacks during breaks and lunch at the new Riverside Student Store. They also kept records of stock and sales and when inventory was low she took them on shopping field trips to the local Costco. Growth in the areas of reading and math skills were anticipated for those students working in the student store, but we also noticed an appreciable growth in confidence and self esteem among the students working in the student store. May of our students couldn't afford school supplies, consequently profits from the student store were used to buy supplies for each classroom to be handed out freely to needy students. Our new student store was more than successful, it was an inspirational breeze. I knew Ms. Rhinehorn had the age and temperament for that business class and store the first few minutes of her interview.

Isaiah, a tall thin dark skinned brother was also a new hire to replace Mr. Cannon who moved to the bay area at the community day school. Controlled, thoughtful and caring he seemed to be working out quite well with his students at community day. Having grown up in Pittsburg and knowing the families of many of the kids in his class made for a smooth transition to his new job. Another important positive was that Isaiah had played basketball on the Pittsburg High School basketball team during his high school days. Annnnd he still claimed to have some skill on the basketball court. On the whole I was very proud of my new hires and things seemed to be going well in my 2nd year as Principal of Alternative Education for Pittsburg Unified School District. I put lots of time and energy into that 2nd year as a means to keep my mind off the horrible tragedy that dominated my being. To think only of work made it easier not to think about other things in my life. That other overwhelming thing which I find to this day, very difficult to put on the page; for all practical purposes destroyed my family and forever changed our lives. And those changes decades later are still inexorably working their unyielding pain and circumstance.

The Worst Day!

Absolutely, the worst day of my life! Of this I was certain; at the time. Pictured here is my younger son Neemie; after much thought trying to decide how to blunt the pain of writing this, I'm afraid it can't be done so here goes. On October 30, 1999 during my first year at Pittsburg, it was a Saturday morning. Rather than ring the bell someone knocked on the door of the family home north of Petaluma, CA. I'd just finished my morning run and was consuming liquids in recovery mode. Peering through the peephole, it was a policeman who asked if he could come in. The police in my house, of course I said No! "I have some important information about your son Neemie." Reluctantly I opened the door and let him come inside and without notice or preamble he just said it; "The Los Angeles County Coroners Office notified us that your son Neemie was found dead in his apartment this morning." How would you respond to such a statement? How does a father, any parent respond to being notified that their child is dead? Dazed, slowly sitting down on the stool at the kitchen bar; "Tell me he is being treated at a Los Angeles hospital, not dead!" The cop just looked at me as Neemie's mother walked in the front door, he then asked, "Do you need me to stay?" Shaking my head no, I watched the cop walk out the open door. Silently, Barbara looked at the back of the departing cop and then at me as I closed the door.

Death is a sledgehammer; and there is no way to soften such a blow; words must be used and there are none in the language to substitute for those bringing unimaginable pain. Pain to someone you love. "Neemie is dead." Helplessly I watched his mother lose all strength in her legs and crumple to the floor with moans and tears. Just like that our baby, our last child was gone forever. I fixed things; it was expected, I did things to shield the family from grief and sadness. But then, through my tears I realized there was nothing, absolutely nothing I could do. This I couldn't fix, in a whisper, just like that no longer a family of four, we were now a grieving family of three. There remained the task of convincing Sulo who lived a couple of hours away;

Neemie

without giving the awful details that he was needed at home. We daren't tell him by phone, they were very close and Sulo had issues. Driving from Berkeley with several stops alongside the road for encouraging phone conversations with his mother, another crisis averted, Sulo finally made it home. We met him in the driveway and that saddest memory of the three of us, without Neemie, missing him, and so alone, standing at the top of the sloping driveway clinging to each other, shedding uncontrollable tears is unforgettable. Tears, like words on a page didn't even come close to mirroring the overwhelming despair, sadness and confusion in our hearts. Funeral arrangements, memorials, cremation; I was in a stumbling useless daze. Death, is a word with such power and so, so personal. Thank God older brother Sulo stepped up and filled the vacuum of responsibility; he was a tower of strength. Neemie's mother wanted me to join her and Sulo for a last viewing of the body. Wanting to remember him as he was when he was alive; I refused to join them for that last look at THE BODY. Sitting on that lonely curb outside the crematorium in San Pedro watching the two of them slowly walk inside without me I yelled at them, at the world, at no one at all; "I don't want to see a 193am body, I want to see my son!" Somehow we survived the drama while continuing to work at our jobs. Some folk say that work is therapeutic during a crisis, maybe.

Appreciating the beauty of each new day, sunshine, plants, animals, and morning breezes; life; all were constant reminders that my son would never feel or see those things again. I had to get over this; I had to move on, but how? Over the years in education I had been in situations as an advisor, a counseling witness, and/or observer, with students considering taking their own lives; suicide. Sitting in with those students, parents, counselors I often thought, who in their right mind would want to kill themselves. What would possibly make one feel so bad that they would choose not to live? Yep, they'd have to be pretty crazy! Then too there was that common mantra that I had heard since childhood; "Black people don't commit suicide." I knew that! Such a bizarre idea never crossed my mind. That very same discussion I had with my oldest Sulo years earlier when he shocked us to the core by attempting to take his own life. Suddenly without a specific name or identifying thought for such personal feelings, surreptitiously my own life was no longer an important consideration. Daily, driving across the San Rafael Bridge on my way to work I couldn't help but notice the one open spot to the right of the on ramp. The space was just large enough for my car to fit on any morning that I might possibly decide to end the pain and drive into the San Francisco Bay. And there were other days; when I thought with just a flick of the steering wheel to the left; I could hit an approaching semi head on. God had taken my son's life and now mine wasn't important to me at all. Work and other daily duties were simply habitual motion. Somehow that first year ended with other life changes.

Sulo & Neemie & Mocha Making Music

Family Life, Year Two: Yes, things were going well with my new hires and their classes, and all of alternative education was running smoothly but I still looked forward to finding some kind of holding pattern, Somehow within the year following my son's death I managed to leave the mother of my children and companion for more than forty years. I wasn't a drinker or on drugs, but one morning I woke up and found myself living in a hotel far away from home. The wife didn't know what the hell was happening nor did I. I was an angry suicidal, confused, walking automaton who worked very hard to present a 'normal' front for the public. One day before the wife came home from work I packed my most cherished books, a few clothes and drove away. Reckon I always assumed it was so, but after walking away, I realized for the first time in my life that the wife really loved me. In one of our last conversations she said to me that she had, "…lost both, a son and a husband." At the time, unhearing, I was uncertain of the meaning or importance of those words. There were other insurmountable issues; such as the overwhelming melancholy brought on by just the thought of continuing to live in the house, on that street, near those schools; in that town among so many reminders of my son, the life that no longer was. Having no idea where or how I was going to live without my family, I drove to the place that helped me maintain that false front called sanity. 'Home" became a hotel in the city of Pittsburg, the town where I worked. Since that drive away more than twenty years ago I've been back to the town where my son was born and grew up briefly a couple of times. The few times I've been as close as fifty miles; the nearness of the town brought back all those saddest memories weighing heavily on my emotions. After a few weeks of life in the Pittsburg hotel; Natalie, a teacher in the home school program upon hearing of my homelessness said she had a spare room for rent. Renting a space in a home with a stranger and her two children was a new thing for me, but indicative of the time. It worked until the drama of her two strange children became overwhelming. The teen aged boy slept in and cut school daily. Most nights he climbed out the window of his second story room and roamed the streets of Pittsburg. His mother didn't think it unusual or strange. The daughter attended school daily, came home entered her room and was not seen until the following morning. On weekends she wasn't seen at all. "Aren't you worried, how do you know she is even in that room?" I asked the mother. Mom just smiled. During the few months I lived there not once did I hear the girl speak. A couple of times I heard her speak through the door to her mother. When I hinted that the child might be a bit odd, again the mother smiled. How could I not compare and contrast my very bright kids to her very strange slow witted dumb kids? My wife Barbara was very smart, this woman didn't come close. Talk about apples not falling far away from the tree, much like her kids she too was not very stable. Invited to attend a barbecue at a local park with the family; I found myself holding the spitting cussing woman back trying to keep her from beating up her mother.

This was happening in front of her kids, her students and other parents who happened to be in the park. Was this my dose of the real world? I missed my wife and family as I started that 2nd year in Pittsburg.

The first meeting of district administrators a few weeks after the start of school was very tense. Over the summer months the black superintendent who hired me and a host of other black administrators, teachers and staff had been fired. The former assistant superintendent Reid Sanner, who had always maintained a low profile, lurking in the background, was now the new superintendent. Four of the eight black administrators hired by the former superintendent D. Landon had already been fired. Needless to say we four remaining Dr. Landon hires were concerned. Now outspoken and assertive Reid Sanner was taking steps to consolidate his new status. Also surprising was seeing Mr. Cannon, the former community day school teacher at the meeting. It seems he had been promoted and was now an administrator. Mr. Cannon was now my assistant principal. Did I ask for an assistant principal, no? Did I need an assistant principal, no? Having no experience or proper credentials, Mr. Cannon was a former football player for Pittsburg High School and a friend of Reid Sanner; those were the only necessary credentials for the job. Suddenly all my 'watch your back' alarms were blasting.

Mr. Cannon: Was quite an experience from his very first day as an administrator, he was late, and continued being late every day until the end of the school year. A nuisance, he followed no rules or procedures, his conduct was so appalling I began keeping a record of his activities. It was a useless record to be turned over to his boss and friend superintendent Reid Tanner. In retrospect they probably should have been turned over to the local police, but in such a small town they too were probably in Reid's pocket. Some of the entries included September 8, 2000 Ms. Rhinehorn found Mr. Cannon inside the student store taking money from the cash box. When questioned he told her that he was "short of cash." On September 9, 2000 Ms. Rhinehorn called to report that Mr. Cannon was "hanging around" in her classroom and refused to leave. On September 20, 2000 Ms. Rhinehorn reported Mr. Cannon stole three bags of potato chips from the student store. On September 29, 2000 Mr. Cannon took several student tickets for our Marine World trip from Ms. Rhinehorn's desk. I sent reports of his activities to Reid. Finally I had the locks changed to Ms. Rhinehorns classroom and the student store. Things got even stranger; suddenly every afternoon one of my alternative education teachers had appointments down at Reid Tanners office. When I asked what was going on no one shared information. Ms. Rhinehorn more than any of the other teachers seemed to spend the most time down at the superintendents office. After having bent over backward to hire that woman now she was

Student Store Workers

Dr Williams and the Student Store Crew 10/13/99

working against me with the superintendent, that's gratitude huh?

Getting Jumped: Possibly things would have gone smoother absent several personal crisis. On the job front in the middle of the school year two of the four remaining administrators from the former superintendent's era were suddenly gone. So I and one other administrator were the last of the Superintendent Landon bunch. Upon returning from a conference in Baltimore I found that my office had been ransacked by district personnel. No explanation was forthcoming from my secretaries or the superintendent. Then too the dismal home front found me still mourning the loss of m y son while going through a divorce. All of the above were being considered when I received a frightened tearful phone call from Ms. Rhinehorn's downstairs classroom. "Kyree won't take his seat and he is threatening me!" She said between sniffles. In the background I clearly heard Kyree's voice; "Put that phone down or I'll kick your white ass bitch!" Typically my vice Principal Mr. Cannon was off campus so I headed down to Ms. Rhinehorns's classroom. Peering through the small window on the door to here room I saw students quietly watching as the thin barely five feet tall Ms. Rhinehorn furtively slumped and cowered keeping the desk between herself and Kyree. Meanwhile the tall thin Kyree moved from one side to the other of the desk as he yelled obscenities. Glancing my way as I opened the door and stepped inside the room, gauging the possibilities, Kyree turned facing me with both hands in fists and a defensive pose. "Come with me to the office." Waiting a few ticks, Kyree quietly followed as we left the room. The concrete steps from the basement classrooms were divided into two sections. About 12 steps led up to the 4X4 platform at the halfway point and from there 12 more steps finished the trek to the first floor. Walking ahead of Kyree as I raised my foot to step onto the 4X4 platform I felt a hand on my right shoulder pulling me backwards. At least six feet above the 12 concrete steps just covered; a fall would guarantee major injury or possibly death. Slamming my right foot down on the platform while reaching back and grabbing Kyree with my left hand and jerking him onto the platform, I landed with both knees on his chest. "Are you done?" "Sorry doc, sorry doc..." He kept repeating as I dragged him to his feet and pushed him up the steps ahead of me. Kyree walked cooperatively and quietly to the office area where several students were sitting on the benches across from the secretaries. Seeing and audience suddenly he became loud and aggressive when I told him to take a seat on the bench. Ignoring my instructions Kyree followed closely behind as I walked toward my office. "You think you're big shit now that you're down here where people can help you." He said this as he firmly grabbed my shoulder. Turning and gently removing his hand I said again; "Kyree, take a seat on the bench." With a fistful of my shirt he pulled me backwards. Both secretaries were standing; looking over the counter with the three students previously waiting on the bench. Nearly stumbling as he pulled me toward the bench, I was getting a little angry. Slapping his hand off my shoulder I turned to face that crazy kid. Sensibility prevailed; as I silently pointed to the bench and again turned away from Kyree. "You just another chicken shit scared motherfucker." He said as he again put his hands on me and jerked my right shoulder. Unfortunately, not thinking, I just reacted, spinning to my left and delivering two quick punches to his chest; Kyree went down hard. Or that's what the custodian told me later, I just remembered him jerking my shoulder and the anger that I felt. Both secretaries, although standing at the counter witnessing the entire scenario said "...It was to fast." And that they didn't really see what happened. Landing on his back Kyree was having trouble breathing. Following him to the floor, poised to strike again a strong hand grabbed my wrist. Turning quickly, I saw the face of Sonny the custodian etched with fear and worry shaking his head, "No!" Pulling me away from the gasping kid on the floor; "He's had enough doc." Standing and looking at the shocked faces of the students and secretaries I was so embarrassed. Straightening my tie and tucking in my shirt as Sonny helped Kyree from the floor, I sad to the lead secretary, "Call the police." and walked into my office. Soon the police came and with looks of respect and admiration, police like fights and killing; asked a few questions about the fight before taking Kyree to jail.

Later, thinking back, I did consider the possibility that maybe I overreacted to Kyree. But I couldn't for the life of me come up with an alternative solution. How would you have reacted? I do remember thinking as I brought him up the stairs to the office why should this kid be alive and here causing trouble when my son who followed all the rules is dead? Was I really angry at Kyree for being alive or just angry at the circumstance where my son was forever gone? Possibly, although I don't remember actually hitting him, I do remember an overwhelming feeling of uncontrollable rage. Yes, a blinding rage; I couldn't see or think, I just reacted to a faceless attacker. Well after that fight with Kyree things were never the same. What could I have done differently? Should I have ignored his hands on me, jerking my shoulder? Should I have just walked into my office and closed the door? If I had done either could I have continued working in that district? Probably not, but reacting to his actions may have created that very same impossible situation. I wonder. Regardless, afterwards teachers and especially students treated me differently. Many just looked at me in an odd distrustful manner, while others acted as if they wanted to test me. The bigger students showed a measuring curiosity, wondering whether they could kick my ass. After so many years in education it was very disconcerting to see those looks on the faces of my students. How long before one decided to see if they could give me a first class whipping? Sure enough, two of the bigger former football players actually came into my office uninvited and stood before my desk in a threatening manner. "We won't be as easy as Kyree was." The larger of the two hulking figures said. Stupidly they thought I would fight them then and there in my office. My comment; "You'll be easy for the police to find when my secretary makes that call." changed their minds as they made a hasty retreat from the building. More painful than physical threats, I could feel the loss of that connective bond of trust between educator and student, sadly it was gone.

Gone too were the relaxed jokes and humor I had shared with faculty and students; all seemed suddenly uncomfortable around me. No longer were there spontaneous conversations, change was in the wind. Those winds of change included a notice from the woman where I was living asking for an increase in rent or I could move on. Fine with me I wasn't paying more and it would be a relief not having to deal with her strange kids. A few days later Reid Sanner the superintendent showed up at my office with two burly policemen. The cops in plainclothes stood off to the side with hands on their guns as Reid told me that I had been relieved of my job. Later I received a letter from the district office stating that I had been placed on involuntary administrative leave without cause for the remainder of the school year. Not surprised by Sanner's act, however I thought he could have at least waited until the end of the school year. Thinking back, before the final Reid action, the office search was just one oddity. Tyler, a teacher from the home school; I found sitting in a car, a newspaper supposedly hiding his face, watching as I pulled out of Natalie's garage one morning. His report to Sanner that I an administrator was living with a female teacher in the district may have caused a bit of gossip and hastened Sanner's action. Only Reid knows; but with three months remaining in the school year, my only question was whether my three months of administrative leave was with pay? Reading the forwarded legal paperwork from the district I noted that the Education Code gave the school district the right to vacate my contract early so long as I was paid for the full year. Good, so three months with pay was ample time to find a new job. Beginning the search, I found myself living alone in a downstairs apartment near a trailer park for seniors. It was great that I no longer had to deal with Natalie and her bizarre children.

The job search alone was stressful but adverse publicity in the town where I still lived was an additional burden. Front page newspaper headlines implied that I had broken numerous rules and possibly even committed crimes while principal of alternative education. The false accusations from my days at Renton High School were also front page news, thanks to Reid Sanner. A small town, when checking my box at the post office, grocery shopping or doing laps around the track; the unwanted attention was uncomfortable.

Having my usual Sunday breakfast at the local Denny's, while reading the morning paper; I noticed the waiters and waitresses reacting to my presence. I saw Isaiah at Denney's; he said that Reid fired him on the same day I was placed on leave. Was it a black male thing with Reid, or simply the fact that I had hired Isaiah? I had also hired the white Ms. Rhinehorn who was still working at Riverside Continuation High School. Isaiah had gotten a lawyer and wanted me to join him in a lawsuit against the school district. Administrators are hired on a year to year contract and I was being paid for the year. I couldn't see a cause of action, so I wished him luck and told Isaiah that I wasn't interested. Not for a minute did I consider staying in that town; if I wasn't wanted I certainly didn't want to work there. Using each day as a work day and relying heavily on the on-line education job site Ed-Join; I rose early and worked until evening preparing and mailing job application packets. Not missing a beat, by the start of the following school year I had moved to the East Bay town of Walnut Creek and was working in Sunnyvale School District.

Adair School: Was a one room school house sitting between the Sunnyvale School District Offices and the transportation yard. It was a school for those students no longer welcome at the junior high and high schools. One teacher, a counselor, a custodian and never more than 14 students; what an amazing teaching/administrative experience it was. Mornings were spent on reading/writing and arithmetic and the afternoons were for other activities. Other activities included Monday and Wednesday working in the garden we planted alongside the building. Shovels, hoes, rakes, seed and plants were purchased from the nearby Home Depot. Those city kids were so surprised to see for the first time in their lives, potatoes, squash, tomatoes and other vegetables growing from the earth. And they could actually take the grown vegetables home. Tuesdays and Thursday afternoons were spent singing old Do-Wop and rock and roll songs and playing African Hand Drums. Several district office administrators who just happened to drop by the class on a Tuesday couldn't wait to join us and the music. Several even showed up with their own recently purchased drums from Amazon. Always and Forever, In the Still of the Night, Sixteen Candles, The Bristol Stomp, The House of The Rising Sun, Come Together, and many other songs from my distant past we sang and played. Don't ask me how, but the kids knew most of those songs. They must have been listening to their parent's old 45's or something. Annnd a couple of the kids really had voice, they could sing. In addition to the do wop and rock and roll I also introduced them to a little light jazz with Moon River, The Work Song and of course Fever which was the most popular of the jazz songs. Fridays were reserved for physical education. Tennis at the nearby city park after a walk through the neighborhood to the courts and/or basketball was the usual Friday activity.

Hoop: Much like the few people I've met from Indiana over the years, male and female all who claimed to be excellent basketball players; alternative education students, much like those liars form Indiana regardless of skill brazenly made the same claim. The following poem Hoop was co-written by Wadell, an alternative education student at Adair School who along with his fellow students made the same claim.

Hoop

Red orange circle, hanging ten feet high; going up for a jam,

I almost touch the

sky.

Backboard glass, see through veneer; a light kiss

off the square, two points here.

Cotton net hanging, way up in the air, three point

jumpers; I can swish it from anywhere.

Long black pole, flowing down from the square,

driving hard to the hoop; remember that it's

there.

The district office supplied several old tennis rackets; I suspect the administrators brought them from home. Somehow it all worked. There, at Adair School with a comfortable salary as teacher/principal and lots of hands on learning activities it was just plain fun and a win, win situation.

Walnut Creek: Abercrombie & Fitch, Nordstrom's, Sax 5th Ave, Tiffany and other high end shopping haunts are all found in Walnut Creek, CA. Living in a downtown apartment, each day was an unending show; especially on weekends when upscale shoppers from all over the bay area came to visit. The women wearing hats and summer dresses were pushing babies in $900 strollers; while their men stuck to the traditional brown boat shoes, khaki pants and blue knit pullovers. Walnut Creek was another one of those towns where if I wanted to see another Black person I had to look in the mirror. Not one other black person did I see, other than the ones visiting me during the four years I lived in Walnut Creek. But that's Cali, if you are a brotha with a few Benjamin's and choose not to live in a major city; you'll be out there breaking new ground in suburbia. Walnut Creek is listed among the top 20 richest cities in the country, while neighboring Danville and Alamo; home to several retired 49ers, is in the top 5.So, yes I was in interesting territory; but beyond all the negative typicalities; I liked it and enjoyed living there. Wherever I am living, I run or walk daily; consequently the mostly indirect hostile interactions with white citizenry; becomes a part of the workout. Stares were common, but on a few occasions racists were more direct.

One bicyclist I saw on the running trail from Walnut Creek to Danville often. It would have been impossible to miss that, "What are you doing her nigger?" look on his face. The 'look' was there the first time I saw him on the trail and every time thereafter. One may easily get used to 'the look' but it is the possibility of action following 'the look' that causes you to be on guard. Each day, the guy heading in the opposite direction would steer his bicycle closer and closer; forcing me to step a little bit more off to the side of the trail as he passed. The final straw was the day when he with both arms waving pretended to lose control of his fast moving bicycle. With a phony I am so sorry I hit you smile already pasted on his face; he headed straight for me. Waiting until the final second, in case he might steer toward my movement; I jumped to the left. Disappointment showed on his hateful face as he rolled past without hitting me. The following days on the trail after that incident we seemed to have reached an understanding. My look said; "If you hit me with that bicycle one of us is going to the hospital or the morgue." His face in return, all pretenses aside showed undisguised hatred. That was fine with me so long as he stayed on his side of the trail controlling the direction of his bicycle. Other than the aforementioned hate stares while shopping at nearby Whole Foods and other venues;

Walnut Creek

the bicyclist was the most direct confrontation in Walnut Creek; except for the skateboard kids. Las Lomas High School is located directly behind Whole Foods and right along the Danville/Alamo Trail. On most days I did my run while school was in session thus avoiding the after school crowds. On this day however I was late getting off from work in Sunnyvale, so I met several students on the trail during my return run. The two skateboarders were noticeable from a block away. On the isolated trail we were the only three. With backpacks, riding skateboards and heading away from the direction of Las Lomas High School; obviously they were students. Fairly big kids, at first blush I thought maybe they were high school juniors or seniors, but juniors and seniors usually had cars. The unblinking hatred contorting their young faces was unmistakable. Such hatred has always been confusing to me. I suspect that I too have hated, but never because of color, race or religion; which makes no sense. Nor has my hatred been directed at complete strangers; that too seems rather senseless. It's all seems so stupid. Hatred takes much energy, so wouldn't it be wise to keep it non generic, momentary and if personable directed at a particular person, place or thing due to some hostile action. Or why waste life's energy on hatred at all? Naively, it is surprising to see powerful hatred generated merely by observation of my color. There has got to be some heavy duty mental issues there. Ten feet away running towards the kids; they were maintaining their hateful glare as they picked up their skateboards. The shorter kid now carried his skateboard at his side in his right hand while the taller of the two had raised his board like a club holding it with both hands. He would be the one, I was ready. I suppose they thought I would stupidly run past and turn my back to them, I did not. Keeping my pace as I started past, I also kept an eye on the tall kid with his skateboard raised to hit me from behind. The shorter kid now stood off to the side of the trail watching his friend. Stopping on the trail right next to the kids I also did a little waiting and watching. I was waiting for the tall boy to take his shot; to swing his skateboard and attempt to hit me. Staring at me watching him, he wordlessly lowered the skateboard turned and continued walking with his short friend. If that kid had hit me on the back of the head with that board it could have killed me. Did he consider that, did he care? What kind of homes do such kids live in and what kind of parents raise such killer children? Were they just typical of whiteness in the Walnut Creek –Danville area or of the country as a whole? Let us hope and pray that those kids were atypical. Yeah, living in Walnut Creek was interesting. After an early morning commute to Sunnyvale for work, I was home in time for a late afternoon run. Alone, that was my life, but there too in Walnut Creek were surprising reminders of the past. Police stalking (surveillance) I'd come to accept as a part of that being black thing; although there in the creek it wasn't as intense as in Sunnyvale and other places where I had lived and worked. Standing in line at the supermarket one Friday afternoon I tried to ignore the guy two places in front who kept staring.

The Danville/Alamo Trail

Even after paying for his pack of Camel cigarettes; remaining in the store, he moved off to the side and kept staring at me. Who is this weirdo, I thought; and then it hit me Yellen and Newell were the two cops who took me from my classroom at Renton High School in Fieldsburg and dragged me down to the local police station on bogus charges more than a decade before. So there in Walnut Creek nearly a hundred miles to the south; over ten years later, making sure I saw him stood officer; Yellen staring. Showing no sign of recognition; paying for and collecting my groceries I walked to my car and drove to the apartment. Very, very strange; although the local police would periodically park outside my apartment I never saw Yelllen again. Happening before public awareness of the depth of police hatred of blacks and people of color; I was left wondering whether Yellen was a routine occurrence or did he have a plan. Meanwhile the most important things in my life work, continued.

Students Rule: Royal Sunset Continuation High School: Learning that Adair School was funded by grant monies which were to be exhausted at the end of the school year, suddenly I had limited options. Enjoying my work with the kids at Adair School I failed to notice the hints from my bosses. In my early 60's and in great health I simply had not considered a future beyond the present job. One option suggested at Sunnyvale, who offered a very generous package, was retirement. Other administrative jobs in the district were not available, I could retire or leave. Walking away from that nice Sunnyvale retirement and choosing to continue working I simply found another job. Another job another interview, this time it was at Royal Sunset Continuation High School with the principal Ms. Falk. A black woman standing about 6'1, she would have been attractive if she didn't have such crooked teeth. Of course I was hired, I discovered later because the school was facing accreditation; and a faculty member with a doctorate would look good to the accreditation committee, and that's why she hired me. Letting her know during the interview that I was thinking about going back to graduate school I said for certain I was good for a year. First day of school for me at Royal Sunset, noticeably mine was the only open door and I was the only adult monitoring the hallway as students changed classes. Standard procedure, especially at continuation and other alternative education sites to prevent conflict, drug sales or fights; teachers and administrators stood outside their classrooms and offices between the changing bells. Without saying, all knew that working in an alternative education environment meant never for a moment forgetting that the kids were in alternative education for a reason. Savvy alternative principals modeled proper teacher conduct by opening their office doors during class changes, but not so at Royal Sunset Continuation. A critical eye was no way to start but I saw what I saw, yet initially remained silent. A second oddity, teachers arrived on campus before the students and remained in their classrooms, doors locked before, during and after class thereby avoiding all unnecessary contact with students during the work day. New man on campus, seemingly there at Royal Sunset Continuation; teachers and administrators were afraid of the students. Even more distressing was finding out soon thereafter that the students knew the teachers and administrators were afraid of them, not a good thing. Teaching, more than anything else is such a learning experience. Another shocker; never would I have imagined finding myself working at a place where students were so surprised that I wasn't afraid of them. After a few weeks observing the student teacher dynamic and talking with the staff, I concluded that as a group they had been afraid of students throughout their careers. How ridiculous, the students were just kids for God's sake! Even the bigger ones still had only the brainpower and experience of the children they were. The end of the school day after the students had left campus was like the first day of spring following a cold, cold winter. Smiling teachers opened their doors; chatting and drinking coffee they ventured out of their classrooms for the very first time during the school day. Such closed door behaviors seemed rather odd and counterproductive. If you don't like and are afraid of kids, why teach? How the hell you ended up in this business, I wondered. Looking out for all students during the school day an integral part of teaching; is an impossible task to perform while locked inside your classroom and/or office. Just hired and knowing that I should maintain a tactful "blind eye"; but being an unreformed creature of habit, I couldn't ignore the most shocking discovery of all when I returned the papers from my first assignment. "You don't know how we do things here!" "This is crazy!" and other such comments were voiced as I handed out the papers. "What's wrong?" I asked, "You'll get better grades next time." I said. Arnold, leaning his wide frame on my desk told me in no uncertain terms; "At this school you give us a passing grade for turning the papers in, you don't correct them!" Standing, I loudly announced, "That's absurd! In this classroom I grade the work that you turn in. How else can you improve if your mistakes are a not corrected; folks that's called school." They were not pleased. Then too there were the other student day to day activities.

Doris: Wide and stooped, sitting with gigantic legs tucked into a too small mini-skirt Doris was big for her age; she had just turned thirteen. A different one each day, I was constantly breaking up arguments between Doris and girls sitting in front, behind or beside her. Changing Doris's seat didn't stop the bickering. Most likely for reasons having nothing to do with school, Doris the youngest and the biggest didn't seem to get along with any of the girls in class. One day it all came to a head when Latris, sitting one row across and to the front of the classroom got out of her seat, walked down the aisle and began pummeling Doris. So big she just barely fitted into the school desk; Doris was trapped, she couldn't get her gigantic body out of the seat.

Knowing this and standing close enough to block her exit Latris continued pounding Doris until help arrived from the office. After calling the emergency number several times I finally sent a student to the office for Ms. Falk. Irked at having to leave the comforts of her office, Principal Falk finally arrived and took the fighters away. Still talking about the fight, students said that Latris was angry because Doris was pregnant with Latris's boyfriend's baby. There was more, it seemed Doris already had a one year old child at home being taken care of by her mom. Amazing stuff, I listened. Regardless of who started a fight all parties received the same punishment, after a brief suspension Latris and Doris were back in school. Latris returned to my class but Doris was wisely assigned to a different class by the counselor.

Ms. Burton: The following morning Ms. Burton, the teacher next door, leaving her class unattended; rushed into my room. Crying and visibly shaken, she sad; "Someone pushed me from behind." Blood was oozing from her stocking covered right knee. "Did you call the office?" She had called but typically had gotten no response. Giving her some Kleenex to stop the bleeding and telling my curious students to be cool for a minute, with Ms. Burton in tow I stepped into the heavy silence, now lurking in the room next door. Pissed and assuming a hostile pose, I gave the known bad actors in the class who I observed daily acting up in the hallway a hard stare and asked; "Did anyone see who pushed Ms. Burton?" The two or three male students who dared look at me, showed fleeting arrogant smirks but no one spoke. Standing at her desk before returning to my classroom I quietly reminded Ms. Burton, a relatively new teacher, of a tried and true inner city teaching rule; "Never turn your back to the class or any student in the classroom. Always stand at an angle where all students remain in view at all times." Then I left her with those thugs. At our after school faculty meeting I waited for Ms. Burton to mention the assault and battery in her classroom. But fearful and new on the job she said nothing. Maybe she was aware that it was not uncommon for teachers, especially new ones to be blamed by poor administrators for student misconduct in their classrooms, regardless of circumstances. I too was a new teacher but still asked, "Ms. Falk what are you going to do about the assault on Ms. Burton today? Actually it was an assault and battery, look at her knee." The others in the room immediately looked at the torn, twisted bloody stocking on her bruised knee. Ms. Falk did not look at the knee but asked, "Ms. Burton was there a problem in your classroom today?" I was the only one surprised at Ms. Burton's quick "No." Any fool could see the bruises, and her bloody torn stocking. Immediately pointing out that assault and battery was a crime; I also mentioned that I had called the office twice to report serious incidents and got no response. "As well as the assault I tried to report a student with a gun in the hallway forcing another student to empty his backpack and pockets

." No one answered the emergency phone either when I called." "Next time I'll just call the police." Unsuccessfully trying but failing to hide her flash of anger Principal Falk said; No police! Here we work with our students."Undeterred, I became even more of a nuisance by telling about the students trying to convince me not to grade their papers, saying I was only allowed to check for completion of the work. The youngest teacher on the faculty, who I later learned was Ms. Falk's best friend, then added a bizarre absurdity. "You just don't understand our kids, most are poor and come from broken homes." Excuse me! (I thought what the fuck?)But I didn't say it. "And what does that have to do with an assault, and armed robbery and refusing to do school work?" After crazy man looks and a long silence from my fellow teachers Principal Falk chimed in with, "Give it time doc, you'll get used to our system." I didn't get used to their "…system…" but gained a clearer understanding of how it worked. The unspoken agreement between faculty, students and the principal granted blanket immunity from all disciplinary proceedings and classroom grading so long as nothing was done to attract the attention of Ms. Falk's bosses, the school district administrators downtown. For helping Ms. Falk maintain that false image of a well run school kids were allowed to continue their student charade. The majority being illiterate still if they continued to play along with Ms. Falk graduation was guaranteed. Having four and five period day's students attended classes in most of the teachers' classrooms. Sadly I witnessed many entering my class could barely read and write yet they ignored my homework suggestions. During our open house those illiterate seniors failing my classes steered their parents away from any contact or conversation with me. At the end of the school year those failing seniors did receive their justly earned F's in my class, although I later learned that Ms. Falk changed those F's to C's. I expected no support from the principal or faculty cowering in their rooms and office during the day. Aware of student needs; it was time I clarified my positions as a teacher. Yes, teaching, monitoring and shaping the pulse of the future. Working with students who fought tooth and nail against the idea of schoolwork and proper classroom conduct was especially difficult with no assistance from the office. So there I was in a place where I was ridiculed and penalized for doing what teachers do, teach. Grading, and correcting papers is not a crime! Nearing the end of a very long teaching career this 'crazy man' had been a few places and seen a few things, thrived and survived. Hence I knew it was time to clear the air.

Statement Morning: Arriving early on 'statement morning' with extra supplies; concrete blocks and boards, the classroom was ready by the time the students arrived. The three boards were placed on top of the four concrete blocks on the first desks in the front row. Ignoring the questions and comments; "Dr. Williams, what's that stuff for?" "

Doing a little building today doc?" I sat at my desk taking roll. Finished I stepped to the desks with the extra supplies at the front of the room. An open palm downward thrust with my right hand halved the board atop the first concrete block and with my left I shattered the board on the next block and continued moving slowly across the front of the room to the double boards on the next block which I shattered with both hands. The stunned silence of the students only served to accentuate the sound of crashing, cracking wood and flying splinters. With quiet footsteps; loud in that silence, I returned to the first desk and started the concrete block breaking demonstration. Students then witnessed my right arm and fist enveloped in the gray dust from the smash and thud of concrete pieces of the broken blocks flying to the sides and falling onto the tile floor. Methodically moving from left to right with both fists I began pulverizing the concrete blocks which had held the boards on my first pass. In minutes the front of the room was enshrouded in gray; with splintered boards and chunks of concrete covering the floor. As the fourth and final concrete block fell in broken pieces Ms. Falk burst into the room. Seeing her, I thought it much more amazing than the broken boards and stone that something finally got her out of her office. "What's going on here, Dr. Williams?" Looking strangely at me, the splintered wood, concrete and students sitting in frozen silence she asked. "I heard the noise from my office; it sounded like your students were tearing down the building." At least now I knew that tearing down the building would get a response from the office☺ "Just a little class experiment, we'll get it cleaned up." Ms. Falk left the room shaking her head in confusion, I sent a student down to the office with her to get a broom and a dustpan. Not much changed around the school during my remaining time there. The bumping, thumping, cussing and other noises were still clearly heard from the classrooms across the hall and on both sides; but upon entrance students maintained a cooperative, attentive, silence in my classroom. They spoke when spoken to and worked diligently on the assignments which I graded and returned. Yes, I was teaching and we were doing school! His first day in class; Carl the new student began chatting with his classmates. Ignoring the bell and my verbal instructions regarding the day's assignment Carl's conversation continued. Giving me a hostile glance he seemed irritated by the silence. "I'm from the ATL and we don't take no shit!" He said in an overly loud whisper to Harold. Reckon I was supposed to hear that as was the rest of the class. Turning to look at Carl, leaning back in the seat, arms resting on his empty desktop, legs stretched across the aisle; I couldn't hear what Harold, the student sitting directly across from him said, but Carl immediately changed his posture and attitude. Not having to explain the rules or have conflicts with students was a positive; borrowing paper from Harold Carl immediately began working on the assignment.

Block & Strike

True to the typical clientele of continuation schools and alternative education, many times our new students were a little rough around the edges but all managed to fit in.

Connor: Following the board and brick demonstration several of the bigger fellows in my class decided that I was in the words of Connor, "All right." Connor and his friend Micah, well over 6 feet tall and together tipping the scales at over 500 pounds, started doing their schoolwork and hanging around after class. Now juniors at continuation school, they'd played high school football as freshmen and Connor said he would like to play again. Having no athletic teams at continuation both Connor and Micah wanted to return to regular high school. So what's new I said, most of the kids at continuation and in alternative education aren't there by choice, for whatever reason all want to return to regular school. Following my suggestion Connor and Micah talked to their old high school football coach about a return to the team. With skepticism Coach Waterman, who needed help on his offensive line; decided to let them return to the team in the fall if they created no problems and took care of their academics. Early fall they both returned to the high school and the football team. Proud of themselves they dropped by continuation a few times wearing their football uniforms.

Unfortunately, happy endings are rare jewels when found in alternative education. Wellll, a few days before Thanksgiving vacation Connor, this time not wearing his football uniform, dropped by for an after school visit. "Shouldn't you be at football practice?" I asked. Refusing to look at me, after a long pause Connor said it; "I got kicked off the team." Maybe to many years in the business, but I wasn't surprised. "Was it drugs?" "Coach came into the locker room and smelled marijuana, I was the only person in the room and he blamed me."Well so ended that experiment. "I'm glad you were brave enough to come back, I'll see you on Monday."When Connor got kicked off the team again Micah quit, so we saw them both on Monday. Continuation was a good fit for Connor and Micah but I wondered whether continuation or any school was a good fit for Jordan His best friend Oliver also was a Royal Sunset Continuation School student.

Oliver: A tall thin former basketball player at the traditional high school with a tiny mustache, dark brown eyes a big smile and one gold earring, Oliver was cool and the girls loved him; all of the girls. He traveled from class to class with a small crowd of female admirers. Laughing and joking down the halls and out on the school grounds, Oliver even found time for schoolwork. At least he turned everything in; although I suspected that Alexandra, one of m y favorite students helped with (did) his schoolwork. Oliver like many of our students wore a police tracking device on his ankle. The device was a source of pride for most of the young men, second only to having

Jordan

Jordan, Jordan so scattered and lost, fluidity of incompleteness,

parts without body, questions never asked,

always undone, an unfilled

task.

Directions to be read, you skip every third word and

every other line, comprehension, impossible to

find.

In a forest of words,

who knows what Jordan sees, blinking blinded by the

trees.

"Jordan, look at the page, look at the word…" think what

it means, that's reading my man, easy and clean.

Take that tongue in Jordan, that other fellow you're not, this isn't about

basketball and taking a

shot.

Head down, it's easy just take a look; there you will find the open

book.

Think through the sentence, every word in the line;

meaning will come with focus and

time.

fathered a child. On this day heading back to class after break I heard someone yelling; "Dr. Williams, Dr. Williams; help me!" Help him? Oliver seemed to be in his usual preferred predicament, surrounded by a bevy of smiling young ladies, so I kept walking. "Dr. Williams they'll get me in trouble!"Then I noticed the girls laughing at his protests and frantic yelling; were pushing Oliver closer and closer to the campus fenced boundary. By now, fear in his eyes Oliver was leaning hard into his pushback attempt to stay on campus. "Dr. if I step off campus my monitor will go off and I'll be put back in Juvy (Juvenile Hall, aka kiddie jail). Help me!"Finally I got it. The girls thought it would be funny, a great laugh to push Oliver off campus and watch police and/or probation come charging in and take him to jail. "OK break it up, go to class." Walking back to the building I couldn't help chuckling with the girls and his best friend Jesse, at the always cool Oliver; now visibly shaken fearfully walking beside me. Yes, it was just another day in the neighborhood that made me appreciate the profession I had chosen.

Alexandra: She was undoubtedly one of the brightest students I had ever met, an 11th grader Alexandra was in my American History class. Not a good liar or actress; with very little success she pretended to be stupid to fit in with her fellow students. Her first day in class we were discussing the Reconstruction Period following the Civil War and I asked members of the class to name at least two of the states being reconstructed. Forgetting to play dumb, Alexandra rattled off each of the states with additional information about Junteenth. Alexandra was embarrassed by the quiet in the room and the looks she got from her classmates. Thereafter she never responded to general questions and if called upon she often pretended not to know the answers. Checking Alexandra's records in the counseling office I discovered that she had earned A+ grades in all her college prep classes at the regular high school; so why was she here at a school for dropouts and petty criminals? Was it her attitude? Alexandra was smart with a cute face and well built; about 5'9 and a fighter. Boys or girls she took no shit from either, and was quick to throw the first punch. Calling here aside one day I told her she was one of the sharpest students I had ever taught. I went on to explain that intelligence and education could be used to change a person's life. This was followed by a question from Alexandra. "What kind of change?" Well I said, "Smart people are paid money for being smart."This I surreptitiously explained in the hallway between classes so she wouldn't be seen kissing up to the teacher. "That's why folks go to college, so they can make more money when they graduate." Briefly listening to this kid I could sadly see her present reality; having spent her entire life in a world without hope. She had never seen her father, her mother was in jail and her grandmother had just gotten out of jail. Staying with various relatives over the years Alexandra expected her life to be no different from the lives of her mother, grandmother and other relatives.

At the end of our furtive hallway conversation Alexandra gave me a copy of the following very insightful poem written about Jesse, a student trying to hit on her. Alexandra liked me enough to try and hook me up with her grandmother. She introduced me with a big wink; one day after school while I was standing outside on yard duty. Of course I was courteous to grandma, who didn't look or sound half bad; but there was no way in hell I was going to become a part of that historic family jail drama. I never shared it with Jessie but her short poem, *Jesse* hit that proverbial nail, Jesse on his head. Alexandra left her poem on my desk and asked whether I thought Jesse might be offended if she gave it to him. I told her yes, it was offensive and Jesse might want to start a fight if he saw it. "I already kicked his ass the first week of school." She said. News to me; that must have been a helluva fight, Jesse was a fairly big dude who considered himself a 'badass' Trying a different tact I explained, without telling her he was recently homeless; that Jesse was going through some tough times and the poem would just add to his misery. Jesse was fairly typical for alternative education and no surprise, but Alexandra was in a way depressing. Maybe it's just California or an inner city Black thing but I absolutely could not understand the hopelessness of my students, especially Alexandra. She was smarter than I was at that age and had clothes, food and even lunch money each day. In my house and the homes of my friends; we went for days without eating because there was no food. Food, clothes, lunch money; there should be no limit to how far California kids can go; but they don't, go. Somehow, somewhere inner-city kids have lost the will or belief in a better future. I kept working on Alexandra, her friend Jesse and others. Although she never said it, I did suspect that Alexandra had a crush on Jesse, but Jesse may have been reluctant to spend time with a girl who had beaten him up. Besides Lupita also really liked Jesse; she was not as bright and she didn't fight boys.

Lupita: She was heavy into gangs, Nortenos. Teachers received a special notice when Lupita was transferred to the school. She was only fifteen but a rougher older looking crowd met her at the end of each school day. During her first week on campus I stepped outside the building to find Lupita in the middle of a group of hostile older female students. Shirt and backpack on the sidewalk; wearing black pants, black shoes and a black bra, fists balled she was slowly turning and facing the surrounding circle. "What's going on here?" I asked approaching the crowd. Getting only hard looks and no movement, I pushed my 6'2 one hundred eighty pound frame into the circle. "Break it up, schools out, go home." As the kids slowly moved away, Lupita put on her shirt and walked with me to the other end of the building and joined her friends. But not before I asked, "Who were those kids?" "Just some crazy scraps." She said. "Surenos?" "Yeah" The kids supposedly in the know claimed Surenos wouldn't dare set foot on our school grounds.

So much for the rumor that ours was a Norteno school; reckon those 'scraps' wanted to change that. Next I asked her why she took off her shirt. Lupita said it was new and she didn't want tomess it up. Odd, but it made sense, I guess. Although later, the cynic in the classroom next door, Ms. Burton said Lupita "…Just wanted to show off her big titties." I thought, in a fight? Not sure how to respond to Ms. Burton's statement I said nothing. The next day Lupita asked me, "Can I trust you?" Laughing, "Yes, but if you kill somebody, keep it to yourself." Thereafter, I don't know why; Lupita felt it necessary to inform me of all gang activity at the school and in the surrounding neighborhoods. She also explained the schools and the various boundaries for Nortenos and Surenos in the city. After meeting her mother, a very nice lady and her three younger siblings I wondered how Lupita managed to be away from home so much. Maybe those stories about her roaming the streets at all hours weren't true. Walking down the hall with Lupita on Monday following the campus confrontation she said, "We messed over some scraps this weekend." How's that I asked. "It was really bad; I can't tell you this one." That's OK with me Lupita. She must have felt guilty about it because the following day it all came out, she had to tell me. It seems that Lupita and three older male friends broke into the car of a man she says was a Sureno. Once inside the Cadillac Escalade parked in front of his apartment they cut up the leather seats and door interiors, ripped out the carpets, poured sugar into the gas tank and took the music system. I listened and prayed that she had made up the story to impress and really wasn't a part of that. Of course the real solution for this added unnecessary drama in my life was to hang out in my room or the teachers lounge during breaks and avoid Lupita. That seemed to work.

Jesse

Moving, rocking, poking, pinching; chair leaned back ever unflinching.

Stop! Did you do that? Tripping; Michaela as she walked by.

"No, no teach twasn't I", a phony English accent for the quick lie.

Lie, lies first, lie fast; never admit the truth, if you expect to last.

You'll pay, regardless what they say. So tell the quick lie and maybe doubt will sway. Conversation is the key, keep the words coming and school will never be.

Talk about colors, where fighting is the game; pound any Blood, Crip is your

claim.

Mat

French citizen, with Latinos and Blacks, claiming to be a Red, sitting way in the back.; ready to please, do what others ask; fetch this, get that, perform any task. Even crawl on your knees, to treat the color Red, like your main

squeeze.

Please, please, please let me fit in; I'm here to do anything, anything for a friend. Talk about me, laugh at me, do what you do; call me a red neck; that's OK too. Quello rojo, that's what I'm called, cool with me if I can hang with

y'all.

Gang member, a French white boy's dream; his one goal in life is to know what it means. Jose suspended, let me do that too; I can model bad behavior with the best of

you.

Attempted to cause, willfully used, possessed or sold, unlawfully offered, bartered or stole. What of education, that's important too; but not if you want friends around

you.

Weed, alcohol, bullying, theft, sexual harassment are just a few, of the things that speak loud, and attracts the 'right' crowd. Wanna have a good time, you must be fast, for 'home boy' friendships; school's gotta be

last

Considering the overwhelming positive number of years, classrooms and students encountered, I felt a sudden discomfort working in an environment of threats and fear. Had it always been that way or was it just alternative education. Did I unintentionally present a rough South Central LA Compton kind of exterior? Was mine just a reaction to the environments in which I found myself or just my approach and way of dealing with any environment? I wondered. Although different from San Francisco County Jail #7; at times there were similarities. It' was kinda strange having kids do what they' were supposed to do, i.e. schoolwork only because they were afraid of me. Was that OK? In schools; directly and indirectly we teach children how to prepare for a work environment and how to become better citizens. Do the ends justify the means? Looking at the bigger picture; balancing the jail environment that I directly witnessed with the jobs and good citizen's environment in public schools, I suspect that it did. However, in other classrooms at the school in hallways and outside on the school grounds those very same students from my class did no schoolwork and were lawlessly out of control. So were some of our students including the ones from my class headed for my old classrooms at the county jail? The year ended, the accreditation committee awarded the necessary accreditation and the school no longer needed a teacher with a doctorate, so I was again on the move; restarting that seemingly never ending search for that oftentimes mythical 'better' place. Should that word that pops up often when one reaches a certain age in any profession, also be a consideration, retirement? It is a fearful and powerful word with numerous implications; reaching into our pasts and directing our futures.

Retirement

Retirement: How does it happen, where does it come from? You're still enjoying the thing you've done most of your life when you notice co workers and even students treating you differently. You wonder whether the odd treatment is because you parked in the wrong space, or maybe sat in the wrong chair. Like my first marriage 'never having done it before' maybe it was time to try that retirement thing, why not? Retirement, meant still receiving a monthly check without having to report to work, unbelievable, but that's the way it really worked I discovered. No strings attached, the check comes. But retirement meant fewer dollars, which I hadn't found the need to think about in years. Still mulling over the dollars I took that leap.

Very Different Circumstance, Arkansas Again: Talking to my brother about retirement, he of course suggested that I should come 'home' to Arkansas upon retirement. I reminded him of the rampant racism in Arkansas while we were growing up, but Lee Willie assured me that things had changed.

He also reminded me that we were the last two survivors of the seven kids in our family who grew up in Arkansas. Although he called it home, I had only lived in Arkansas the first 18 years of my life and joyfully left for California; where I had lived for more than 40 years, so where was home? But maybe it was time to listen to my older brother, that's what younger brothers do isn't it; and move back 'home'. No way was I going to move back to the town of fewer than a thousand people where we grew up. Still uneasy about the new adventure, Cabot, Arkansas was the city where I bought a house. Feeling the need to be near a major airport for a quick exit if necessary, Little Rock Airport (Bill & Hillary Clinton National) was nearby.

A little over $90,000 for a four bedroom 2 ½ bath brick home only two years old on one acre was quite a steal compared to California prices. Meanwhile moving slowly into that retirement idea I continued working in California and visiting my Cabot house for a few days every 6 months or so to get a feel for actually living in Arkansas. In a middle class neighborhood near an Air Force Base it was much like living in California with neighbors from all over the country and very few Arkansas natives; which was a good thing. I even saw a couple of black men with white women. The couples looked furtive and afraid but smiled and said hello when they saw the California license plate on my car in the parking lot. Near the time of actual retirement, rather than a couple of days here and there; I decided to spend two weeks of day to day living in Cabot to get used to that "...changed." Arkansas. During my short visits to Cabot I often shopped at the local markets including Wal Mart. The 2nd week of my two week test visit before retirement in Arkansas I again found myself at Wal Mart. There were two check out lines; one manned by a twenty something checker and the other by an older woman maybe in her mid sixties. Judging from her hard looks at me and her age I figured she had to be from the time of legalized segregation and lynching in Arkansas. Yep, looking and acting her part, the lady had to be Arkansas 'old school.' Avoiding the historical hatred and drama, I of course chose the other line. But just my luck the younger checker closed his station for lunch. Consequently I found myself exactly where I didn't want to be, in the older white woman's check out line. The customers ahead of me were greeted with a smile and, "Good afternoon, did you find what you were looking for?" My turn came and the old woman with unkempt gray hair snatched my shopping cart forward and silently began checking and bagging my groceries. Returning her hostile silence I waited. Looking at my check when I paid, the old racist went off; saying in a loud nasal voice, "I get so sick of you boys trying to pass these out of state checks here!" Over 60 years old I was certainly beyond the "boy" stage of my life. Trying hard to maintain a semblance of courtesy I said; "I've been shopping at this store for more than two years and this is the first time my check has been questioned."

Cabot Arkansas

The look on that hags face was priceless, if she had a gun she would have shot me on the spot, instead she pressed a buzzer underneath the counter. Soon a fellow looking to be in his early thirties appeared wearing an assistant manager's name tag. Looking at my check handed to him by 'Ms. Confederacy" the assistant manager said; "You boys should know you can't cash out of state checks here." Leaning close enough to nearly touch his lopsided nose, "I am not your fucking boy!" I said as I snatched my check from his hand and slammed the empty shopping cart into the adjoining check out stand. Furious, and ready to kick some white red neck ass; but remembering I was in Arkansas, I walked to my car and drove the six miles to my house in Cabot. Glancing in the rearview mirror as I pulled into the garage I saw two fellows in a Wal Mart security van stop at my driveway and watch me get out of my car. Those sons of bitches had followed me home. Being followed home in Arkansas was dangerously significant. Leaving the garage door open and the car engine running I ran into the house and grabbed my Walther PPK. Fortunately when I returned to the garage with one in the chamber Wal Mart security was pulling away from the curb. They followed me home, so now they knew where I lived. Putting two slugs in their departing rear window did cross my mind, briefly. Back inside I called my brother and explained what had happened. Brushing the whole thing off as inconsequential, he said it was just an isolated incident. Yeah well, "...isolated incident" my ass; the very next day I contacted the broker and told him to sell the house. Of course he asked why and I told him that I had been living in California to long to live in Arkansas. He diligently began working to sell the house that I had foolishly bought at the urging of my brother Lee Willie. As far back as I can remember Lee Willie always managed to get me involved in one dubious undertaking or another. Although I blame him for the initial house buying and possible retirement plans in Arkansas; there were other contributing factors, there too was Inez.

Inez: On one of my trips to Arkansas before the retirement conversations with Brother Lee Willie I happened to run into Inez, the older sister of one of my best friends from high school. Her brother Hearsie Dee AKA known as 'Top', and I grew up together; playing basketball, chopping and picking cotton around Gould, Arkansas. Seeing Inez in Arkansas I remembered the first party I ever attended at age 16. Inez was there and looking soooo good. For some reason I ended up walking her home but was to shy and scared to do anything but stumble along with little conversation and wave good night. After so many years she still looked pretty good. Then a widow we managed to get together a few times during my Arkansas visits. When I returned home I invited her to spend the summer with me in California. She agreed and came to live with me in the city of Walnut Creek. Having never been to the bay area she enjoyed visiting Alcatraz, The Golden Gate Bridge, Chinatown, and Fisherman's Wharf and other tourist attractions.

At summers end Inez returned home to Little Rock, Arkansas where she owned a home and I went back to work. However, we maintained a relationship and I flew back to visit during holidays and other occasions. Preceding Lee Willie's input she and I had first started the retirement location discussions. Inez was looking for a house per my instructions in and around Little Rock. I told her to look outside the city and not in a ghetto. She found several houses that I checked out on the internet and they all were in the ghetto. After reminding her again that I didn't want to live in a ghetto she finally looked outside the city of Little Rock and found a new housing development that was also in a ghetto. Finally remembering how I had to insist that she not stop to let whites go ahead of her in lines at the supermarket, theatres and other places in California; I saw that she couldn't shake her racist southern indoctrination. Bottom line Inez, like many Black southerners, including my brother Lee Willie; are afraid of white people. Having left the South as a teen ager it surprised me to witness that fear in her eyes and in the eyes of other Southern Blacks. Her fear and refusal to look beyond the ghetto for housing was one of the major reasons our little relationship fell apart. Certain that I was going to marry his sister Inez, when I didn't her brother 'Top'; formerly my best friend, stopped speaking to me; and to this day, hasn't spoken to me since. Yes brother 'Top' is still pissed, although her personal relationship and mine was none of his dam business. So that Arkansas retirement idea all started with Inez, and when she dropped the ball Lee Willie picked up on the idea. After bailing out on Inez and Lee Willie's Arkansas plans, California retirement returned to the forefront.Seeking a house that I could afford and wanting to stay as close to the bay area as possible, my internet search started in Walnut Creek and moved south. The search eventually took me to the central valley town of Merced where I found a house being built on the west side of town at 451 Brittany Way

Merced Life: Settling into my new home town right away I began to notice certain familiar housing patterns. Like many cities in California's Central Valley Merced is divided along racial lines. This I first noticed over the years visiting my Bakersfield cousins. Merced, like Bakersfield; reminded me of my hometown in Arkansas where white people lived on one side of the railroad tracks and black people on the other. In Merced the downtown shopping areas and most white homes are located on the east side of the railroad tracks. When I bought my house of course I was unaware of the racial boundaries and delineations; something realtors don't mention to prospective buyers. Finding myself on the west side; still a working man; I started my new life deep in the San Joaquin Valley in the town of Merced, California. A drummer since the late sixties at Venice Beach in Southern California I immediately sought out drummers and drum circles in the area.

Main Street Merced, California

I met numerous folk in my eight years; damm, did I live there that long? Yep I did live there longer than any other place since my divorce. Upon leaving leaving Merced after those eight years I realized I had had many interactions but only one true friend in that town, Frank McMillon. Soon after first meeting him during my first few months in the city he introduced me to other drummers. Frank also arranged for me to teach a class at the local community college, Introduction to Hand drumming. Using my drum collection the students met twice a week to make sounds at Merced College. My very first college teaching experience was great fun. With members of the class we formed a musical group with an emphasis on drums called the Merced Marauders. On weekends we played in bay area parades, at schools, downtown on the streets of Merced and other venues. Individual participants varied in number depending on the days and times of scheduled events. Sometimes we marched with other groups in street parades and other times we played while riding on vehicles or floats. On several occasions we had gigs at local bars, coffee shops and clubs, which was quite a learning experience. There is nothing like entering a crowded bar when the lights are dim and hearing the bartender say, "There's the talent!" In the beginning we were using my drums exclusively but after a while students started purchasing their own instruments. We even convinced one local music store manager to give a special discount on drum purchases to The Merced Marauders. One Saturday afternoon while taking a break from playing at the local Farmers Market we spotted a booth for the new University of California Merced. Naturally we all wandered over to talk to the fine looking young lady manning the booth. At first she seemed mostly interested in the older white fellow in the band as her eyes flickered between the two of us talking our heads off to gain a foothold. For whatever reason; the young lady finally seemed to settle and give me all of her attention. Reluctantly noticing my looks and hearing my suggestive throat clearing the other band members got the hint and wandered off leaving me with Ms. Fine.

Angela Modair: A recent graduate of UC Santa Cruz's Theatre Arts Program, manning the UC Merced information booth was just one of Angela's summer jobs. Exchanging phone numbers we set up a lunch date for the very next day. By the 2nd week of introductory activities, still moving with watchful caution Angela seemed unsure of where we might be headed, I wasn't. Is life so complicated? She was with me by choice because she liked something or some things about me. I was with her because I liked some things about her. "That's called attractiveness; or I like you and you like me." In the simplest terms I explained our budding relationship to a seemingly confused Angela. No confusion on my part, fine ass woman was headed for my king sized bed ASAP. Her living situation was unusual. The 'baby' and the only girl with two older brothers in Los Angeles; Angela lived in her new house recently purchased by her doting father.

Merced Marauders Group I

To help with the house payment she rented a room to an older white fellow. It felt strange seeing him there when I visited so we spent most of our time at my house. Angela kept her dogand her old room at her parents' house as well, she was spread out. Morning runs, movies, theatre in Sacramento and San Francisco, overnighters at Yosemite were typical outings.Being more than twice her age didn't bother me and since she was with me I assumed it didn't bother her either. But there were important outsiders in her life. Working for Planned Parenthood was Angela's 2nd job and she insisted that we both be tested for HIV before having sex. But when I visited Planned Parenthood for testing Angela's boss nearly had a cow, the woman was upset. A grunted hello when introduced and several hostile glances later I decided she didn't like me and/or our situation. She obviously didn't think I was a wise love interest for Angela. Angela was well over 18, in her mid twenties but her boss treated me like I was robbing the cradle. And she wasn't the only disapproving outsider.

Enjoying each other in a healthy relationship after weeks of preparation Angela decided it was time for me to meet her parents. I was cool with that but she was a little nervous. We didn't stay; it was just a drive-by meeting. The father standing in the front doorway peering up at me with a look of disapproval paused before deciding to shake my offered hand. Remembering Angela's pre warning I just gave him my best smile. Moms didn't seem bothered as she smiled graciously and shook my hand. Later I understood the father's concern; how would I feel if my son brought home a girlfriend old enough to be my mother? Not good; unless of course she was quite fine☺ Angela's parents were maybe late 40's and I was flirting with the 60's. Getting past the meeting of the parents thing we got on with the important parts of life. Even though he was "just renting a room" I was still bothered by the fact that Angela was living with some old white guy. Often together at my house until very late Angela ignored my suggestions that she stay over. Although I had two guest bedrooms she always drove home. Having done all the pre sex things that she suggested including meeting her parents and HIV testing I thought it past time that she share my bed. During another one of our getting to know each other talks Angela asked if I had ever smoked marijuana. Although I had stopped smoking marijuana and drinking when my son was born. I told her that if she wanted to try marijuana I could get some.

Well, the relationship was about to change. The following morning found us on the road for that four hour drive to Los Angeles. I'd called my former road dog Charles and told him we were headed his way. I didn't have to ask whether he had marijuana because Charles started each day smoking a joint and stayed high until bedtime. He had lived that way for more than thirty years. Arriving at Charles house in the early afternoon, he rolled us a couple of joints and in no time at all we were on the road for the return trip home.

The King

Excited, Angela couldn't wait to try marijuana. Preparing for the after smoking munchies we stopped at the local supermarket to buy cookies, ice cream, hot dogs and other goodies. Here we go! Sitting on the floor sharing a pillow next to the coffee table, I lit up. Telling her to observe, I took a big puff off the joint and held the smoke inside as long as possible. Her turn came and she sucked in the smoke and held her breath like a pro. Soon we were giggling and chomping on cookies, ice cream and hot dogs. Between one and two AM the time Angela often chose to leave she said, "I have to go home." Smiling I reminded her; "You can't drive." Looking at me like I was a crazy man she responded; "I don't see why not!" "Uh, honey bun, I don't think you'll be doing any driving tonight, you're loaded, high."Watching closely and anticipating as she leaned on the coffee table, stood and took several steps toward the door, I followed. Walking alongside Angela; at about the third step I caught her as she crumpled toward the carpeted floor. Finally she was in my bed, the sex was good and the following morning began a new chapter. Sex is always an important part of any relationship, most often a very good part; it cuts through all the bullshit, and ours was no different, at first. The first few times I noticed mutual enjoyment then the shit got strange. Why me I ask? Why must I find these weird sex females? First I noticed her rushing to climax before my ejaculation and stopping. Other times she had a look of anger on her face as if my giving her sexual pleasure and my own displeased her .Questioning her about past sexual experience Angela mentioned Gunter, her first who she met in South Africa when she was an exchange student. Then she showed me photo albums of her two prior boyfriends, they too were white. Thinking back I wondered whether her fathers' hostility was more because I was black rather than because of my age. Along those very same lines I remembered that both her brothers were married to white women. Was there a family pattern? Things got even more interesting when I noticed three or four calls a week to Germany on the phone bill. Then at a Black History Week Picnic in the park she disappeared for three hours with a woman I didn't know. I also noticed her spending hours with the underage daughter of a band member while we were playing a downtown gig. She was so interested in the daughter that she decided to find her own ride home. The shit was getting weirder and I was beginning to think about ways of easing out of the situation. First I asked about the calls to Germany and she denied making any calls to Germany. OOOOOOOOOk. Then I showed her the phone bill, that's when the tears came. Through the snotty nose and the tears she said that her relationship with Gunter was over and she would never speak to him again. Agreeable me I told her that if she wanted to be with Gunter, the mystery woman in the park or the underage blind female; it was her business, just let me know when she was ready to move. More and more tears with promises of lasting love etc. "Yeah."Nearing summer's end the surprises and other drama did not end they seemed to multiply.

Living cozily together in my west side house things were getting a little shaky, although she had helped me shop for a new house on the 'proper' east side of town. Angela had forgotten to mention that she had applied and been accepted at NYU's Graduate school for the coming fall semester. She said she would be leaving for New York in a couple of weeks. Gunter her "former" boyfriend had also been accepted at Columbia and would be in New York as well. The lady was moving to Times Square, Broadway and New York City! I wrote a poem about a comment made the night before I dropped her off at the airport.

So suddenly Angela was comfortably in New York and I was anxious to visit, I hadn't been there in a while, but no invitation came. In one conversation after she sent the following picture Angela suggested "phone sex." What the hell, that sounded pretty damm bizarre to me; but reckon I was out of touch, or maybe she was, no pun intended. "How does one have sex over the phone?" I asked. Listening to her explanation I then understood those long conversations she had charged to my phone talking to Gunter when we were living together. Thanksgiving I was invited for a weekend visit. Listening to her talk about opportunities on Broadway and seeing that look I'd seen on the faces of so many Hollywood hopefuls when I lived in Los Angeles I wondered whether Angela was more interested in Broadway and New York City than her coursework at NYU. It was a beautiful fall weekend; we did Times Square, Central Park and other tourist haunts. Following that weekend we went our separate ways. Before writing this section I did a little Google search and lo and behold I found Angela with pictures looking a little thicker and older, with a German last name teaching at a major California University. Her husband also seems to be teaching at that same university. I assume he is her husband, his first name is Gunter his last the same as hers.

Well enough about that woman and back to life in my new town of Merced. Events in our lives are housed in certain mental and physical spaces. And it just may be nearly impossible to tell those stories without considering those physical and mental spaces where they happened. Other than the brief Angela fling, she was the first woman I had lived with since my divorce over six years before. I was also living in my first California house since that divorce. Although living in a new house in a new neighborhood, maybe it was just a west side thing but all the rules of ghetto living seemed to apply. Or maybe it was just me and a black thing. Periodic break ins, car thefts and excessive police scrutiny were all a part of the west side package. Police stalking was so intense; especially after I started attending and working at UC Merced; I kept a daily record titled "Chronicles of Harassment." My very first day in the city a friend and I decided to go for a walk alongside the almond trees irrigation canals.

"Like Your Poetry"

"Like your poetry," she said. Honey tI's not new; the

Source of my expression should be familiar to

you,

My poetry is life, pages of my pain; words are bullets, ripping, tearing and twisting; explosively quiet

refrain.

My poetry, is it not common, do you not recognize a line, each a gift

from you to me; passed over

time.

You sit there and make such a statement, bold as can be, oblivious to your presence writing the words for all but you to

see.

"Like your poetry" you say, tightening straps on your backpack preparing to go away; California to New York with the coming day. So many loose pages you never read, but on this day you managed to see just one, lying on the

bed.

You are the words I squeeze and dribble onto the page; the essence of all the

thoughts, tastes, smells and colors I see, that makes what you call, my

"...poetry.

Angela Modair

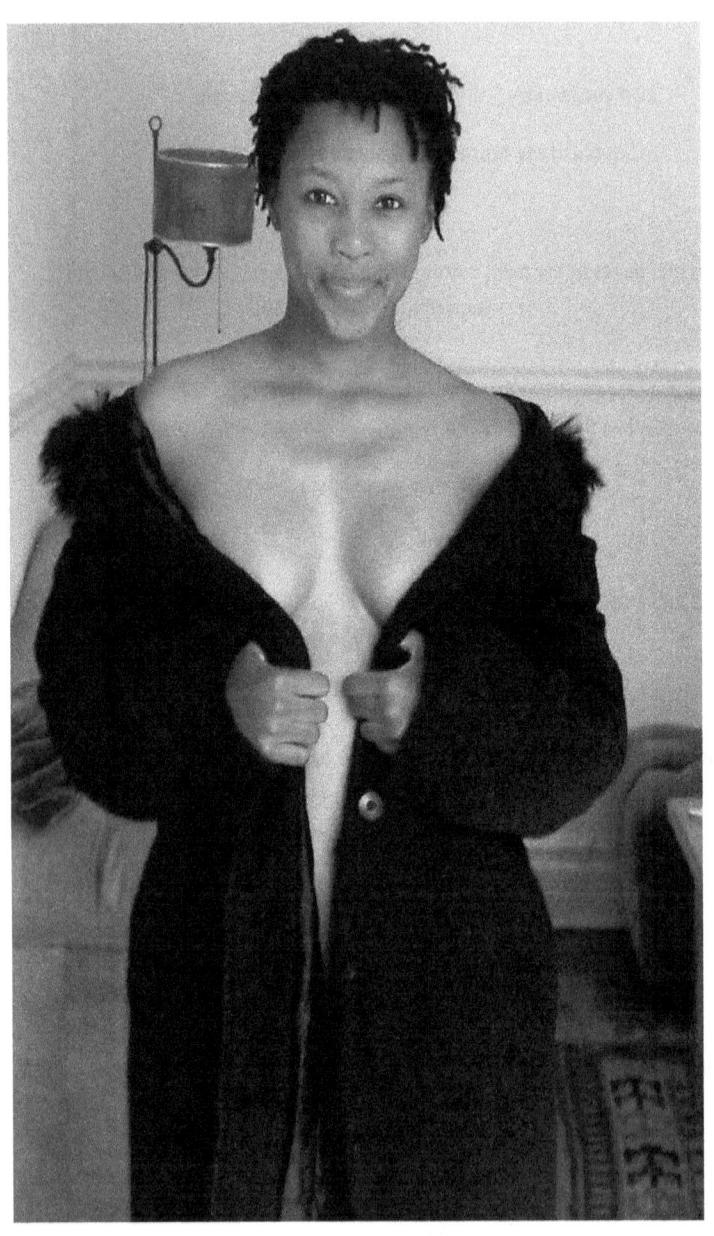

Central Park, New York City

There are tons of almond trees and canals in the area; and upon our return there were two marked police cars waiting alongside the isolated canals. Both cops gave us the "police stare" as we walked past. Welcome to Merced, The very next morning backing out of my garage, there were two guys in yellow hazard suits sifting through my two garbage containers. Reading that common look in their eyes, they didn't try to hide the fact that they were police. Pausing and looking at them as if they were nuts, I remembered that stereotypes are the rule with slow witted racists. My black skin meant that I had to be dealing drugs to be able to buy a house, and stupid enough to put drug paraphernalia in my trash. What assholes! On another occasion I pulled out of the garage and found a marked police car idling in front of m y house. Thank God I listen to the news daily and read the local papers. You gotta stay informed; your life may depend on it. Anyway a black guy had killed a highway patrolman in a neighboring town the day before. Slowly pulling out of my driveway on Brittany Way, I knew present conduct would determine whether I lived to see another sunrise. From the moment I pulled out of my driveway following just inches from my rear bumper in his California Highway Patrol Cruiser with his brights on he stayed right on my tail for the entire two miles to the freeway on ramp. If I had hit on my brakes, made a sudden turn or speeded up; it would have given the cop the excuse he was looking for to take some killing action. Moving with utmost care and caution; I knew he was waiting for any reason to kill me then and there on the road, knowing he would get away with it. His small minded racist cop logic said a black person killed a cop so a cop had the right to kill a black person, any black person. He knew where I lived and the time I left for work. Privy to police stalking records he also knew I left very early, at a time when the neighborhood streets were still deserted. There was just him with an urge to kill a man with black skin and me. Cautiously rolling onto the freeway I pulled away. On yet another occasion I went away for the weekend and unlocking my front door upon my return I heard running footsteps inside my house and a large vase falling onto the marble floor. There was no evidence of a break in and nothing was taken which in my book meant an illegal police presence in my home. When a much younger man I thought the stalking and harassment was personal, maybe there was something I was doing or not doing to attract police attention. But after a few years I realized that it wasn't personal it was just my color; seeing black was just like waving the proverbial cape at a bull, police will take some negative action. Driving past one or two police; on or off duty; the immediate thought is 'There's a black guy let's fuck with him." Riding together in their marked police cruiser, look at their faces; they're having fun, a grand old time. You may have money, a nice house, a nice car and all the things we strive for in America but when attained by Blacks, those things serve only to further infuriate racist KKK minded police. Be yourself, being the courteous, smiling, shuffling "good nigger" won't change a thing, you still

West Side, 451 Brittany Way, Merced, California

black and that's all they see. But enough about those stalking wizards of racism wearing blue rather than the usual Ku Klux Klan white sheets. And there were the west side civilians. One night I heard a noise coming from my rear patio in my 8 foot high fenced back yard. Cocking the Walther PPK and sliding open the rear door I decided to take a peek. With a look of horror, staring at my gun hand, a young Latino fellow ran down the side yard glancing fearfully over his shoulder and with one leap swung over the 8 foot fence. I don't know what he wanted, maybe to steal the patio furniture, or just a peeping tom? My neighbor on the right side owned three junker cars; two he kept in his garage and the other he parked in front of his house. His fourth vehicle, a truck he decided to park in front of my house. My cars were parked inside my garage. But to maintain my home space; I had to start parking one of my cars in front of the house. After about a week of parking one of my cars outside; thinking surely by then the neighbor would have gotten the hint, I again started parking both my cars in the garage. He didn't get it; he started parking in front of my house again. That was the last straw! "Stop parking your fucking vehicles in front of my house!" He got the hint, or felt the threat and stopped parking his truck in front of my house.

After about a year I started looking closely at neighborhoods on the east side of town and put the Brittany Way house up for sale. Remembering the one lesson learned from my brother and Inez trying to resettle me in Arkansas, the state of my birth, I was too old for ghetto living. With the job and money to move, why would I continue living in the west side ghetto? Construction finished; I moved to the east side of town. Properly housed with three large bedrooms, family room, den, library, office, dining room and 2 ½ baths I was set for life. Long distance relationships, Arkansas houses, California houses, retirement; seemingly I had a very full plate; but was so busy living it (Eating it?) I hardly noticed. What would be the most practical next move? Would I have enough income to pay for the new living space? Should I seek out a new lady to share the new space? The most important relationships in my life all started while I was working or attending schools. If no longer working it seemed reasonable to hold off on expectations of companionship until I returned to that well known comfortable environment, school. School became the major objective as the higher mortgage rate and retirement loomed. With time on my hands I was thinking I could pursue another advanced degree; possibly a Masters in American History, or a PhD in African American History or Medical School. My university attendance only included schools in Southern California and Northern California; consequently I had no knowledge of schools in and around Merced. There was The University of California Merced which was within blocks of my new home but it had yet to open its doors. So California State University Stanislaus in Nearby Turlock seemed the reasonable option.

East Side, 4623 Hutchinson Lane, Merced, California

California State University Stanislaus: Just a short drive down the road from Merced I registered for the fall term to pursue a graduate degree in history. Communicating with Professor Louganis, who happened to be on campus during the summer I applied to the university and registered for three classes during the coming semester. Looking at my resume; BA History Pepperdine University, MA Educational Management Sonoma State University, Secondary Teaching Credential University of Southern California, High Intensity Language Training (HILT) University of Southern California, and a JD from New College of California School of Law; Louganis was impressed. He was certain that my admission to the graduate program was in his words "...a no brainer." So I registered, purchased and pre read the books for my classes and started the fall semester. After more than twenty years since attending a California University I noticed that things hadn't changed. Just like back in the day when I was a beginning undergraduate, no other blacks were in any of my three classes. Yep, here again I was the only 'one'. Nor were there any other blacks visible on campus. Some without color, the white privileged might ask why is such oneness noticeably important?

Well in situations where there are few blacks or only one, whites who've never interacted with blacks, which I daresay would include most whites; react. Consequently, blacks preferring the same anonymity granted other students are burdened with the necessity of responding to those reactions. The 77% white majority population expects blacks to be the same as or similar to the blacks they know from rap songs, TV and the movies. But surprise, surprise; just like other students blacks want to attend class get good grades and move on to the next class. Unfortunately, such neutrality is not an option. Many whites, at university or wherever encountered; expect the obligatory, stereotypical poor, ignorant, smiling joke telling idiot. If one doesn't fit the stereotype; never to admit that their beliefs and expectations are not only wrong but bizarre; white folks get angry, downright huffy. Blacks having suffered through the experience so many times in the "only one" situations, instinctively prepare for the coming onslaught of active racism. Beyond those observations, a few weeks later I was called into the office of the History department chairman, Dr. Metz. Contrary to what I had been told by Dr. Louganis during the summer, Dr. Metz informed me in no uncertain terms that I hadn't been accepted into the graduate program. I mentioned the acceptance letter I received from Dr. Louganis, but ignoring me he went on to say that since my BA in history was more than twenty years old I would have to earn another BA at Stanislaus before being admitted to the graduate program. Of course at the time I was already enrolled and attending classes three times a week. One look into that man's eyes showed what he wouldn't verbalize, "Nigger you ain't getting into my program!" After several weeks of listening to his bullshit I told Metz,

A black Male You Will Always

be

Not a real person, no individuality, a black male you will always

be.

Climb the highest mountain and swim that proverbial sea; a black male you will

always

be.

Be aware; yes there is a plan, to make you less than a man; just a black male,

and all that that

entails.

So remember my son, the visions you

see,

and the good that you do, is only

important to those who love you, and always to

me.

To thrive, to survive, you must realize, that no one else; only you can

decide,

altitude and distance, how far. Yes only you can choose to be the person you

are.

"Fuck off! No way will I repeat a degree just to get into your chicken shit graduate program! Put on your KKK pillowcase and go burn a cross!" Amazing the obstacles racists create to block the simplest actions goggled Metz and wasn't surprised to discover that I have more degrees and education than he does. Been black all my life and one thing you learn to do is move on to the next obstacle, keep on stepping.

California State University East Bay: Checking on line I discovered California State University East Bay, formerly Cal State Hayward. Moving from a San Joaquin Valley to a bay area university was like that proverbial night and day. Other than the commute Hayward sounded like the perfect spot. Perfect mainly because the cost of the commute was offset by tuition free attendance for persons over the age of 60, that was me. So I applied and was immediately admitted to their graduate history program. The university also had an agreement with Cal Berkeley's History department facilitating the completion of the PhD in History while attending Cal State East Bay. It was good to keep on stepping instead of kicking Metz's ass back at Stanislaus. There in the East Bay certain nearby cities have had high concentrations of Blacks for many years. Oakland, Richmond, Pittsburg, San Leandro and Hayward have large Black populations. In years past I had even taught in Oakland, Richmond and Pittsburg, California. Sooooo foolish me, bring on some chitlins; I looked forward to being knee deep in Black folk at Cal State East Bay. But when moving around campus and attending seminars, lo and behold again I was 'the only one' in my classes. I suspect that such only oneness is typical of colleges and universities throughout the country. Yet there at Cal State East Bay professors and staff didn't exhibit the outright fear of blackness and patronizing racism witnessed at Stanislaus and other colleges and universities I attended. One afternoon I spotted a couple of fine sistas during my break. We chatted for a minute or so about the university but they werer in between classes as was I. On another occasion I met Dr. Truncas, a black professor who taught in the Education Department. Dr. Truncas said there were at least two other Black professors she knew who worked at the university. Three black professors, comparatively, that was a host of black folk. Except for the commute all was good at Cal State East Bay, but when blessed with a little patience things get even better. During my afternoon workout I happened to run past the new University of California Merced, just a few blocks from my home. Folk were milling about so I stopped and asked a few questions about what was up. What a pleasant surprise to discover they were open for business. Yes, another university; looking back I don't know how I maintained any kind of balance dealing with so many people in so many places in so many schools; but on to Merced. Praying that I wouldn't have to go through any Stanislaus racist bullshit I figured it would be wise to apply. God is good!

California State University Stanislaus

California State University East Bay

The University of California Merced: California State University Stanislaus, California State University East Bay and now the University of California Merced, what the hell? Was I to spend my retirement bouncing from one to the other; touring California Universities? Regardless, only about a mile from my home surrounded by open fields and dairy farms UC Merced was my next stop. Sailing thorough the application and admission process, it was nice being at yet another California University. Did I mention that I like schools? An excellent letter of recommendation from my History of Japan Professor from my days at California State University Stanislaus helped. It seems her friend taught Ancient Chinese History and was the chairperson of the history department at The University of California Merced. Soon I was to learn how the friend to friend, family to family manipulations worked within the university system. Here it could be said to work to my advantage, but I wasn't a friend or relative; instead I was the best student in the aforementioned professor's class at Stanislaus earning an easy A+ grade. During the next seven years as a student and teacher at the University I would learn that connections and friendships are first; hard work, intelligence and all else take a back seat. Well anyway I was in and next on the agenda was meeting my PhD committee and scheduling classes and seminars.

The TA Surprise: Finances were also a part of the registration process. After making arrangements for tuition payments at the registrar, I headed to a meeting with my research committee chairperson. On my way to her office I just happened to walk past the group of 14 other, all white, PhD students headed in the opposite direction. "Where are you guys going?" Renee yelled, "To the meeting for Teaching Assistants (TA's)" Graduate students hired as teaching assistants had their tuition waived and were paid a monthly salary for teaching supplemental classes at the university. Immediately returning to the registrars office where two days earlier I had been told that there were no open TA positions; I asked why ALL of the WHITE graduate students had TA positions and I did not. Within ten minutes I was assigned a TA position and told to go to the TA meeting that I had just by chance discovered. Following the meeting, TA position settled; next on the agenda was meeting my PhD committee.

During the latter part of the 1960's and early 1970's I was intrigued by groups of African American street brothers wearing black turtleneck sweaters, black berets and leather jackets. They were hanging around college campuses selling copies of Chairman Mao's *Little Red Book*. Watching those guys being rousted by the police in the bay area and on the streets of Los Angeles; I remained curious here in the 21st century about the history of the short lived Black Panther Party I was specifically interested in the link between communism and the Black Panther Party. The plan was to research those armed street brothers quoting Mao Zedong as they prepared for a coming revolution in the United States of America.

University of California Merced

Finding professors for my committee with interest in my area of study was problematic. There were no African American Historians, nor African American, Latino, Asian or any teachers of color at UC Merced. Two white teachers claimed to be, maybe 1/10 Native American. Really! What utter nonsense! The USA is such a mix that anyone can legitimately claim to be 1/10 of any ethnicity. Watching the assembly of a 40 foot high structure from my classroom window in the 2nd building on the left, the first is the library; I asked my students; "What's our new campus art piece called?" Samantha said that it was called the vagina. When I doubted Samantha the other students in the class agreed with her. Hmmmmm Guess it did kinda look like a vagina but I walked over after class and asked the construction crew and was told that the piece was called "Beginnings". Vagina, beginnings one could easily make the connections but it all depends on perspective where you could go with that.

PhD Committee: So I ended up with a Diplomatic Historian, An Ancient China Historian and an American Literature Professor on my PhD committee. Rail thin standing about 5'9 Professor Dalton the Diplomatic Historian lived in the heavily minority populated (Black) East Bay city of Richmond, California. Pleased to have him on my committee I relaxed a little bit, judging from where he lived I figured he would be comfortable with blacks. I also felt comfortable with short chunky black haired Ruth Motern the Ancient China Historian and the chair of my committee. After all it was her friend's strong letter of recommendation that facilitated my entrance into the PHD program. Thinking I had two of the three committee members on my side was a good feeling. The two other members were to come from outside of the history department. American Literature professor Garth Chuner, about 6'3 fit and well known in literary circles was the third member. One of his students said at English and American Literature Conferences Chuner was treated like a rock star. In later conversations as he checked me out as I checked him out, once he fought past his racist stereotypical assumptions and decided I could read and write; Chuner mentioned Douglas, Wright, Ellison, Dubois, Baldwin, Malcolm, Martin and other African American Writers. Having read them all and lived much of what they wrote was really pushing the envelope for a man who assumed I was illiterate; he was shocked. Students, especially students of color and women; know that perceptions and assumptions affect grades. It is always wise to be aware of how you are perceived. For a 'normal' college experience some may have to pressure racist professors just to have the same day to day college experience as do other students. So how does one deal with the ever present racist dilemma? When possible the first alternative is to ignore the bullshit and do what must be done in your area of study. Even when facing surprising and shockingly unfair circumstances; you gotta survive and work through the brambles, ignoring the minor cuts and scratches, that's what we do!

Ruth: Once past their patronizing racist assumptions I got to know the three committee members quite well. From the beginning Ruth, the Ancient China Historian directed my research into areas which had nothing to do with the Black Panther Party. She suggested, without clarification or reasons, that I would be better served by concentrating my research on Modern China. **(1) Modern China** seemed interesting but beyond Chairman Mao's Little Red Book, I wondered where the connection to the Black Panther Party was. What's up with that? New on campus, I had no reason to distrust her; after all she was the department chair and the friend of my favorite professor at Stanislaus. What did I know I did as I was told and plowed into researching the history of Modern China from 1949 to the present. Unasked, maybe to gain my trust Ruth just happened to mention that her husband had a PhD in African American History. That said, I assumed she had my back until doubt and the police began to creep into the mix. During my first week on campus I was looking for a space in the staff parking lot and found the 1st lot full, so I continued to the 2nd lot. Driving from lot 1 to lot 2 I noticed a campus police car following closely behind. He stayed on my tail from lot 2 to lot 3. At the entrance to lot 4, I walked back to the driver of the police car and asked, "Can I help you with something?" Saying not a word the policeman rolled up his window and sat there watching until I parked my car in lot 4 and walked into the main building. The next evening another of our three campus policemen watched me park and walked a few paces behind me from the parking lot to the stairway at the entrance to my classroom. Still standing on the stairway at the end of class he followed me to my car. Foolishly thinking that as my committee chairperson Ruth was my campus advocate, I reported the police harassment. After a couple of weeks of listening to my reports of daily harassment Ruth responded as if I was some naughty child; **(2) "Stop complaining and do your work!"** Doing the work wasn't the problem; "the work" was easy I carried a 4.0 during my time at the university. This was the 2nd hint that the woman wasn't on my side. The third and strongest hint came during my first faculty party. Walking past Ruth in the refreshment line I said, "Hello." The woman; saying not a word, jerked her head to the right; away from my direction and quickly left the serving line. **(3) Ruth pretended she didn't know me.** By no means a newcomer to racism and its irrationality, still was I surprised. UC Merced was a very small campus and Ruth not only saw me but worked with me every day, very strange; but it got worse. In another class, my Sociology Seminar; we were discussing a reading assignment about whites going on a lynching rampage through a black community in the south. I facetiously commented that maybe I should avoid white people.

Beth: Who didn't participate in the classroom discussion; I later discovered she hadn't even done the assigned reading; started to cry and said, "What a mean thing to say."

What the hell is wrong with that crazy white girl I thought as the class ended? Beth in her 2nd year of graduate school I soon learned was close friends with many of the faculty members at the school. She was also the research assistant for the 'rock star' on my committee, Dr. Chunner. A week or so after Beth's weirdness I was summoned to Dr. Chunner's office for a meeting. During our meeting Chunner said that **(4)** I might **"...be dropped from the school because of my racist comments in ...sociology seminar**. Sitting in his office listening I soon realized the man had no knowledge of the circumstance or what was said in my sociology seminar. Beth's strange "...hurt feelings." Seemed more important to him than the facts and/or anything I had to say. Here we go again, you'd think by now I would be used to the fight that comes from racist whites every step of the way when trying to accomplish any goal. They pop out of the woodwork so often that they are expected as an ingrained part of the process. Leaving Chunner's office and feeling that I had no support I remembered Professor Dalton, the professor who lived among Black folk in the East Bay, at least he was still in my corner. Meanwhile, beyond the additional heavy load of meetings and racist machinations; I continued to attend classes, research and write papers and teach my TA sections.

"It ain't over until it's over." After a couple of weeks with no strange meetings I was back into my routine until I received a notice **(5) telling me to report to a 2nd meeting to determine whether I should be dropped from the school for my comment in the discussion of an assigned reading in a university required Sociology Seminar.** The remaining two members of my PhD committee Ruth who had shown her true colors at the faculty luncheon and Dalton the Diplomatic Historian would be presiding over this 2nd meeting. As the meetings and the absurdity grew, I wondered where the teacher of the Sociology Seminar was; it was her class and she was the discussion leader who also heard my comment and the comments of all the student participants? Reckon facts weren't a part of the process when kicking me out of the university with no basis or reason, other than the color of my skin.

The NAACP (National Association for the Advancement of Colored People) Yes, I was surprised that people who really knew nothing about me; people who smiled in class and at committee meetings; were seriously going to kick me out of the school for no credible reason, other than my blackness. This was real and happening at the University of California in the 21st century. White people are strange and crazy. Having been a member of the NAACP since my teen age years in the segregated south I contacted the local branch. When asked by the local NAACP president to explain why members of my PhD committee were meeting to decide to kick me out of the university, I could not. I did tell him about the classroom discussion in my Sociology Seminar but he didn't see how that could possibly have a connection to a meeting for dismissal from the university. With no advance notice, the appearance of a Black man from the NAACP wearing a suit and tie, carrying a briefcase and taking notes, surprised those racists. Thanks to him not only was I not summarily kicked out of the university; but no mention was ever again made about my Sociology Seminar comments. Maybe still a bit naïve, but I was hurt to discover that my success and well being at the university was so unimportant to my committee members who obviously hated me. Not once or twice but at least five times that I was made aware of and recorded they pushed hard t o kick me out of school. Without the NAACP presence they would have successfully, thoughtlessly, kicked me out of the university on a whim. Why? Again while still hefting that extra burden of having to contact the NAACP and arrange meeting times with the committee members bent on kicking my ass out of the university; like every other student enrolled I still had to study, prepare writing assignments, participate in class discussions and prepare and teach my TA classes. One wonders how many run of the mill politically unaware Black Students without NAACP or ACLU connections are railroaded out of colleges and universities each year by uncaring racist white professors and administrators. Truly; "There but for the grace of God go I." Additionally, outside of class, on campus and in the neighborhoods, still a black male, consequently police stalking remained a constant. Some folk don't like the NAACP, fuck em, not the first time the NAACP saved my ass. Yes, there are still a majority among our 'white privileged' American brethren who vehemently argue that Black, Latino and Americans of color are not treated differently because of their color. Following the 2nd kick Williams out of the university meeting I again looked at my PhD Committee, the folk to help with my research and to facilitate my university experience.

How could I not notice that for a year my committee chairwoman had directed my African American History research specifically toward the history of Modern China? Having done a year of reading and research papers, turned in to Ruth; with no mention of the Black Panther Party I foolishly expected at some point to concentrate on African American History and the Black Panther Party. No such luck, at the end of the year Ruth after unabashedly taking advantage of my research for personal gain resigned from my committee. The following year, after her resignation from my committee, Ruth introduced a new course at the university, and guess what it was called; yep Modern China. Checking the reading list for her new class I saw that every book on that list I had read outlined and reported on for Ruth during my year of modern China research. Not only was she using the very same books but she still had my papers and book reports that she never returned. Regardless of my area of interest and my student needs the bitch had used me to do the preparatory research and reading for her class Modern China which she knew she would be introducing in the fall.

NAACP

This is the same hussy who just months before would have kicked me out of school if not for the assistance of the NAACP. The racist bitch fucked me and there was nothing I could do about it. **What balls, (chutzpah) without even taking the time to read the books herself she had used me to do the research and reading for her Modern China class. What to do, move on I couldn't even call her a racist bitch**☺

Thinking good riddance to Ruth, now I had to figure out how to work with my new committee chair, Dalton the Diplomatic Historian. Having to put aside the fact that he shared the meeting to kick me out of the university with Ruth; I had no choice but to work with the guy. Sitting in his office for numerous meetings; smiling and courteous; not once did he mention the plan to kick me out of school. One racist is as good, or bad as another. On the positive side at least his area of specialization was American Diplomatic History, and much closer to my research interests. Another positive I noted while sitting in on a couple of his classes, never failing to point out American self interest, he didn't try to sugar coat American History for his students. But then seeing the police pacing back and forth past his office during our conferences he knew of the harassment but said nothing. He didn't even get up to close his office door. Of course an American Historian living in Richmond, once a hot bed of the Black Panther Party he had some knowledge of my area of research. Annnnnnnd when convenient and not conflicting with any of his racial stereotypes Dalton tried to be fair and impartial, bless his biased heart. He often reminded me that he lived in Richmond, although he failed to mention that he lived in an all white gated community. Regardless Dalton seemed certain that living in Richmond alone made him a caring liberal. Dealing with those white folk on my committee was much like dealing with racists in any other part of the community; all were "Fuck you!" and exclusively out for themselves. I felt justified in my harsh conclusions when out of the blue I got a Ruth-like request from Professor Chunner.

Chunner the American Literature professor suggested that as a part of my dissertation I research an American literary figure totally unrelated to my Black Panther Party studies. So that was how the game was played, it was his turn and he wanted to use me as Ruth had done, that is to do his research for him to use in his class or for another book. Without saying no, I just gave him a look, and he mumbled something about it just being a thought. Working with the members of my committee supposedly on my side was most certainly hard ass work. At least I was finally concentrating on my area of study The Black Panther Party. After much reading and numerous research papers I gathered a hefty amount of information about this unique group. Having shared many of those BPP experiences in many of those particular places added a personal reality to my research and writing.

The Black Panther Party: The Black Panther Party was founded in 1966 with an avowed purpose to patrol and monitor the activities of the brutal police force in Oakland, California's Black community. Originally called The Black Panther Party for Self Defense; this group at great cost, changed attitudes toward police and police misconduct throughout the nation. The Black Panther Party was a product of the shift in the civil rights movement toward more active protest and revolutionary ideology. The year 1965 had seen the Watts Rebellion (Riot) and the beginning of this new phase of the civil rights movement. This new phase witnessed a time when the elders and the leaders of 'turn the other cheek' non violence were pushed aside by younger African American brothers and sisters living mostly in cities outside the South. They insisted on meeting violence with violence, regardless.

Huey P. Newton and Bobby Seale two students at Merritt College in Oakland, California choosing a Black Cat, a panther as their symbolic representation organized The Black Panther Party for Self Defense in1966. Disgusted with the constant talk and inaction of The Black Student Union and other campus organizations they felt the need to start their own. One certainly could understand the reluctance of other students to join Huey Newton and Bobby Seale who suggested that they should first arm themselves, and then follow and watch the police as they moved about the black community. Monitoring the armed police who absolutely don't want anyone to see their dirt; many thought Newton and Seale not only insane but suicidal as well. Following the police; was a dangerously crazy idea then and now. Much like their peasant hero Mao Zedong featured in "The Little Red Book; both Newton and Seale were the sons and grandsons of American peasants from the south. Their families were descendants of subsistence farmers and sharecroppers who moved North, East and West during the Great Migration. African Americans moved during the Great Migration to escape the poverty, lynching and racism in the South. Newton and Seale sold copies of Chairman Mao's "Little Red Book" on college campuses to earn money to buy guns for members of the party to carry while monitoring the police. At the time it was legal for citizens to carry guns in California without a permit so long as they were unloaded. Loaded or unloaded; seeing groups of gun toting young blacks in the neighborhoods on the evening news; convinced a panicked Governor Reagan and the legislature to immediately push through a bill changing that law. Seeking Black Panther Party members Newton and Seale felt the ideal Black Panthers were their fellow descendants of that American Peasant class, sons and daughters of the Great Migration now living in the cities; the jobless, the hungry hustling pimps and petty thieves whom they called "Brothers off the Block" or lumpen.

"Brothers off the Block": Who were those "Brothers off the Block"?

The Black Panther Party for Self Defense

They were brothers from the streets of Oakland, Los Angeles, San Bernardino, Chicago, New York, Detroit and other cities throughout the country who dared choose Malcolm X, Robert F. Williams, Mao Zedong, Chou En Lai, Frantz Fanon, Ho Chi Minh, Kwame Nkrumah, Che Guevara and Fidel Castro as their role models and heroes. They were the brothers I saw out of the corner of my eye on the streets of Los Angeles when going to and from my classes at Pepperdine. Wearing black turtlenecks, leather jackets and black berets I saw them watching policemen arresting black men. Here decades later I still wanted to know how those street brothers ended up with programs copied by governments including our own around the world. Free clinics, free food programs, free schools, and firearms training for interested community members were all a part of the Black Panther Party agenda. How did those street brothers develop a foreign policy agenda which led to negotiations and discussions with the governments of Morocco, Algeria, Cuba, North Korea, North Vietnam, China and other third world countries? With no formal diplomatic or foreign policy training, and no government financing; how did they do that? J. Edgar Hoover the head of the FBI personally vowed to eradicate the Black Panther Party. It seems with a trained military wing, a foreign policy, public safety, free health clinics, schools and food programs the Black Panther Party directly threatened the legitimate government of the United States. This was serious business! As police attacks intensified and the Black Panther Party body count grew many survivors fled to nearby Cuba. So here in the 21st century I decided to interview the surviving members of the Black Panther Party who by hijacking planes and other means found ways to Cuba. Those party members who fled to Cuba were an integral part of my research. My focus was on the several former members of the Black Panther Party now living in and around Havana with their Cuban families. Since the United States did not have diplomatic relations with Cuba and it was considered a hostile communist country how would I get there? Of course a secondary reason for my interest was Cuba being one of the two or three remaining Communist countries, I wanted to see and experience firsthand a communist government. So first on the agenda was getting there; and once on the island how would I find among the 70 or more fugitives living in Cuba, the former Panthers? And if and when I did find them; aware of their political situation in Cuba; what questions could I safely ask? African Americans, Civil Rights Activists and Panthers of note who spent time in Cuba included Eldridge Cleaver, Huey Newton, Assata Shakur, Robert F. Williams, Elaine Brown, Stokely Carmichael, William Lee Brent who died there in 2006, Anthony Bryant, William Potts and others. Being hunted by the police and racism in the United States was a driving force behind the Panthers rushing to Cuba; I also thought it would be interesting getting their take on racism in Cuba. Again for that discussion I had to get there first. American citizens were not allowed to travel to Cuba, but there were exceptions.

Panthers up against the wall, USA

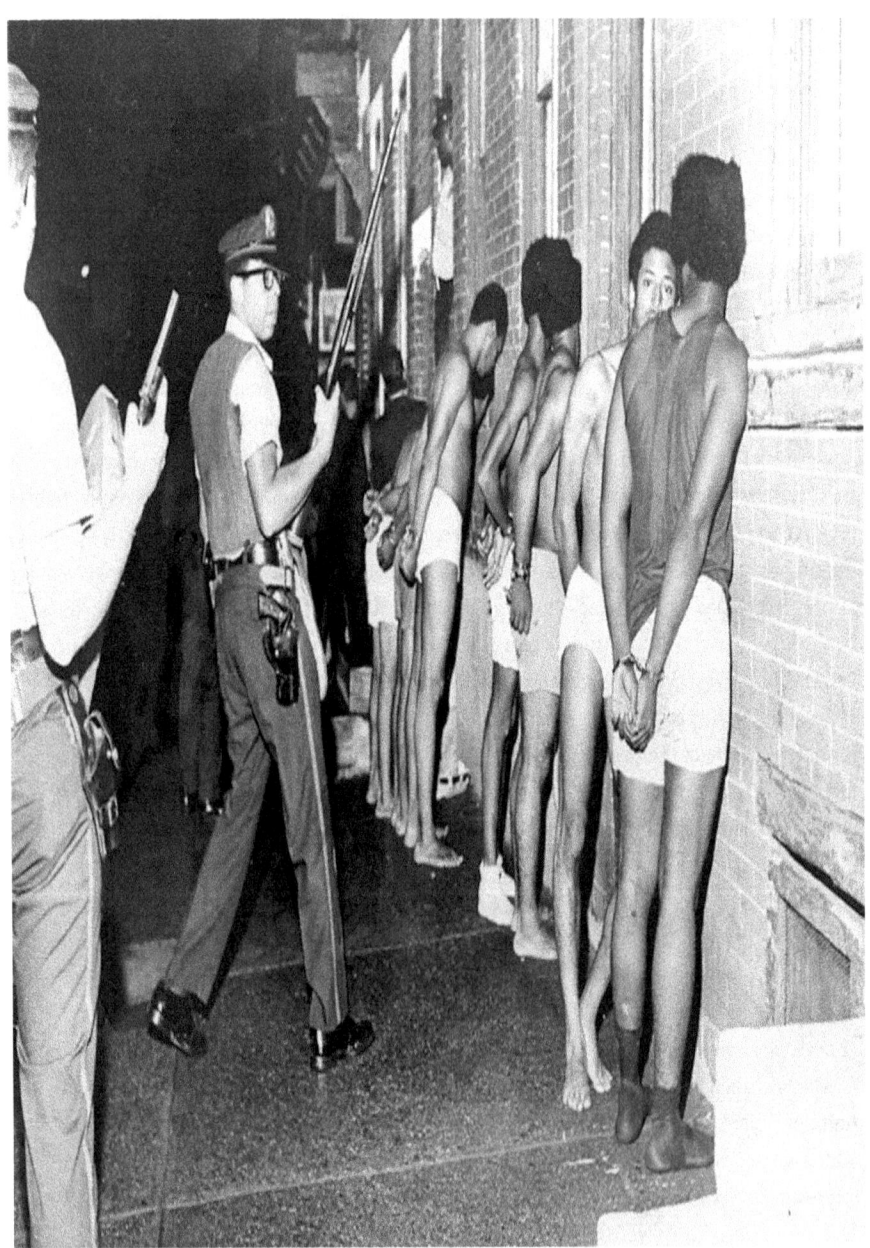

One exception allowed educational researchers with prior authorization to travel to Cuba. Researching former members of the Black Panther Party now living in Cuba seemed to fit the aforementioned rule. Relying heavily on Google with a little help from Professor Dalton I found the authorizing agents for educational travel to Cuba. A letter from the headquarters of the University of California in Oakland, which no one ever asked to see, verified my educational travel interest. I also stumbled upon a reporter for the Miami Herald, Tracey Eaton who had interviewed former Black Panthers in Cuba, including Assata Shakur. Thinking he might be able to give me a few contacts I tried to reach him. He acted as if I wanted to do harm to the former Black Panthers. It was clear that Tracey Eaton wasn't giving up any of his contacts in Havana. He was no help at all! Wandering into uncharted waters I found a couple of small educational grants for the trip. All new lessons, in no time at all I was making reservations for travel and hotel for a couple of weeks or more in Cuba. Again relying on Google, I found the names and room prices for several hotels in Havana. Deciding on the Hotel Colina, at $40 a day located just across the street from the University of Havana; it seemed an ideal location. Having read that American credit cards were not accepted in Cuba, I called first and was surprised when the clerk at the Hotel Colina willingly accepted my American Express credit card information over the phone and made reservations. Flight arrangements followed hotel reservations and with reluctant UC Merced approval from Program administrator Trainor I would be ready to roll. Somehow I must have offended the man who to this day I have never met. I say reluctant approval because along with his hard looks when walking past on campus for days he managed to be out of his office, have the day off, or visiting classrooms when I came by. Nearing departure time for Cuba, after more than a week trying to track the man down I finally sat in his office for an entire day until his secretary brought out the signed form.

Of course the constant stalking by police and school administration lackeys remained apart of my daily routine, with surprise breaks now and then. Most days approaching my car in the faculty parking lot; they would be clearly and noticeably parked nearby. Knowing my schedule they would pull out behind me and follow me home, daily. On the day I got the signed travel form from Trainor I saw the license plate on the following car. Talk about bold arrogance TRANR was the name on the personalized license plate of the car that followed me home. Pulling into my driveway and letting her pass I then followed her and took a picture of the license plate. Asking around campus the next day I discovered the woman following me was Trainor's wife. Talk about nerve! There were times when I had to pinch myself to verify the reality of my obsdervations; it really wasn't a bad dream most of the time. Doing what we do, smile,be strong and keep on stepping.

Vice Chancellor Trainor's Wife & Car

Exit Gate Cancun, Next Stop Havana

Cuba

Cuba: more than ready for Cuba, I flew out of San Francisco International to Cancun Mexico. Havana being just a short hop from Cancun, now there was no turning back, Communism here I come. Those fearful stories about communism read in textbooks and heard in discussions since elementary school came to mind as I studied the faces of my fellow passengers. All were waiting patiently and fearlessly in line at Cancun to board the flight to Havana's Jose Marti International Airport. Most folk were quietly sitting or standing around gate B11 except for one group of about 15 college age Americans. They reminded me of my students back at UC Merced because they were loud and boisterous. Having been made aware of the penalties for visiting Cuba without US government approval, fines and/or imprisonment; I asked whether they were visiting Cuba for educational reasons as was I. "Approval, you don't need any of that shit, just pay $50 dollars for a Mexican Visa and you're good to go!" I was told. Well! Son of a gun, new knowledge; but knowing if I tried to go to Cuba that way, with my luck I would be the only one fined and imprisoned for illegal travel. So along with my loud young fellow Americans we left the palm tree lined streets, the multicolored silver and glass buildings, cultivated greenery and Mercedes Benz taxicabs of Cancun to board the flight to Havana. Just like that, in less than an hour I would be in a country of people and a government which all of my life I had been taught to hate. There is mainland China where nowadays the almighty dollar seems to blur the lines between communism and capitalism. Also North Korea is a place where it is said that outsiders, especially Americans are not welcome. Cuba, one of the last communist governments; just 90 miles off the coast I had to see before it to passed into the all encompassing world of capitalism. Arriving at Jose Marti International Airport, Havana, Cuba in the early afternoon; who would have thought that such a short airplane ride could provide so many lessons. As expected the visuals were most striking; A U.S. Air Force veteran stepping from the plane first I noticed the no frills militaristic runways at Jose Marti.

Secondly, the often seen multicolored trucks and smaller vehicles, towing planes, and hauling baggage were nonexistent. Those long gray flight lanes with the single blue tower were matched inside with dividing panels, desks and walls of the same blue gray colors found on the outside buildings and runways. The all female customs contingent wore uniforms of the same dull blue gray colors with matching gender neutral Soviet style military caps. In the United States those women working customs would have been called African American or Black; but I was to learn that in Cuba technically and debatably, all regardless of color were Cubanos. Hmph. Anyway, beyond the Soviet style drabness of dress and surroundings, those ladies were beautiful.

The government surely had a hand in their selection because they were fine enough to make one ignore the shortcomings of Communism or whatever the political regime. Through customs I had to find a cab to the Hotel Colina. Looking for the refurbished cars from the 1950's that I'd read about and seen pictures of I was surprised to see shiny new American cars waiting at the curb. Of the five or six waiting for customers I chose the only Black driver among the bunch. He was dressed pretty much as was I, which I discovered was a rarity in Cuba. On the drive into town he told me about life in his country, which he wanted to leave. He first mentioned that his American clothes and shoes due to the embargo cost more than twice as much as they would in the United States. His dream, the same as every Cuban I talked to during my time in country, was to earn enough money and influence to move to the United States. For government permission to leave the country I was told that one must have a relative in the United States and pay a substantial fee. For the last seven years he had been saving money and writing letters trying to track down distant cousins in the United States to fulfill the relative obligation. "Where in the United States would you choose to live?" I asked. Surprisingly, "New York" was his response. I had expected him to say Miami; where the largest Cuban population in the USA lives? True, but I learned my first Cuban lesson from the cab driver, reinforced by others.

Repeatedly I was told by white and black Cubans that color was meaningless in Cuba, "...all are Cubanos..."Yet during my interactions with various Cubans I noticed things. As previously stated many Cubans wanted to leave for America; but overwhelmingly only white Cubans chose Miami as their destination while Black Cubans chose New York. Questioning my driver on the long ride to the hotel, mostly from things left unsaid I got an early glimpse of life in Cuba. He would not discuss the government, other than restrictions on his plans to leave the country, even when I asked direct questions. But he did say that Black Cubans traveling to the United States wished to avoid those racist Cubans living in Miami. Well! Paying the $40 cab fare, more than four times the average monthly income for Cubans, I wished the driver success in his attempt to come to America.

Getting out of the cab in front of the Hotel Colina, I couldn't help but notice the church like edifice across the street with more than a hundred moss covered steps leading up to its entrance. It was indeed The University of Havana founded in1728. Later I was to learn that teaching salaries at the university, much like the salaries of non professional jobs, are minimal. This I learned from two professors off for the summer out hustling coins from tourists by showing them around Havana. First I didn't believe they were professors, but they took me to their classrooms and showed valid identification to get into the buildingFor 75 cents each I had two very educated guides.

Jose Marti International Airport, Havana, Cuba

Turns out I had overpaid them and bottom line they couldn't find the places, such as the local bank, where I wanted them to take me. After wandering about for more than an hour I paid them and told them I'd manage on my own. Happily well paid they wandered off to find another sucker. Viva la revolucion!

Arriving a day before my reservation at the Hotel Colina I checked to see if I could possibly get a room. The Black desk clerks both wearing white blouses, black skirts and speaking excellent English explained that I would have to wait until the day of my reservation to get a room a the hotel. So on my first day in my very first Communist country, I was homeless. A little worried, but not yet panicked I needed to find a room for the night. Leaving the Hotel Colina I saw another hotel within the next block. I also noticed room for rent signs hanging on fences as I walked past private residences in the neighborhood. All was not lost; I only needed a place to stay for one night so it was the other hotel or knocking on the doors of the houses with signs on their fences. Walking past the University of Havana still operating it certainly looked its age. My Spanish was good enough to read the fence signs, but the thought of staying with strangers overnight in a private home in a strange country was disconcerting. Looking back I had stayed in a private home in Amsterdam years before; but in a Communist country, hmmmmmmmmmm? So I was off to the next hotel. Entering the hotel and walking to the front desk, I noticed a group of white Cubans talking in the lobby. Turning my way when I spoke to the desk clerk they immediately recognized my American clothes and poor Spanish. By then the desk clerk also had that universal look, mentally counting the dollars she would take from the rich American, me. A room at the Hotel Colina cost $40 a day whereas with a beautiful smile the clerk told me that a room for a day would cost me $85. That was absolutely out of the question, as I again walked past the group in the lobby talking excitedly in Spanish one asked in English, "Are you looking for a room?"He told me that he would call his cousin who might have a room. Standing in the lobby as afternoon turned to early evening I listened while he made several frantic calls and still couldn't find a cousin, friend or anyone else with a room. Not wanting to offend, I eased away from that group of Cuban hustlers in the hotel lobby and hit the streets. Concerned and forgetting my inhibitions I stopped at the very next house posting a room for rent sign. The owner took the time to show me a very nice room on the first floor renting for $30 a night. Very relaxed, Indeed a rarity in the country at that time and an unending source of curiosity fo all; I reckon she just wanted to talk to an American.Sfter chatted with me for more than an hour before telling me that the room was already reserved for the night. Her regular tenant from Mexico was coming to the island for the weekend. Ooooooooooooook, I was back on the street and moving on to the next house with a for rent sign out front.

The University of Havana

Having read of free government supplied housing in Cuba and other Communist countries, over the years I had seen pictures of the decaying apartment buildings with multicolored laundry hanging from the upper balconies. Just as had been pictured, walking down the streets there in Havana I saw the real thing. Row upon row of multi storied decaying apartment buildings on one side of the street with hanging laundry while on the other side of the street sat well kept Victorian era private homes. Just saying.

On an interesting other note, by the time I left the 2nd hotel I had a small following of Cuban teenagers and preteens. A weekday, guess it was the teacher part of me kicking in, I wondered; "Why aren't these kids in school?" As they moved along the sidewalk with me, I answered their questions as best I could; using my limited Spanish vocabulary. Are you an American? Where in America are you from, Florida? They really perked up when I told them I was from California. Do you live in Hollywood? Where did you get those sandals? I like your shirt were typical questions and comments. Fresh out of the USA, even with everyday things the contrasts were fascinating. Wallking along I couldn't help but notice what the kids ignored; reckon they were used to them; but the he sidewalks were very different. They were mostly uneven broken concrete and at each corner there were no pedestrian Wait or Walk signs. Just stepping down from the sidewalk to the street was an unasked for adventure. There was at least a 1 foot drop stepping down from the sidewalk onto the street. Handicapped; to bad you were on your own; there was no such thing as handicap access. Speaking of which crossing the street took quite a bit of chutzpah as well, God be with you otherwise you were very quick. Pedestrians walked rolled or ran across the streets weaving through moving cars. There were no traffic lights and stop signs were rare, especially on the major streets; so cars traveling at full speed didn't stop. Thinking back I don't remember actually seeing one stop sign during my time on the streets of Havana. Wheelchairs avoided the high sidewalks and rolled on the streets with cars; crossing at their own risk with other folk. They were made of thick heavy wood, squeaky, slow, hard to maneuver and much like the cars on the streets of Havana very old. Just the short time I was in the country I witnessed two or three near misses a day sitting outside at the hotel Colina Café. At any rate, following and surviving the visual show on the sidewalks and the streets it was nearing sundown when I stopped at Ramon's. An ideal location, no worries about getting lost, his home was just a few blocks from the Hotel Colina. Ramon's house looked to have originally been one storied until he added a room on the roof. His rudimentary building skills showed in the electrical work, the plumbing and in all areas. The poorly constructed room had a rickety stair and a bathroom with one barred window. In case of fire there was no emergency exit, but maybe I could survive one night. Welcome to Cuba.

Apartamementos Habana

All was good, $35 dollars for the night and the following day I would check into the Hotel Colina. Agreeing on the price Ramon stood in the room waiting for me to pay in advance. Advance payment was fine with me but I wasn't going to take money from my backpack while he was standing there watching. Following several uncomfortable words in Spanish and English Ramon finally got the hint and went down the rickety stairs to the lower part of the house. Then I took the $35 from my backpack and carried it downstairs, he smiled. I didn't get much sleep but I was inside and the night was interesting.

A very special event, I didn't know what to say; the whole neighborhood seemed to know an American was at Ramon's house. So late into the night young folk gathered on the sidewalk below; talking among themselves and staring up at my window. A few times I waved, but couldn't speak to them because the window was nailed shut and barred. Across the street in one of the neighboring apartments someone was blasting 1950's do-wop songs. Music matching the years of the 1950's cars prevalent on the streets of Havana, I suppose it shouldn't have been surprising. The time frame of the music and the cars matched the beginning of the Castro regime and the US ban on trade with Cuba; still those tunes from my childhood were a bit disconcerting. Deep into the 21st century they were playing Chuck Berry, Fats Domino, The Rondells, Carla Thomas, Sam Cooke, and others from that 1950's early 1960's era. With pauses between each song, allowing time to change, I assumed they were playing 45's. There aren't many folk left who remember those stacks of 45's and/or the machines on which they were played. Surviving the night with a few hours sleep I looked forward to my first full day in Cuba. Breakfast came with the room, so a sandwich with coffee fulfilled that obligation. All sitting at the downstairs dining room table I met Ramon's wife, cute young lady. Again even the Black Cubans claimed that it didn't matter to other Cubans, but in the coming days as I suspected, I was to discover that it does matter, especially to white Cubans. Ramon's wife was black, I noticed. Following thanks and courteous goodbyes I was on the streets again and headed for the Hotel Colina. Generally, the few cars on the streets of Havana are cabs, mostly for tourists. There are subsidized buses but folks did a lot of walking. Then too there were those who seemed to be aimlessly wandering the streets. Is there such a thing as homelessness in a Communist society? Yep.

Assuming it was the American clothes; and I wasn't wearing anything unusual mind you, just khaki shorts a t-shirt and sandals, they were a beacon. There was a rush to see who could get to me first as I closed the front gate leaving Ramon's house. A muscular black guy standing about 6 feet wearing an old sport coat and slacks pushed two women and a shorter fellow aside as he approached.

"Don't these people have jobs?"I thought. Later I realized that was their job hustling tourists; that's what they did each day to make a living. Uninvited the guy started walking alongside me as I headed for the hotel Colina while showing me a large book he was carrying. "Sir this is a great Cuban History Book and it is in English." He said, leaning toward me with a hustlers smile recognizable in any language or culture. I was trying to figure out how to tell the guy to "Fuck off!" without creating an international incident. Opening the book he began showing the historical pictures from the early days of Cuban History to the present. "Senor, normally this book sells for $20, but since this is my last one I will sell it to you for ½ price; $10. Stepping into the hotel lobby, under the hard scrutiny of the desk clerks and a white Cuban; I noticed a subtle change in the booksellers' attitude. As I moved to the front desk to register; nervously looking about and finally taking a seat in one of the comfortable leather chairs he said; "I'll wait here for you." Certainly NOT what I wanted; my plan was to register and then make a mad dash for my room. "Is he with you?" The clerk asked. "No he followed me here trying to sell me a book." Nuff said, by the time I finished registering hard looks from the white Cuban in the lobby had persuaded the bookseller to move off the premises. Locals, with various scams hang around hotels, night clubs, banks, beaches and places where tourists gather. Generally, they are not allowed inside or on hotel property unless invited by a guest. Finally at the right place and time, and rid of the book hustler I now faced a more serious crisis. Contrary to what I had been told by a clerk at the Hotel Colina when I called from back in the USA; who said I could use my cards and checks; while registering I discovered that my American Express, debit card and checks were useless, unacceptable in Cuba. Exactly what I first read but when told they were good; I foolishly ignored the prohibition and counted on using my cards and checks. Thinking I could use my American Express and debit card, I didn't bring enough cash for the planned months stay in Cuba. Immediately I had to make some schedule readjustments. Paying cash for everything, if careful maybe I'd have enough money to last 15 or 20 days with limited food and entertainment. Initially paying for two weeks, the clerk assigned me a room on the 4th floor and directed me to the elevator. I felt comfortable with the two Black female clerks handling the front desk and managing the hotel. But the white Cuban wearing a black suit, white shirt and black tie; observing the clerks and all activity in the lobby activated my alarms. He gave me 'the look', the very same one he had given the guy trying to sell me a book, as I wallked past him to the elevator with my backpack. Even in Cuba a cop was easily recognizable. Reckon I'd see how the cop thing is done in Cuba; cultural observation too was another reason why I was there. While waiting for the elevator, I noticed water puddles on the floor by the doors. It was food for thought, an electric elevator, with standing water by the doors hmmmmmmmmm

Hotel Colina

Tossing my backpack on the bed by the window in my 4th floor room I saw painters scaffolding just outside. So they were painting the building, I was cool with that until I saw that there were no locks on the windows. Supposedly Communism, according to the years of propaganda, was a crime free society; but it made me a little nervous knowing that anyone could use the painters scaffolding to climb into my room through the unlocked window. Again I was fighting to control those suddenly alert South Central Los Angeles alarms when I discovered that the door lock also didn't work. New in the country and not wanting to make waves I reluctantly called the front desk and mentioned the windows and door. The desk clerk said mine was the only vacant room they had, so be it; I settled in for a cautious nights sleep. Up with the sunrise coming through my unlocked window, I showered and headed downstairs for breakfast in the 2nd floor cafeteria. There in Cuba to examine all aspects of the society in which fugitive members of the Black Panther Party and other African Americans lived; the cafeteria workers were also interesting. On that first morning I saw white Cubans working the line dishing out food and collecting payment from customers. On the 2nd or 3rd morning the waitress barely spoke English so I ordered in Spanish. Upon hearing my American accented Spanish a couple of black faces peered at me from behind the curtain in the kitchen. The following mornings they smiled and waved but never left the kitchen area. Black faces back in the kitchen and white faces serving out front. Todos es Cubanos; but that's not what I was seeing.

So where do I start? First I asked the desk clerks for directions to a café mentioned in an article about Black Panthers in Cuba by Tracey Eaton. In the article he told of meeting those former members of the Black Panther Party at the café. I couldn't really get them to respond because the lobby cops ears perked up every time I started a conversation with the clerks as he moved closer to the desk. Ignoring him, the tropical blue skies with few clouds soon lured me out the door. Glancing over my shoulder as I turned the corner and headed downhill from the hotel I could see the lobby cop leaning out the front door watching. About a block around the corner past the hotel I was in the neighborhoods which are another world. No tourists and cars were a rarity; and most importantly, to the folk walking the streets I was just another Black Cuban. Being able to blend in was a good thing and I liked it. While out I also wanted to find a market to buy groceries so I wouldn't have to pay for dining out each day. Stopping an older fellow with a grocery bag in hand I asked, "Donde Es Mercado?" Answering in English he said he would take me to the market which was a couple of blocks away. So what was wrong with the market he just left with a bag of groceries? During the walk he wanted to talk in English and told me that he was a retiree from the Cuban Army. Of course I wanted to ask if he fought with Castro, and if he was at the Bay of Pigs. He seemed to be about the right age.

New in the country and thinking that might be a touchy subject I asked a simpler question instead. "IHow much is your monthly retirement check?" "El mes, siete dolares." He said. Knowing my Spanish was poor, I thoughtmisunderstood so I asked in English, "Seven dollars a month?" "Si" Thanking him for directions to the market; I went inside wondering who the hell can live on seven dollars a month even with subsidized housing and transportation, it sounded so absurd. New knowledge gained, that's why I was in Cuba. The only customer I looked around the store and saw dry goods, no fresh fruit or vegetables. Stocking up on cookies, dried fruit, oatmeal and crackers I returned to the hotel. On the streets of Havana, seeing no fat or obese folk; most with that noticeable aboriginal, African and Spanish mix; I thought what a beautiful and physically fit people But later after watching the cafeteria workers bagging leftover food scraps to take home to their families; and assorted beggars and hustlers on the streets I quickly changed that false perception. By the time I left Cuba I realized that I had mistaken starvation for physical fitness, those people were so thin because they had no money and no food. The government leaders put up a good front and talk a good game; but one can't help seeing that sadly, the common folk are living just barely on the edge of survival. Daily, living under those borderline conditions the citizens refused to criticize the government and were accepting of things as they are. Accepting while there in Cuba but the solution for most is to by any means move to the United States. All knowing that just by setting foot on American soil automatically grants USA asylum is added incentive to leave. Of course asylum in the United States, for Cuban refugees only, automatically includes employment, housing and living assistance. Oddly enough there are millions of American citizens living in the inner cities who could certainly use those perks granted to non citizen Cuban refugees. Again, just saying. By early afternoon I returned to my room and dumped the groceries and headed downstairs to the outdoor café for lunch. Bordering the sidewalk the café was located at a major intersection; Calle L numero 23 e/27 y Jovellar Plaza de la Revolucion, and across the street from the bus stop. Surrounded by a four foot high decorative fence, it was the perfect spot to sit and watch everyday Cubans going to and fro. Sitting with my back to the wall facing the street I couldn't help but notice the only other Black in the café sitting to my left. Curious I assumed he was maybe another American tourist because generally locals especially Blacks weren't welcome at the hotels. I saw Blacks walk with their white 'friends' to the entrance and wait for them until they finished their meals. So I was pleasantly surprised to see someone sitting across from me at the hotel restaurant with a color matching my own. Pompous and wanting to be seen, the fellow made a great show of shaking and placing his napkin, sipping his wine; lighting his cigar and spreading his feet into the aisle after lunch. Then I saw a look rarely seen on the faces of Black men looking at other Blacks.

Calle L numero 23 e/27 y Jovellar Plaza de la Revolucion Havana, Cuba

." **Hotel Colina Outdoor Café**

Those looks I saw growing up in Arkansas on the faces of racist whites, the brotha was giving me the classic 'hate stare'. I asked the white waitress, "Who is that Black guy?" I nearly fell off my chair when she said to me, "He's not Black, he is whiteThe man had kinky hair lips and color from the homeland, Africa; yet he and the waitress, claimed he was of European ancestry, white. Well he may have considered himself white but during the time I was in the country everyone talked that we are all Cubanos nonsense, but again that wasn't what I was seeing on the streets. Race too had been an issue for those first members of the Black Panther Party who fled to Cuba and I suspect that it remains an issue for those former Panthers and other African Americans now living in the country. However those still living in the country will not discuss the issue. Assata Shakur in her book Assata danced around it and avoided and mentions of racial issues she may have faced while living in Cuba. In my research I found that Robert F. Williams was silent as well during his stay in Cuba from 1961 until 1966. But the minute he got out of the country with his family he said that the so called "racial democracy" in Cuba meant power in the hands of the white middle class. Both Stokely Carmichael and Eldridge Cleaver also found racism prevalent in Cuba.

Just an old LA Street Dog in Cuba: On the scene I was there for a first hand look and got it. The Malecon, a pier fronting the ocean in Havana is a major gathering spot for tourists and locals alike, especially on weekends. Women dressed in their finest stroll up and down the Malecon as young men sit watching the parade of Cuban beauties on Saturday and Sunday afternoons. One Thursday afternoon I decided to go down and get a firsthand look and pictures at the Malecon. Peering from the tinted windows on their air conditioned buses I am sure the European and Canadian tourists thought I was just another Cuban wandering the neighborhoods heading for the Malecon. In those neighborhoods, much like New York, Baltimore, Chicago, Detroit, Los Angeles and other American ghettos I saw groups of unemployed Black Cubans sitting on the steps of apartment buildings. Their faces showed those very same looks of hopeless despair I had seen in South Central Los Angeles and Compton. I quickly hurried past. Well the distance from the hotel to the Malecon turned out to be about three miles and I was exhausted at the end of the walk. The Malecon was deserted except for a lone fisherman about a mile down the shore. So I decided to stretch out on top of the 6 foot high barrier and rest for a minute. I must have dozed off, feeling someone very close; I thought it was a bad dream. Turning to my left I saw a hard eyed 20 something fellow standing below the wall within inches of my face. "What the fuck!" Quickly standing to my full height, eyes on the lurking creep, he slowly backed away before I climbed down from the wall. Walking along the sidewalk across the street from the Malecon after nearly being jumped; I saw other tourists and several bicycle cabs.

Black Folk in Havana, Cuba

The Malecon

One offered to take me to see Ernest Hemingway's house for a mere $30. Laughing, I told the fellow that I wasn't a Hemingway fan and besides; "Here in Havana I can buy a bicycle for much les than $30." Spotting an open coffee shop along the sidewalk I thought it might be a good place to buy a soda. The middle aged waitress was talking to her only customer, who seemed to be a friend sitting at the bar. Both women perked up when I asked in English; "How much are your sodas?" "Five cents," She said. When she handed me the soda I saw beer in the same cooler so I asked the cost of the beers. They too cost five cents. Smiling at the price, several beer guzzling friends back in California came to mind. Finished with my soda and preparing to leave the waitress asked, "Aren't you going to buy us a beer?" Both were highly offended when I said, "No." Reckon I could have easily bought them a five cent beers but I was getting a little irritated at every Cuban I met unquestionably with absolute certainty assuming because I was American that I was rich. It was further assumed that I was obligated to share my American riches. Cuban anger when I refused to share those imaginary American riches only added to my irritation,

Continuing down the Malecon away from the angry women and starting back to the hotel, I realized I was lost. Asking directions at another café along the roadside, upon hearing my English, two policemen having lunch called me over. Instant LA police mode, I thought here we go, in Cuba no less; to suffer some harassment and maybe a little police violence. And to top if off there I was in a foreign country where there was no American Embassy. Accepting the offered seat, I joined them at the outdoor table and answered their curious questions. Turns out they were just two nice (Did I just call a cop, no two cops nice?) working stiffs driving and older beat up Toyota police car; wearing threadbare uniforms and scuffed boots. Frustrated and exhausted, I told them that I was lost and asked for directions to my hotel. I was completely surprised and relieved, when Antonio and Juan agreed to give me a ride to the Hotel Colina. I do wish I had gotten a picture of the looks on the faces of the hotel workers when they saw me getting out of the back of a police car. Probably just a coincidence, but the day after the encounter with my new police friends I was moved to a much better room with a lock on the door that worked, newer furniture, a TV set and locking windows. Watching a little Cuban TV, it was interesting to note that there were very few programs in Spanish. Not only were most of the programs in English but they were from China. The evening news was presented with a Chinese newscaster speaking perfect English accented English. I was trying to decide whether the news was from Beijing, Hong Kong or Taiwan. Politically, I thought Beijing, but then there were tourists and container ships from both Mainland China and Taiwan in Havana

Finca Vigia: Hemingway's House, where he wrote *The Old Man And The Sea* and *For Whom the Bell Tolls*

Comfortably back at my base, the Hotel Colina I found myself again people watching from the outdoor café. Located at a plaza and major intersection with a bus stop just across the street the cafe was a perfect spot. There were a couple of instances where I discovered by uninvited responses; that the people were watching me as well. On one occasion I was looking at this fine, fine white Cuban standing just outside the surrounding café barrier. I noticed her because she was staring at me. Later I decided she was staring because she thought I was a Black Cuban sitting inside the café boundaries. But I assumed she was staring because she found me interesting and wanted to hook up; maybe she wanted to be with me for a while. The bubble burst when I saw her excitedly talking to the guy standing beside her and pointing at me. "Oh shit!" Must be a husband or boyfriend, the thought crossed my mind as he looked in my direction and started climbing over the barrier. What to do, a fight with a Cuban was a guaranteed a lose lose situation. So I kept looking in the general direction of the Cubana; but raised my gaze a tiny bit to stare at the apartment buildings across the street behind her. Halfway to my table the disgruntled husband/boyfriend must have decided that I wasn't looking at his wife/girlfriend; because he turned and climbed back over the barrier to rejoin her, Bitch! She was trying to set me up. Looking at me over his shoulder as he returned to his spot; I gave her a wink and a smile, which really pissed her off. Meaning no harm I was a people watcher, even back in the good old USA; but in a foreign country what better way to become familiar with the culture.

Unfortunately that wasn't to be my only uncomfortable encounter from my people watching position from the table by the wall at the Hotel Colina's outdoor café. I assumed that most folk walking past or waiting at the nearby bus stop rarely noticed the tourists sitting outside at the café; but some like the woman with the jealous boyfriend did notice. The tall black Cuban; she must have been at least 6'4, well built with a nice body and OK face walked past about 3:00 PM every afternoon and gave me a smile. Walking, erect, with determination and pride she was a pleasant sight. Didn't think much of the interaction from a distance until the fourth day when things got a little scary. Ignoring the no local blacks allowed on the premises policy she boldly walked onto the patio and stopped beside my table. Just she and I were the only two in the restaurant. I don't think she knew a word of English, but her face, her eyes; waited for me to say something. Silence was my response to her bold action. Now you must hear my excuses☺; well, she was a good looking woman but her forwardness caught me off guard; besides every other day during her walks past she carried a baby on her right hip. Frozen in my chair and watching her eyes, she must have waited for an eternity before deciding I wasn't going to say anything; then turned and walked away.

So back to reality; after my shopping spree at the market I still needed fruits and vegetables. I later discovered that the dry goods market was empty because it is exclusively for foreigners. Only the CUC the currency for foreigners equal to about a dollar; and dollars are accepted at that market. The Cuban Convertible Peso is the currency foreigners are required to use. But if you can pass yourself off as a Cuban you may want to use the Cuban Peso instead of the CUC or the dollar. One dollar equal 26 Cuban Pesos. Anyway the ladies at the front desk directed me to a fruit stand down a side street just past the University of Havana.

The open air fruit stand was one large room about 12X12 with roll up tarps and several tables overflowing with a variety of fruits inside. Staring at my clothing, the three dread locked blacks working the stand knew I was an American before I said a word. "Hable Ingles?" was my first question. Neither of the three spoke English but they pointed to their friend standing just outside and said that he spoke English. He did not. The fellow couldn't tell me the prices or the names of the various fruits. They called over a white Cuban walking past and she translated my questions and their answers. I could have done it own my own but I was getting lost with the money conversion from the dollar to the Cuban Convertible Peso to the Cuban Peso. After stocking up on apples, grapefruits and several mangoes the size of cantaloupes I was ready to head back to the hotel. Giving me free samples of their wares and plying me with questions, my new friends insisted that I stay and talk to them. My poor Spanish was not a deterrent as I stumbled through the usual answers about the United States and California. One question of my own caused an interesting reaction. "Why don't I see more Black men, other than the cab driver from the airport to my hotel, you're the first that I have seen working in the city." Looking at me as if I had insulted him the young Cuban responded, "No es negro, es blanco!"Staring at his face and long rasta dreadlocks, "Oh" was all I could say. Not wanting to offend, but after an hour hanging out with those "White" guys I was ready to leave. One fellow asked me to give him my shirt and another asked for my sandals. And what would I wear I asked. They didn't seem to care about my needs. Finally to get away from that fruit stand I had to promise the most insistent brotha that I would mail him similar shoes when I got home. He scribbled his address on a slip of paper gave it to me and only then was I allowed to leave. Whew! Yes, I could have used a picture of the dred locked brothas from the fruit stand, but I think I made the wisest choice with the picture on the following page☺ New in the country I found myself doing as I was told by the hotel clerks and headed for the bank to convert my dollars into Cuban Convertible Pesos (CUC). Cuban women much like the one pictured on the following page are pause and take a good look beautiful. Standing just outside the entrance to the bank stood one such Cuban woman

Havana Fruit Stand

Shoulder length black hair with a slight curl, upturned nose, black eyes, full rounded breasts, short shorts with long light brown shapely legs; she smiled at me and said "Buenos Dias, senor." Seeing no ring on the left hand I thought I might try to hook up with that fine thing. Then I had a second thought, "Why is she standing outside of a bank that obviously caters to foreigners?" Slowly, reluctantly, I came to the conclusion that Ms. Fine was probably a 'working girl'; why else would she be standing outside the bank. Regretfully, I eased on past. Later back in the states I was telling a Panamanian friend about my 'working girl' encounter and she got angry and said that I shouldn't look down my nose at the woman because that was the only way she had to make a living. Food for thought; well as I said I walked past her and entered the bank. Like banks in the states tellers sat inside separate cages facing customers. My turn came and I moved up to the window and told the teller that I wanted to convert $50 US Dollars into convertible pesos (CUC's). Counting out my pesos I noticed the teller taking a $5 bill from my pesos and putting it off to the side. Pocketing my money I asked, "What about my other $5?" She simply pointed toward the armed guard standing by the exit. I got the message and quietly left the bank. So is life in Cuba I thought as I headed back to the hotel

Regrouping, I thought it time to do what I came to Cuba to do, find and interview former members of The Black Panther Party now living in Havana. The desk clerks were valuable sources of information, but the policeman assigned to the hotel came to stand beside me whenever I started a conversation with the clerks. One day he even jammed me in the lobby by walking up close staring me in the face and asking in perfect English, I never knew he spoke the language, "Are you Eddie?" Looking down at the short fellow I answered no; stepped around him and exited the building. Using the hotel phone book I found the last names of several individuals matching the names of former members of the Black Panther Party. The names stood out in the phone book with very few English last names. Getting no answers from my phone calls I decided to visit the addresses of two of the names called. At the first address an apartment building in a modest neighborhood no one answered the door and I got very hard looks from the neighbors sitting outside on the stoop. The 2nd apartment building was near the café where the Miami Herald reporter Tracey Eaton met several former Black Panther Party members. Entering the small café, it didn't feel right. Even before I ordered breakfast every eye in the place seemed focused on me. I asked the waitress whether she knew the family of the former Black Panther Party member living in the neighborhood. She did not. Before I finished breakfast two uniformed policemen stopped by the restaurant and they didn't have friendly smiles like the last two I met. When I left the restaurant to visit the apartment next door they followed me outside.

Standing in front of the café the policemen watched as I walked toward the apartment building. Having gotten used to the lack of 24/7 police stalking that I received back home in the USA, this Cuban reminder was enough to encourage me to keep on walking past the apartment. Reckon I understood, those people didn't know me from Adam; I could have been CIA or any other USA nutso out to do harm to the people the Cuban government was sworn to protect; especially from the USA. Oh well, heading back to the hotel nearing the end of my third week in Cuba I wondered whether I had enough information to paint a clear picture of where and how the former Black Panther Party members lived in Cuba. Even without a face to face I could research current personal information to fill any blank spaces. Stopping by the room for a minute I decided it might be a good time to visit a local market I had passed in the neighborhood. Looking more like a traditional grocery store or super market, not only did I find all the things needed, but saved a fortune by paying in Cuban Pesos; one dollar being worth 26 Cuban Pesos. For 75 cents I nearly bought out the store☺ During my walk to the market I saw the two Cuban policemen who I had just seen in the lobby of the hotel. Since my Panther questions I was getting more scrutiny. Maybe it was time for me to start thinking about heading home. Home, but not before being embarrassed by a young drunk white American female cussing out a hotel employee in the lobby. Barely able to stand she looked like a slutty drunk. I hoped the bystanders assumed as she did that I was a Black Cuban. When she saw my look of disapproval she gave me one of those fuck all you Cubans looks. The idiot was complaining about slow service in the café; she even used the phrase "you people".

Yes, time to go home. Visiting the airline travel center I discovered I could use my American Express card for a flight on Mexicana Airlines to Cancun. On my way back to The Hotel Colina a white Cuban woman was approaching on the sidewalk and just like in Arkansas back in the time of rabid racism; she stepped off the sidewalk to keep distance between us. No racism in Cuba, they're al Cubanos; well I certainly learned that is a bunch of bull. I had my ticket but still was concerned and nervous about getting out of that country. Not a good time but I was remembering several African Americans who disappeared in Cuba and were never heard from again. Backpack ready, I left a tip under the pillow for the woman cleaning the room daily and also tips for the two ladies working the front desk at the hotel. Entering and leaving are very tense times for Americans traveling to Cuba. Upon entry the customs workers try very hard to cover it with a restrained military type courtesy, but the hostile envy is there. At departure one sees the same hostile envy but individual customs workers take advantage of the final opportunities to rip off Americans. It was the same as in the Cuban bank where I was exchanging my dollars for Cuban currency and the teller took $5 of my money.

When I started to complain; without a word she just pointed to the man with the gun, the bank guard standing off to the side watching. Going through customs for departure from Cuba was much the same. There was one line for passport, visa and ticket check before being waved onto the ramp for the departing plane. I finished my customs check and headed for the plane but was stopped at the entrance to the ramp. Not wearing a customs uniform or any identifying clothing the woman blocking my path to the aircraft pointed me to a 2nd line for departing American passengers only. Finally reaching the checkout window for the 2nd line I again showed my passport, visa and ticket to Cancun. The clerk told me I would have to pay a $40 exit fee to leave the country. Damm a final rip off! A Cuban with a gun and a uniform stood right next to her booth, I am certain he was getting a cut of this extra charge. Having only dollars, I was pointed to another window to exchange my dollars for CUC's. This I did and was at the end of the extortion line worrying about missing my plane and being stuck in this country of rip offs and thieves. I paid and literally ran down the exit corridor to the plane.

Cancun being a major vacation spot; especially for Californians; there are numerous flights from Cancun to major California cities. But first I had to get from Havana, Cuba to Cancun. Only about an hours flight away I sat nervously waiting for takeoff with a plane load of relaxed mostly Mexican vacationers returning home. There were no vacant seats on the plane. When finally airborne and I could look back at a fading Jose Marti International Airport in the distance I finally relaxed. No I wasn't home, but I was on a plane with people I felt comfortable with and most certainly heading in the right direction. In no time at all we were landing at Cancun International Airport, Mexico. I felt like kissing the ground; no, it wasn't the good old USA, but still Mexico felt like home. The tension in Cuba is everywhere it is very subtle and grows on you the longer you are there. The people go about their daily lives and one hardly notices that undercurrent of constant worry and fear. Remembering the faces of the clerks and workers in the Hotel Colina, they acted as if they were under constant surveillance even when no officials were present. I hardly noticed until it was time to go then the thought hit me, what if I couldn't leave? The relief was immediate and amazingly powerful upon departure.

Home: from Cancun to San Francisco International and just like that Cuba was a memory for me, but not for some. Now it was time to deal with a more direct racism with which I was familiar. The minute I popped out of the chute unloading from the plane from Cancun two suit wearing FBI police types watching the unloading passengers; Immediately perked up and followed me to the waiting area for transit buses. One remained in the airport while the other hopped on the bus and rode with me to the long term parking area. There he stood watching in the waiting hut until I found my vehicle and drove away. Yeah, welcome home.

Cancun International Airport, Mexico

There really is a life beyond the assorted petty racists some folk deal with daily. Such a life is available for people of color; if they choose to be hermits; never seeing or interacting with white folk and wannabe white folk under any circumstance. Having gathered information for my research while in Cuba; it was now time to face my racist PhD committee. First day I saw Chunner; "Back so soon, did you really use that grant money for Cuba travel? Just kidding" He said. But he wasn't, that racist assumed I stole the money and used it for other purposes, after all that's what blacks do, right? On the bulletin board I also saw a flyer; announcing my committee chairperson was having a signing for his new book, "The Black Panther Party". Coincidence, I thought "This can't be happening again." Maybe if Dalton had told me that he was writing a book about The Black Panther Party, my specialty I wouldn't have suspected that he used my years of research for his book. Maybe if he hadn't been so secretive about his book signing, not once mentioning it to me the one man on campus doing a dissertation on the Black Panther party I wouldn't have been concerned. Maybe if he hadn't scheduled his book signing on a day he knew I had no classes and was usually off campus I would have had no reason for suspicion. Maybe if Chunner hadn't also suggested that I do research in areas that he could use I would have been more trusting. Maybe if Ruth my previous committee chair hadn't done the very same thing I wouldn't have been pissed. Do they have no shame? What kind of people are they, I wondered? Finally, I could only conclude that overriding self interest first last and always is the way things are done at university. There was good news; Ignacio Lopez-Calvo was added to my PhD committee. A shining light of reasonability, Ignacio represented what I had expected from my committee members at the university. Ignacio seemed to think, without the phony posturing and dishonesty; that his function was to be helpful and humane. He was always available for consultation, discussion and assistance when necessary and to this day remains a trusted friend. The uncomfortable subtle and unsubtle racism so much a part of interactions with other committee members, faculty, administration and staff was far removed from Ignacio's fair and reasonable interactions. Intelligent, wise, and caring he is a fine example of the best the university has to offer. Here I must consider whether to go into the 'dark side' the record of being stalked by various representatives of the university on and off campus daily. That alone few (whites) would believe and it would encompass an entire book. The written record I titled Chronicles of Harassment. Foolishly expecting some assistance I gave a copy to the local NAACP president. A longtime resident and business owner in town, he promptly turned it over to the local police who laughing, showed me copies as they drove past daily.

Slow Witted Frightened Racists With Guns: "Pigs" as they were called by members of the Black Panther Party, was a complimentary term.

As a child back in Arkansas we raised pigs and they were very bright and fearless. These folk are small minded bullies who are especially afraid of Blacks, Latinos and poor people. At Stanislaus I dealt directly with a history department chairman who was comfortably entrenched in his racism. Assuming that Dr. Metz assured them that I would soon be gone from the university; Stanislaus police department stalking was minimal. The same could be said for Cal State East Bay where the stalking was limited to parking lots and other nearby off campus areas. Irksome at the time but too soon I discovered that it was nothing compared to the intensity and duration of police and school administration stalking to come at UC Merced. There campus police, administration, city police, county sheriffs and Highway patrol worked hand in hand intimidating and harassing Black and Latinos students and faculty (me). Campus police stalking was a given, but the administration also hired students, driving official UC Merced vehicles to follow me home on occasion; parking in front of my house waiting to follow when I pulled out of my garage. I know this because I confronted two of the students hired by the university' forcing confessions from both. Their racism came in handy, to my advantage; afraid of blacks they thought I was about to kick their asses, maybe I was. One was in trouble financially and the other academically. One was to receive a financial waiver and the other and academic waiver as payment for periodically following me from the campus to my home. On campus non tenured and new faculty directed by the administration literally peered around corners; following me on campus days and evenings. Crazy shit, yeah it happened. When driving on campus I got used to the stalking by campus police as well as the city police, county sheriff and highway patrol the minute I pulled off campus. One morning leaving home with only a few minutes to get to class, failing to notice the highway patrol vehicle on my tail I hurried down the road. Soon the lights were one me and I was pulled over for speeding. The fellow writing the ticket looked vaguely familiar so I asked; "Where do I know you from?" Then it hit me; "Didn't you use to work at UC Merced?" When he answered, "Yes" I realized he was the very same former UC Merced Policeman who followed me from the parking lot to my classroom and stood outside in the stairwell waiting until the end of class and then followed me to the parking lot daily. He typified my harassment but what of the few Black, Latino and other students of color at the university?

The only faculty member of color at the university, I was invited to student functions where the contrasts were amazing. At white activities there were NO police. However, at Black and Latino activities there were our campus police and city police. With so few Blacks and Latinos attending the university at the time; police often outnumbered the students present at those functions. It pissed me off and I wondered what kind of message were we sending to our students of color, but they seemed to accept the heavy police presence as a norm. Also a singer and a drummer I managed to connect with students on that level as well. Most had seen The Merced Marauders at parades and at other venues around the city; so it was suggested that we form a similar group on campus at UC Merced.

The Beat: So I started playing with interested students from my Political Science and History classes and other faculty. Meeting after hours a couple of nights a week Makaylah chose a name for our group; The Beat, and in a very short time all had learned to play African hand drums. Returning to the T-Shirt store from the days of Merced Marauders, I ordered Black Shirts with the group name, The Beat on the front and "When we drum we are one' on the back". Weekends we played gigs downtown at the Yogurt Shoppe, La Casitas Restaurant, The Cave and other spots on Main Street. But most of our shows were on campus where we played for various student organizations. Lunchtime performances in the campus quad were a favorite because students in the group got a chance to play before their friends and sometimes invited family. Pictured on the previous page are some members of The Beat after a campus lunchtime performance. It was of course much easier working with student groups on campus as opposed to some of the groups and situations we found ourselves in performing with the Merced Marauders. Playing in bars with the Merced Marauders we learned that after about 11:00 PM folks got a little rowdy and no one cared about who or what was being played or sung. The Beat lasted for several years with membership changes as students graduated and moved on with their lives. My eventual move signaled the end of The Beat.

Change: Change or Life; I couldn't decide whether there was any difference in meaning between the two so I chose change for a heading. In Merced like in other places lived in California I started my days with a morning walk or run. So it came as quite a shock to discover that I could no longer run or walk outside in Merced. Along with the discovery that I had developed asthma, I also discovered that the air quality in the San Joaquin Valley, which caused my asthma; where Merced is located, is the worst in the country. There are more asthma cases in children in the valley than in any other place in the country. With such air quality and asthma cases one would think that folks would be told or warned before moving into the valley. Things got so bad, that I couldn't leave the house during the day without wearing a mask. Without that mask my chest hurt every time I took a breath. Outdoor activity had been a part of my life since childhood and suddenly I couldn't go outside; especially during the daylight hours. Buying a treadmill helped with my exercise but it wasn't the same. Breathing is a biggie; a very important part of life, but there were other issues. After my return from Cuba police stalking on and off campus increased as did school administrator activity. So busy living and dealing with the day to

The Beat, When we drum we are one.

day issues I never considered the possibility of a connection between Cuba travel and their increased activity, nowadays I do suspect their was a connection. The idea is to frighten and if you ignore them or show no fear it really irritates them. So not being very bright folk they just increase their harassment activity. The stares, following, lurking outside my home, and classrooms I had gotten used to but after Cuba; they keyed both of my cars, poured acid on the hood of my Lexus, broke windshield wipers, let the air out of my tires among other things. When parked downtown or at a place where I was performing they had free rein. Returning to the parking lot I saw the acid fresh on my windshield and the front hood of my Lexus. Looking around to see if I could spot the person who had dumped it on my car I saw only one fellow in the parking lot. He wanted me to know he did it; parked directly in front of my vehicle, he sat watching and waiting for my reaction. Yeah, I wanted to confront him and kick his ass but all of my instincts said cop, I got in my Lexus and drove home. Now I was dealing with my asthma, increased police activity, and UC Merced administration; other than that life was pretty 'normal'. Thinking back I was trying to decide what was the absolute last straw, when did I decide that it was time to leave Merced? After all I had lived there longer than any other place, 8 years, since my divorce back in 2000. Any one of a number of incidents could have been the catalyst.

The female student planted in my class by the administration, class was over yet she refused to leave until I told her I was calling security. Or it could have been the underage students following me from campus to the parking lot daily? There were many incidents but the action that made me realize I had to move was when Merced Police started stalking visitors to my home. When visitors left my house the Merced police in marked police cars; would follow them to their homes or to the freeway. That really crossed the line, whereas I was used to them and unafraid; single women of color some traveling alone from the bay area was very frightened. Once they left my house there was nothing I could do to protect them. Could any one man take on a whole police department? Seeing no positive future in the coming battles, and tiring of the fight it was time to move. Knowing the police stalking came with the territory, being black territory; maybe I could find an area where at least I could breathe while being stalked. Practical considerations included my job at UC Merced and my house. By no means thinking of leaving the state; looking on the internet I found the cities with the best air quality. Still receiving my State Teachers Retirement Check, by dumping the $2200 monthly house payment I wouldn't suffer any major life changes wherever I moved. Checking the ethnicity of inhabitants as well as air quality; naturally the cities with the best air quality are 'white' cities.

Monterey, with the best air quality in the state listed NO Black residents

Judging from the shocked looks on the faces of tourists when they saw my black face walking the beaches I guessed that they must have Googled the same information I did about no Blacks in Monterey. But after moving there I discovered several Black families although most lived in neighboring Seaside, CA. So, I got rid of the house quit my job at UC Merced and found an apartment in Monterey. With awe and admiration, I looked forward to living within the stomping grounds of John Stienbeck and seeing firsthand the areas referred to in his books, *The Grapes of Wrath, Cannery Row, East of Eden, Of Mice and Men* and others reflecting the area and its people. But first of course I had to survive my welcome to Monterey. Just before the city limits with my last load for the newly rented apartment; a Monterey County Sheriff's Department vehicle pulled alongside and shined a hand held light onto my face. Then he dropped behind and turned on his flashers. I wasn't speeding so pulling into the slow lane I thought, "Here we go!" But when I pulled into that lane the guy turned off his flashers and followed me into the city limits of Monterey. Oh well, on to my new living space, located in an all white section of this city claiming to have no black residents. Later I was to discover that I was living in an older Italian part of the city called "Dago Hill" or so I was told by one of the locals. The older Italian American owner acted as if she was doing me a favor and some great civil rights good deed by renting to me. Although paying to stay I was expected to kiss her ass with gratitude? Choosing to live in safe, beautiful places people of color learn to put up with a lot of such racist bullshit. A tourist mecca I learned to smile at the shocked faces of whites from the inland cities on vacation at Monterey when they saw a Black person walking on the beach, me. It was so nice to be able to breathe and do my morning walks again. Except at Monterey I was walking past seal habitats, the Monterey Bay Aquarium, Cannery Row and Fisherman's Wharf on the most breathtaking beaches in California. There seemed to be an overabundance of seals along the shore. In one spot where I walked each day a large group of seals lives along the beach. Walking past I saw babies born and some abandoned right there on the seashore. I also saw a seal that I didn't know existed. One day routinely walking past I couldn't help but notice this gigantic creature about the size of a small whale lying off to the side of the rest of the herd. Checking Google later I discovered that it was an elephant seal. Not quite the size of an elephant but kinda big.

Monterey is a military town; the US Army bases and, schools are the dominant presence in the city. On my morning walks the Army base and guards were on the hill up from the beach and the Coast Guard boats and sailors were on the water. Surviving that gauntlet was interesting but the Monterey Police went above and beyond. Settled into my new apartment I took my first morning walk and stopped in the park for my after walk Tai Chi.

Cannery Row, Monterey, CA

Monterey seals & Elephant Seal

Suddenly a police helicopter was hovering just above the tree line. I moved and the helicopter followed. The next day the very same thing happened except the police helicopter followed hovering overhead for the entire four miles, out and back, of my walk and again hovered over the park as I did my Tai Chi. The police helicopter was with me for my first week living in Monterey; after which the stalking fell into the category of usual routine activities. A major part of the routine activities included pictures of any new Blacks moving into a town or city. I learned to quickly sidestep, change direction, and stop on the sidewalk along the beach to avoid undercover cops trying to take my picture. Once the picture is taken of course it is hung in police department 'ready rooms' and shared with all members of the department. It never fails to impress me how hard those racists in blue work; they will go to any lengths to intimidate and harass Blacks and people of color. Knowing I was paying with my tax dollars for my stalking and harassment was disturbing. Looking up at that helicopter and the two men inside; each with salaries more than six figures per year; and knowing that they were wasting time, fuel, and working hours stalking me was very irritating to say the least. Just a couple of guys having fun doing what they enjoy doing; stalking and harassing Blacks. But then too on second thought that's exactly what the white majority wants them to do. Sorely disappointed at the Monterey/Salinas area not living up to my romanticized John Steinbeck expectations I was soon ready to leave.

During the few months living in Monterey I continued working on my first book; *The Killing of Mr. Floyd & Other Stories* which is available from Amazon.com and Kindle. Also; missing teaching, I applied for a position at Cal Poly San Luis Obispo. After seeing the opening for a Political Science teacher on an internet job site; I thought, why not. After filling out the application and mailing the necessary paperwork showing my degrees and experience I was offered the job in a letter from the head of the Political Science Department at Cal Poly San Luis Obispo. Checking the air quality for the area I discovered that it was very good, so I sent a letter accepting the offer of employment. Over the phone and in his letters the head of the department sounded most welcoming. One of his instructors in the department was taking off for a quarter. Once our contract had a valid offer and acceptance I thought end of story until the fall quarter. A couple of months before the start of the quarter I moved from Monterey to San Luis Obispo and waited to hear from the department head about class assignments, books to be ordered for student purchase from the bookstore and other details. For two months prior to the start of school I heard nothing from the guy. Luckily I found the Cal Poly orientation schedule on line and that listed the reporting date for new teachers. On that day I walked into his office and introduced myself and the jerk acted surprised.

Cal Poly San Luis Obispo

Uh Uhhhhh I'd seen this before so many times; usually when the powers that be discovered that I was Black after hiring me. Fumbling on his desk he produced a paper contract for my signature to supplement the on-line contract that I had already signed. Damm! Talk about racism on steroids, that place took the cake! At the orientation all the new teachers picked up their introductory packets with parking permits, classroom assignments, classes to be taught, books to be used, etc; but surprise they didn't have one for me. While the new teachers divided into discussion groups I had to wait for the clerk to make up the necessary packet and scribble a name tag for me. Surviving orientation day, I still needed my room assignment, list of classes and student lists for me and the bookstore. As the start of classes was quickly approaching, I finally confronted the department chairman who seemed to be hoping that I would just give up and go away. Reminding him that we had a valid contract; and if he made it impossible for me to teach my classes I would stay home and still be paid. "The courts if necessary are available to enforce contracts; along with my salary for the quarter." I also mentioned that I would seek damages for intentional infliction of emotional distress. By the end of the day I had all the necessities to begin work the following Monday. Miraculously the bookstore had the books for each class days before the start. The quarter started; and of course here too again I was the 'only one' teaching on campus. As always being a novelty adds interest to the subject matter. What can I say, I enjoy teaching and after so many years I am pretty damm good at it. During that time I was also writing my first book which covered much of the time being discussed in our Political Science classes thus adding a surprising reality to the classroom experience. The students in my Political Science and History classes provided the impetus for me to publish my writing. In my teaching to keep my students alert and awake; I told stories from the times we were studying. One student suggested that I might publish those stories and I did. The stories may be found in my books; *The Killing of Mr. Floyd & Other Stories* and in my 2nd book *There Are Times When...*

San Luis Obispo: I do wonder whether I should continue to chronicle police activity, it's pretty much the same with interesting, I think they are; variations. San Luis Obispo a town with few if any Blacks didn't quite know how to react. Clumsily, at first they tried to get pictures when I did my morning walks; then it got more intense as my landlord allowed them free rein on the premises. I saw them taking the apparatus down after I moved, but he allowed the police to install cameras, recording and listening devices through the attic into my apartment. When I read what I have just written it sounds too crazy but it actually happened. My suspicions were aroused when I saw the hole from the attic in the corner just above my front door. Having googled likely spots for cameras and listening devices I knew where to look.

A camera in the attic through a hole just above my front door monitored folks entering and leaving my apartment. I found other tiny holes in the upper corner of the bedroom, the living room and the bathroom. Then I ordered a "Bug Detector", yes there is such a device; of course I ordered it from whom else but Amazon.com. Easy to operate, you just charge it and point it toward the spot and it gives a buzz for a camera monitor and a different sounding buzz for a recorder. But once located I was left wondering what to do next. I thought about going into the attic and taking the equipment, but I would have to go through the landlord for the attic. The only entry was directly in front of the landlord's apartment. Yeah it got worse but I won't bore you with details. With a hefty deposit, I had signed the lease for a year, so I was stuck. We do what we have to do in order to survive. I did my walks every morning just as I have done most of my life, walking or running. No nearby beaches, I walked for miles through the neighborhoods seeing the fearful looks on the faces of the white folk. I am talking driving on the street in their cars and seeing a Black man; with looks of fear and horror suddenly slamming on their brakes and stopping in the middle of the road. I just shook my head, white folks are insane, and kept on stepping. Could be the discipline from my military years but my routine was pretty ingrained, walk and Tai Chi in the morning and write for the rest of the day. Ignoring lots of heavy duty police shit I still managed to finish writing that first book and started working on publication.

Open Mics: From the local newspaper I discovered a listing of places scattered around neighboring towns and San Luis Obispo where writers met and shard their work on various nights. Arroyo Grande, Nipomo, Pismo Beach, Grover City and even Avila Beach became regular stops for writers. Those very same places had open mics for other entertainments as well. Week nights I spent with the writers but often weekends found me playing and singing at the open mic locations. One reading and gathering of writers happened an early evening in Los Osos, a small town on the south end of Morro Bay. Although still stuck with my lease for a few more months I began looking into the possibility of finding a place in Los Osos. Cousin Bobby has lived in nearby Morro Bay for years and he often bragged about the area. "You won't have any problems dealing with it because you've spent most of your life around these white folks." Finally the year ended and after a hefty argument I got most of my deposit and went on Craigslist searching for that perfect place to write and found it in Los Osos. Sitting on the coast; you're never more than a ten minute walk away from the beach. Remembering and comparing the cities I would say that Merced is extremely racist, as is Monterey and San Luis Obispo. But Los Osos is different. Yes it is a "White" town like the others but the positives are noteworthy. Most know of Pismo Beach and Morro Bay but Los Osos is an isolated and surprising jewel.

Los Osos

Los Osos: Translated from Spanish, The Bears and as they say along Canadian Highway 1, yes there really are bears in the area. Los Osos is 'different' in that the folks don't seem to really give a shit about color. There are no railroad tracks which separated the black and white communities in other parts of the country, there is no railroad. Even if there were tracks historically there were no blacks in Los Osos to be separated. Hence, that common racist history is missing from the community's past. Racism is learned and generally without that history those folk don't seem to know how to do racism, I know un American and weird☺ They shocked me with their honesty and curiosity. On a morning walk a car pulled alongside and the driver got out introduced himself, and offered his hand "You're the first black person I've ever met, I'm Jonathan Pierce." That and similar conversations happened several times in Los Osos. What do you do, but shake your head, smile and roll with it☺ Yea, I like that town. Most of the people I met and interacted with seemed quite pleased to know and have a black person living in the town. Continuing my morning walks and Tai Chi followed by a day of writing I happened to meet other writers in the community. When I wanted a change of pace I chose to write in the local Starbucks. There I would sit for hours with other writers in an abandoned vault converted to a writing and meeting space for the locals. It seems the building was a former bank before Starbucks took over the premises and made a few changes. One large Rooibos and Chai tea, elbow room at the work table for me and my laptop and I was set for the afternoon. When I wanted to take a break I would wander out into the main customer area and chat with other retirees. Starbucks was a beacon for that crowd as well. The hardest part was; with other than the curiosity, getting used to people reacting to my color in a welcoming and positive manner. What's up with that?

In the quiet isolation with a clear head and positive time I finished and published my first book, mentioned earlier, *The Killing of Mr. Floyd*. After months of dealing with publishing companies, agents, editors and other shady characters; including some shady friends, it was finally done.You might notice in the picture of Los Osos on the preceding page that there is no downtown area, just homes and the ocean. The main drag and major street running through town is Los Osos Valley Road. Alongside Los Osos Valley Road is the post office, a supermarket, a couple of restaurants, a real estate office, a used bookstore and two gas stations. Los Osos sitting at the south end of Morro Bay had fewer miles of open beach than the neighboring city of Morro Bay itself. The beaches in Morro Bay too were more isolated, I liked the privacy. During those years following the seven minute drive to Morro Bay; alongside the seals, ducks and vultures on the miles of empty beach, I witnessed the sunrise each day.

Los Osos, looking north toward Morro Rock

Upon my return from the two miles down the beach and 30 minutes of Tai Chi, other daily walkers and runners began to appear. Over the years we recognized each other and managed to say hello, but I didn't know those people and didn't wish too. It just may be true what some say about writers and writing, it is a lonely isolated pastime. Most folk I try very hard to avoid, and am most comfortable with the nicest person I know, me. I loved that quiet space I also wrote and published my second book; *There Are Times When...in* Los Osos. Upon completion of *Times When* I decided to reward myself and take a trip I had been looking forward to for many years. A historian, I was fascinated with the impact of the **Panama Canal** on the exploration and settlement of the Americas.

The Panama Canal

Magellan and other European explorers had to sail around the bottom tip of South America to reach the West coast of the continents. After the hole; the western United States and North America was suddenly open to hordes of explorers and gold rushers heading for California and the west. The growth of this country;, the slave trade' can all be directly and indirectly attributed to that hole. Wherever you may live in America today would not have been possible without the hole. The impact of that hole was felt; and it influenced the exploration and settlement of the North and South American continents. The gold, furs, crops and other resources also directly contributed to the development of European nations; and to the continuation and expansion of the Age of Exploration and the industrial revolution. Even today many of those very same nations use the canal for trade. Having thought about it and talked about it for years, in the footsteps of many early adventurers and explorers; I too wanted to sail through that amazing historical gap between the continents. Yeah, I wanted to see, touch and smell the hole. So I signed up for a Panama Canal tour. It was my first time traveling with a tour group, Caravan Tours. We had about twelve people in the group for the scheduled nine day tour. On the first day after registration at the first hotel we boarded the bus where we were given 3X5 cards and told to print our names with black markers. The cards we placed above our seats on the tour bus. On the third day I returned to the bus to find my card missing, only mine. It was replaced by another card with my name misspelled and printed with a red ball point pen. So everyone else had the cards they printed but mine had been taken and replaced, OK> The evening after the card change I returned to m y room following dinner and found a Panamanian Soldier, at least he was wearing fatigues, military boots, and carrying an M-16 Rifle; standing by the door to my room. He said not a word, but stood with his gun and watched me enter my room. This tour was turning out to be much like the constant police stalking in the good old USA.

The Panama Canal

The Author & the Alligator in Panama

For the remaining days of the tour we suddenly had this unexplained extra person with us during meals, at performances and other sites visited. I was itting in the bar chatting with another member of the tour group when she asked, "Who the hell is that guy, he was sitting next to us during dinner and at our table before we moved to the bar?" It felt so much like home☺ An aside, those sons of bitches at Carvan Tours still sends me tour information. So back to reality, my only interest was in the canal so I hadn't put much thought into the country and people of Panama. Once there of course I noted the cities and former US Military bases; now just housing in Panamanian neighborhoods. I was very surprised at its size and the commercial and building activity in and around Panama City. It reminded me of San Francisco. My older brother had been stationed in Panama and the stories he told about the country and its' people came to mind. He mentioned that he and his friends often passed for Panamanians when the US military police were chasing all the American soldiers out of the nightclubs.

So I reckon I expected to see more black faces in Panama, I did not. The white Panamanian tour guide talked that Latin American BS; pretending racism doesn't exist when I asked, "Where are the Black Panamanians?" He said, "There are no Blacks or Whites in our country, we are all Panamanians." "So you're telling me that there are no Panamanians with skin the color of my own." His response, "We are all Panamanians." So beyond his nonsense as we rolled about the city from one tourist site to the next I kept looking for those Panamanians with skin the color of my own. At one theatre stop we were told that the African performers, wearing authentic African Tribal Costumes were performing dances of their African Tribes. The other members of the tour group accepted the white Panamanian's statement without comment. But I just had to point out that the dancers were white Panamanians and not African Panamanian. I even suggested that having white Panamanians performing as Africans was a clear indication of racism in Panama. "Maybe all are not Panamanians!" Reckon I was beginning to irritate the fellow, he stopped talking to me after I called over a Black Panamanian I saw on the street; placed my arm next to his and said; "His skin is Black and so is mine, he is a Black Panamanian."

Panama City is a bustling metropolis but just outside and on its borders are thick overgrown jungles. Riding around the city in heavy traffic was reminiscent of any major city in the USA. Surrounded by the daily hubbub of urban life while hanging out in luxury hotels and restaurants; it was hard to imagine that there are large tribal areas with several tribes within minutes of Panama City. Traveling by boat down a river to visit one tribe we saw monkeys and tropical birds hanging from the trees. The guide drove the boat near the beach and stopped in several places   to toss bananas to the expectant monkeys.

Panama City Panama

We were also warned not to put our hands in the water if we didn't want to lose them. It seems there were schools of flesh eating fish and other beasts native to the area. Suppose the boat accidentally turned over, I wondered, guess drowning wouldn't necessarily be a first concern. Hmmmmmmmm. The tribe we visited lived alongside the river. Seeing the TV dishes attached to the huts kinda took away from the authenticity for me. But who was I to judge, we are who we are wherever and however we must live. And there is no charge for that little bit of life philosophy. Anyway, it was summer vacation from school, I asked, so there were lots of kids around. Most of the adults and parents worked. They didn't work out in the forests hunting animals with bows and arrows as the grass huts might suggest but they worked at full time 8 hour a day jobs in Panama City. Glancing underneath the thatch on the roofs I saw tin and the walls of the houses were common wood siding, just saying. I didn't mention those observations because my fellow tour mates were totally caught up in the 'primitive' experience. They were posing for pictures, dressing in native clothing and doing the whole tourist thing. .The kids not participating in the performances were standing off to the side texting on their cell phones. Most striking were the similarities not the manufactured differences in the native Panamanian culture. Those folk lived pretty much as we tour people lived back home in the good old USA. And as I said earlier, Panama is very much like the Untied States. The nine days I was in country I didn't hear one person speaking Spanish, the native language. Maybe it was the planned places we were taken to on the tour; but everyone spoke English, even when they were speaking among themselves. Sitting in the bars we listened to the musical groups singing and playing "Hey Jude" and Santana's Evil Ways. It was an interesting nine days and I found a couple of friends who I still communicate with on Facebook. We'll be getting together the next time I am in Michigan. Returning home to Los Osos I quickly fell back into my daily routine, beach walk in the morning, write until four and hill walking in the afternoon. Book III I had started soon after publishing *There Are Times When* and had planned to have it finished before the end of 2015. But that very crooked knee in the picture on page 386 was a problem; with constant pain and limited mobility I was a bit distracted. Then too there was Sulo. Before moving on here I will respond to a question asked at a meeting of a local women's book club: "Where do you get your stories?" My response, things, good and bad happen; I put mine on the printed page.

Finding a Lost Son

Sulo: During my years living in Merced and all the years following the death of my youngest son in 1999 I had no contact with my oldest son Sulo or his mother, my ex wife. Always closest to his mother they both shared the anger following the divorce. On with my life I continued to work, doing the things that I do; attend schools and teach

Tribal Dancers, Panama

That time of separation from Sulo and his mother I did manage to periodically see my grandson Justice. After retiring in 2012 and writing a couple of books that Sulo happened to read; after more than 15 years he began a cautious communication with me. One phone conversation led to another and he invited me down to a film festival he and his then girlfriend Sufe were putting on. Overjoyed to see him and asking no questions, I did wonder about his living situation. He invited me down to his film festival but did not invite me to spend the night at his home. Later I discovered not much had changed, his mother was still paying his way, and she bought him a house in Los Angeles. Arriving in the city about 1:00 AM after my four hour drive from Los Osos I found a hotel in Santa Monica on ocean Ave for a mere $450 a night. After 15 years it was nothing, a very small price to see my only surviving child. The last time we had spoken he was a much younger man; now much older; in his 40's my son was a man whom I had never really known. Saturday afternoon I found the theatre being used in Santa Monica and waited until I spotted Sulo stepping outside for a smoke. During our unending conversation, trying to catch up on 15 years, I met many of his friends. Snack time with wine and cheese following the short films; moving about the room and participating in the 'meet and greet' I noticed that the majority of the folk I talked to had some sort of police affiliation or connection. Sure there were a few recognizable Hollywood faces but most of those people; although dresse for the occasion were police. My alarms immediately kicked in and I was in that cautionary watchful mode. Enjoying the first meeting with the long lost son I remembered that he and his mother refused to even acknowledge my existence for more than 15 years. Does that take a bit of Hate? Can hate be turned on and off at will? Was this going to be a clumsy police set up engineered by my own son? I wondered. It was odd observing that Hollywood thing which I always thought funny with my son as a participant. All of the look at me people, constantly posing and staring at themselves was creepy. But when you're in a room filled with those people there is no one to whisper; "Can you believe this shit?" There too are members of the group who are looking to hang with the "right" people, people who can get them a part in their next movie or commercial. Those folk, all pretty, the men and the women; will do ANYTHING to further their careers. Their desperation is scary, but that's Hollywood. Sulo introduced me to his Haitian friend Whenda who was photographing the event. Moving about the room taking pictures for the 2nd time I was blinded by the flash. Once maybe for a record of attendees at the function but another picture; OK I let it slide. Having dealt with a lifetime of police and police tactics the most common is to get pictures of new Blacks in town to post in ready rooms and share with other police agencies. Seeing her in whispered conversation with several of the police connected folk; by the fourth blinding flash I kept my distance. I suspect, encouraged by Sulo, Whenda texted me several times after I returned home to Los Osos.

Sulo & his Son Justice

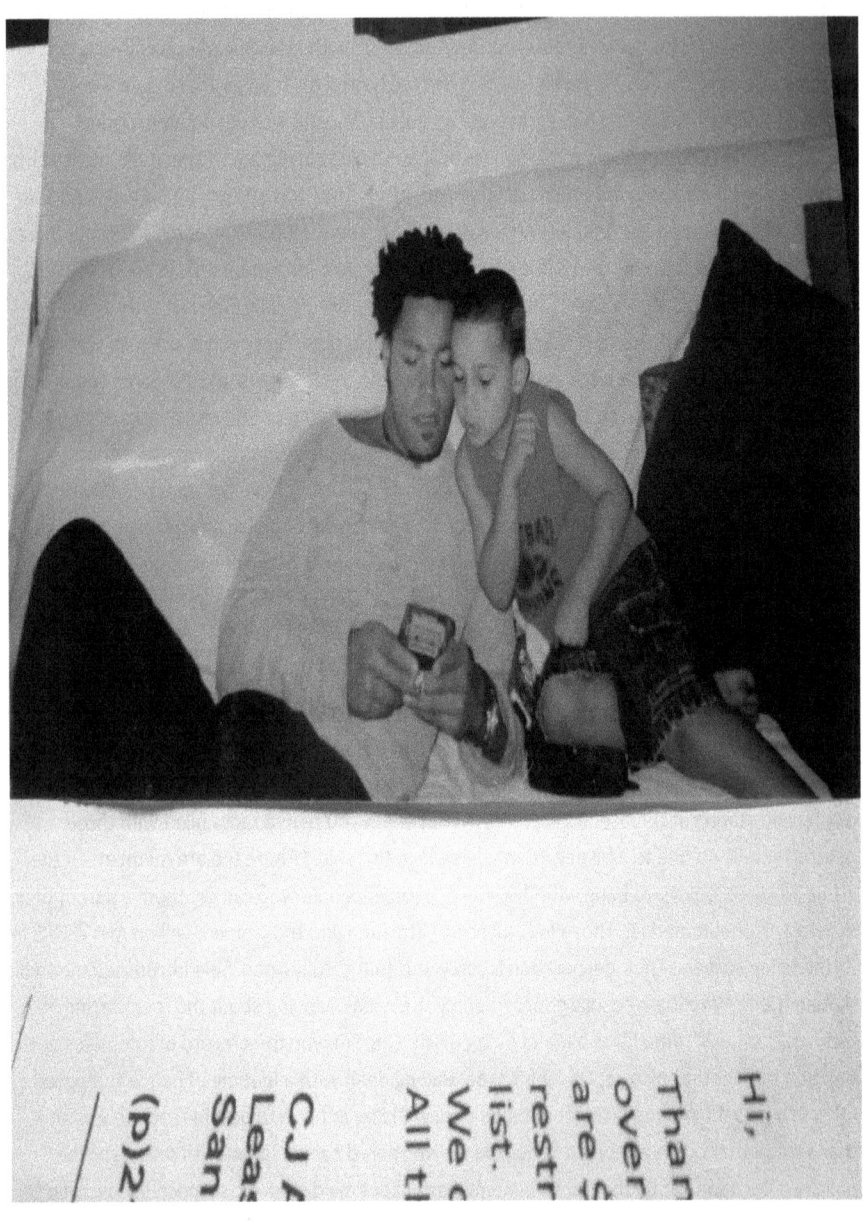

Last picture: of the author, Sulo, Sufe and brother, nephew, and brother

I stopped all communication after she tried to unload an unrequested very large file onto my computer. One can imagine what those files contained, thanks son. Was Whenda a part of my son's plan to set me up and get me arrested for the child porn Whenda tried to download onto my computer? It sure seemed that way to me after his response. When I told Sulo about his friends attempt to download porn onto my computer he down played it saying it was no big deal. What? Was he a police snitch trying to set me up? That seemed to be the case. Listening to his constant conversation; bragging about fighting; he even mentioned that he had fought with his brother before he died. He bragged about and was proud of having been in jail. Was this the son we raised; more and more I wondered about those police connections? The screenplays he wrote and filmed, most glorified police with police heroes. Remembering that regardless of our feelings, questions, pain, guilt, and suspicions we must listen; because if we listen stories will play out, they will tell themselves. Sulo also mentioned the shotgun that I had left when I moved out of the family home. He said he sawed off the long barrel and kept it in one of the rentals behind his house. Did he keep the shotgun out back because the barrel was sawed off or because he had a felony, or both? When asked he denied having a felony, but from my days working in the Public Defender's office; right down to the worshipful fear of police, he sure acted like a felon. What happened to him, why was he like this? We did all the things parents are supposed to do, even down to his Princeton education, but he acted like any other cheap ignorant thug. Continually, cautiously watchful I saw things that would make any parent worry. Each of the four times I visited during the year I saw the daily morning delivery of the ½ gallon of vodka. Having finished the delivery from the previous morning Sulo immediately started drinking from the new bottle. Sitting on the couch in the living room or on the front porch smoking; regardless of the conversation or who was present Sulo drank all day into the night until the bottle was empty. The first time I was to spend the night at his house, I was down for his wedding. His mother refused to attend because she hated the woman he was marrying. Of course Sulo's day was typical starting with the morning bottle. Arriving late afternoon we sat talking into the night. I sat across from him watching him drinking on the couch. Suddenly he slammed the bottle onto the table and stood. Then staring hard at me and pounding the table with both fists; ready for a fight Sulo yelled, "You hurt mom!" Although I was supposed to participate in his wedding the following day, I walked to my vehicle and prepared to leave. With red unblinking eyes, Sulo stood staring through my driver's side window while I tried to back past the car parked behind me. Before greater escalation and/or departure his friend Marcus arrived. The mood changed and Marcus convinced me not to leave. The next morning, the wedding day; I watched this guy; Sulo act as if nothing had happened the night before and start the day with his Vodka bottle.

The wedding went well; their friend Kelly Perrine performed the ceremony. There were several folk from the old hometown who I had known as kids and as Sulo's friends. It was nice to see them, as they too were working in various capacities in Hollywood. However I couldn't help noticing that they kept their distance from Sulo and treated him like he was a little off. Observing and learning; I tried I never to make the mistake of visiting past afternoon again. Any reasonable coherent interactions with Sulo had to occur before a half day of alcohol consumption. The drunker he got the more he wanted to fight any man present. His uncle Charles; who Sulo hadn't seen for more than twenty years; showed up on his wedding day, after a few drinks Sulo started a baiting conversation about fighting ability. I interrupted and he said, "Why you gotta protect Uncle Charles?" The shit got crazier each time I visited. Sitting listening to his conversation when drinking was like listening to some street hoodlum. The shocking stories he told included one he was proud of; he beat up his dead brother's best friend for not coming to his brother's aid when he was dying. Sulo bragged about the kid having to go to the hospital after the beating he gave him. A nice kid who the family had known since kindergarten; he was Neemie's very best friend. There was nothing he or anyone else could have done to save Nemie's life, one would have had to be in Neemie's presence, but he died alone. It sounded like Sulo was angry because Neemie died so he wanted to strike out and fight someone, anyone; and Neemie's friend was available. Why he told me I have no idea, because I was shocked and embarrassed at Sulo's violence and stupidity. How many more stupid stories must I listen to when coming to visit? Later talking to his friends, I was to learn that after doing the most outrageous things to people close to him he habitually acted as if it never happened and/or was no big deal. His best friends who just had a baby girl after trying to have a child for years told me an unbelievably horrible story about Sulo. Two years before they had lost triplets and instead of sorry for your loss Sulo called and said to them that he was glad the triplets were stillborn. Why would anyone say such a mean thing to grieving parents? Go figure. A few days after marriage Sulo and the new wife were talking about having kids. I reminded them that they were in AA although they refused to attend the meetings and that Sulo was bipolar and wouldn't take his medication. "There is no way in hell that you could raise a child." "Besides child protective services would take the child away from the two of you in a heartbeat." On one occasion when I was down visiting, I met a friend from college days in Southern California at the nearby Starbucks. While sitting talking about old times, like a jealous lover Sulo kept calling my phone every 15 minutes or so and hanging up. Odd and freaky weird behavior but no longer surprising as I began to realize that my son was very mentally ill. Another realization was that my son still wanted to beat up his father, the fellow hated me.

Always happy to see my only son our visits had excellent starts. Hoping to make up for years of distance I wanted as much time as possible with him. Although very happy to see him those four or five times I felt so bad as a parent because I could do nothing to help him. Just thinking about it as I write this brings tears; every time I saw Sulo he seemed sadder than the time before.

Remembering when they were kids you could crack a joke, give them candy, ice cream, or tickle them to drive away the sadness. But when the child is suddenly a 42 year old man those things won't work, so you suffer in silence. The excellent morning starts made me forget the evenings of previous visits ending with Sulo wanting to fight me. My final visit, sitting on the front porch wrapped in a blanket about 2AM I listened as Sulo continued his non-stop drunken rant. Marcus one of his childhood friends had attended the wedding, but his very best friend who spent many a night at our house and Sulo at his; was not there. So I asked, "Whatever happened to Caleb?" "He hasn't spoken to me in years." "But you were like brothers from elementary through high school." Caleb introduced me to this girl he was engaged to marry and I fucked her, she liked rough sex." "He married someone else and has three kids. Caleb lives in Ecuador and doesn't speak to me." What a horrible thing to do; and it was even more horrible to share that kind of information with your father. I never figured out why he told me things that painted him in such a bad light. But then there was much I didn't begin to understand. So there we were sitting on the front porch, way past the time I should have been long gone from his presence. But he was my only evidence of a much happier past with a family in a pleasant place and time; he was my son. Listening to his shocking unending conversation, suddenly things changed. Reaching out with his right hand and touching my face he said, "Pop there is something just below your eye." There was nothing there and he ignored my hostile reaction as I pulled away from his touch. Rambling on he pointed out the broken twigs arranged in a ragged rectangle in the front yard. He said he changed the arrangement each day. I thought but did not say why; because there was too much unanswerable why about my son. He told me soon after we reconnected that every morning he had to decide whether he wanted to live another day. Is that not a very heavy duty thing to say to anyone, especially a parent? There again I didn't ask why because there is no reasonable answer to such a statement. Knowing that; I just felt extremely helpless and sad that there was nothing I could do to help my only child. I was just a spectator watching and praying for a miracle to save him from himself. Wordlessly the 2nd time he rubbed a finger just below my right eye, freaky, freaky shit! Looking toward my car and thinking I should be out of here before I have to hurt this drunk, the drama continued. With no reason or explanation Sulo with a balled fist punched me on my upper thigh.

Was this it, I thought, the long planned attack on his father? I am certain he would have continued regardless of any action or inaction on my part but looking toward my hands underneath the blanket covering my legs and lower body on the cool porch, he paused to ask a key question; surprisingly under the circumstances in a reasonably normal tone: "Pop do you still have the Walther (Walther PPK Pistol)?" My answer, "Yes" was enough, with unblinking red eyes Sulo stood, turned and stumbled into the house leaving me sitting alone on the front porch. Yes, he remembered I own a Walther but I didn't have it in my hands on that porch. How does one deal with straight up insanity? How do you reason with unreasonable thoughts, ideas and actions? Is there a proper way to react and be a father to a threatening, psychotic 42 year old son? Just the thought of the pain and suffering it would have caused his mother and me if we had fought; even now is so depressing. What to do, then and there I made a decision. That was the last time I saw my son. With that 20/20 hindsight I do wonder whether/if there was anything I could have done to change the ending. Having no training as a mental health professional; still could I have broken through that barrier and discussed or directed possible future happiness for my son? I got up walked to the car and drove the four hours home to Los Osos and called Sulo later that day. "Until you get the professional help you need, stay away from me." The picture on the following page is one of Sulo and his wife Sufe at the Emmy Awards. Her show VEEP won an award and a rarity, my son Sulo seems really very happy. Why not, he is in Hollywood where he always dreamed of being and at the Emmy Awards. But typically the day to day continued as other issues were pushing to the forefront of our lives.

2016 was hinting at being an exceptional year. Returning home early one afternoon in August I found a realtors card stuck in the front screen with a scribbled message saying to call her. I didn't know her and I didn't need a realtor so I ignored the message. Two days later she showed up and told me that the owner was selling the property and that she would be showing it starting the following week. I said no and suggested that she could show it after three months notice and I had moved. Three months notice would put me out of the place by October 9.

My knee replacement surgery scheduled for September 12 would leave me immobile for at least a month and barely mobile for two or three more. Crisis number 2 was front and center, could I find a place to live and recover from knee surgery before the September 12, operation? Frantically looking around the central coast where I had lived comfortably for the past four years I found nothing. Every realtor contacted was now insisting on month-to-month tenancies whereas I wanted a year lease. Month to month gave every advantage to the landlord who could raise the rent with a month's notice and/or kick you out if you refused to accept the raised rent.

The Emmys 2015

Regardless it was August and I had until October to find a place so I decided I would take a trip home to Arkansas to see my one remaining brother before the operation. The doctor claimed that the operation was routine; but I remembered that my older brother had gone in to a hospital for the very same "routine" knee operation and died there. So the Arkansas trip was on. Yes, my son, Sulo was still very Sulo. Acting as if nothing had happened he was calling and texting daily; even suggesting that I take him to Arkansas with me. Just the thought of his drunken craziness in Arkansas was scary. Receiving no response to his Arkansas suggestion Sulo then texted me that he and his wife were coming to stay with me for a few days. Noting my refusal to respond to his texts or phone calls after the assault and battery; he started using Uncle Charles to communicate with me. He told Charles we had had a minor disagreement at his house. In no uncertain terms I made it clear to Uncle Charles that if Sulo showed up at my home I would call the police. With that settled, in late August a few weeks before my knee operation; I returned home to Arkansas for the first time in four years. Regardless of the years it is always good to see home again; all the streets, places and the remaining folk are poignant reminders of a distant past. From a family of nine just Brother Lee Willie there in Gould, Arkansas; and I are the only remaining family members. So a visit to the family plot and those who have passed on are always a part of the visit home. Choosing to stay in a hotel in the nearby city of Pine Bluff; I avoided the drama of staying at Brother Lee Willie's home. Each time I've visited and stayed with him he's tried to get me to invest in some hare brained scheme or another. When I refused he and his wife would get pissed off and rude until I left their house. My Bro assumes that education and courtesy means weakness. "Street knowledge" which some of us calls street stupidity; in his mind is the only real knowledge; whatever.

Hanging with my brother for a few days I also happened to attend a high school reunion of a class that graduated tens years after me. It was briefly interesting chatting with the much younger sisters and brothers of my high school classmates. They were from a different time and school although in the same small town. By the time they graduated the White school had finally integrated but integration still meant an all black school because the majority of the white kids left for all white private schools. There were no whites attending the reunion, and with a quick look in old year books I saw maybe two white faces in all the yearbook grades. After a few days of driving to Gould from Pine Bluff and spending time with my brother and his wife Charlotte I was ready to say goodbye. On my last day in Arkansas I received a text from DL Johnson, a high school classmate who told me that his brother Andrew had died. I was shocked, just a few days before my trip we were texting regarding the new book he had been working on. Discourteous, unrepentant, and unyielding; death has no respect.

Gould Colored Cemetery: Home to Sister, Poppa, Mother & Brother, so far.

My flight to California was scheduled for the following morning. Early September I was home and Andrew's funeral was to be on September 10, 2016 in Austin Texas. The leg was more painful each day as the operation time approached. Thinking I could dash to Texas and return before my operation, I checked with my doctor and he nixed the idea. So on September 12, 2016 I went under the knife. Using Medicare which paid for three days hospitalization; of course after the operation I was stuck in the hospital until the 15th of September. Although in pain I was way past ready to get out of that place and go home but they refused to discharge me without a ride. Even after I explained to them that the operation was on my left leg and that I drove with my healthy right they still refused to let me leave. After texting my dilemma to two folk from my daily beach walks they took me home. Bob and Barbara picked me up drove me home and practically carried me up two sets of steps into my apartment and to my bed. They were just folks I said hello to on my morning beach walks. Didn't know I had them but what a pleasant and timely discovery, friends

Corinne (2016): A friend from the distant past, from the time when I was married and raising two children agreed to spend a few days with me following the operation. So the very next day after being deposited in my bed by my beach friends, Corinne showed up with her dog Osos. Having difficulty getting in and out of bed and walking in general her presence was appreciated. It was appreciated until she introduced her drama. It takes much energy to deal with drama especially other peoples drama; and at the time I needed all of my energy to maintain any semblance of a life. A captive audience I could only listen with shock and surprise as Corinne railed about "...welfare queens in ghettos stealing her tax money."It didn't end there she also loudly voiced her concern regarding "...black hoodlums whining about police doing their jobs."I had known this woman for years and spent many a Thanksgiving with the wife and kids on the farm where she lived. The kids loved her and thoroughly enjoyed spending time with the cows, chickens and horses on the farm. What could have happened to her, was she always a mean, spiteful, angry racist? During those years when the kids were growing up and spending time with her and other families over Thanksgiving she had never shown her racist side. Following her racist rant on the afternoon of the first day of her visit she insisted that I drive her and Osos to the beach. Feeling obligated for past and present kindness I couldn't say no. Using my walker I hobbled down two sets of steps to the car and wrestled my heavily bandaged left leg inside. Needing only the right leg to drive we set out on that painful drive to the beach. Unable to walk of course I sat in the car and waited while Corinne and Osos romped on the beach. While waiting I got a call from my doctor; and when I told him where I was he was not pleased. In no uncertain terms he told me get home into bed and "...stay there!"

Thanksgiving at Corinnes circa 1986

He was kinda pissed, and he also said it was unsafe for me to be driving. Far down the beach I honked the horn for Corinne and Osos who reluctantly returned to the car and sat quietly as I drove home. It never crossed my mind at the time, but I reckon she didn't give a shit about me or my condition. Unfortunately the Corinne drama didn't end there; thankful to be able to move from my bed to the bathroom and kitchen I had no idea what was going on outside the doors of the apartment. The next day started with one of the neighbors pounding on the front door. In the four years I had lived in that complex the woman had never set foot inside my home or I in hers, but Corinne without checking or acknowledging me in any way opened the door and immediately invited her inside. Knee hurting like hell, I could only lay there listening to the woman in the open doorway yelling at me about Corinne's dog running loose around the complex. While talking to me I noticed her glance to her right. Following her gaze I couldn't miss Corinne standing and posing for the neighbor with her top off and a big smile. Looking at Corinne as if she was nuts as did I, the neighbor continued her rant about the loose dog. Listening to my apology with an explanation that the dog would be gone in a couple of days the neighbor finally left. The neighbor gone now Corrine put on her top and tore into me for "...not taking her side." "What side is that?" I asked. She wasn't listening as I told her that I had to live with the people in the complex. *I* also mentioned that there are rules forbidding loose dogs. On her last day I was so happy she was leaving, Corinne asked for the neighbor's phone number. She said she wanted to invite the neighbor to her home for a weekend visit. Oops, this was getting freaky with more unwanted drama; I could see me in the middle of some confrontation between Corinne and the woman's husband, if the woman didn't kick her ass first. "It's none of my business, but I don't think she is gay and I am pretty sure her husband wouldn't agree for her to visit you." I said. Daily mental drama added to my pain I didn't need; finally Corinne left and good riddance forever.

Recovery: Two weeks out from surgery I was on my own, with a nurse visiting each day to check my vitals. I was even beginning to move around without the walker inside the apartment. Having stocked up the refrigerator before the operation I didn't need to go out shopping. I had also moved most of my furniture and heavy objects to a storage locker with the help of my cousin Bobby before the operation as well. The brotha was prepared. I was even beginning to take short walks on the beach. One morning about 500 feet into my walk, suddenly I was having trouble breathing. Reaching for my inhaler, I discovered that I had left it in the car. The car was just a few hundred feet up the hill but it seemed miles away as I started back. Never in my life had I found it so hard to breathe so I panicked. I knew there was something seriously wrong, especially after using my emergency inhaler and still finding it difficult to breathe.

So I headed for the nearest emergency room in nearby San Luis Obispo. Observing the medical folk as they went through their examination and medical procedures I noticed their relaxed attitude suddenly changed after they read my x-ray and blood results. Their concern only heightened my own, especially when they moved me from emergency to a hospital room. Resulting from my knee replacement surgery I had a blood clot on my lung. I was told if I hadn't come in it probably would have killed me. About the same time Sulo was texting me daily about breathing problems. I told him to see a doctor each time he texted, I don't think he did. Meanwhile I was sent home after heavy doses of blood thinners with a prescription for more. My scheduled nurse visits now also included daily shots of the prescribed blood thinner. They seemed to be preparing for the possibility of one or more blood clots which could possibly be fatal. Things got a bit stranger as I fought off blood clots I was also moving the rest of my things to the storage locker and to my vehicle. I was sick and homeless, sorta, but I had money. I found a hotel near the beach where I took my morning walks and settled in for recovery time. Soon I was taking short walks on the beach again as I looked for an apartment.

Sulo's Mom Barbara: Who I always thought a little insane talked to Sulo daily by phone and/or text. In my book *There Are Times When...* During our marriage I mentioned her habit of locking herself in the bedroom for days while I tried to keep a 'normal' home life for the kids. But there was no reasonable explanation for their mother locking herself away from us. Always especially close to Sulo who rarely spoke to me during our marriage; I wasn't surprised at his reaction to the divorce. So when Sulo started talking to me he mentioned that his mother texted daily but refused to see him. She still made his house payments and sent him money periodically; but when talking about his mom Sulo got this strange angry look on his face. Always the outsider I never understood their relationship. I knew she really disliked me but never contemplated the depth of her hatred. I have never hated anyone as much as the hatred she displayed. So while I was going through my various crisis; Arkansas, death of a friend, knee surgery, blood clot, I was to discover in a most horrible way that Sulo was experiencing the ultimate crisis of his own. He was in a Los Angeles hospital with his mom sitting at his bedside dying. I had no way of knowing since he wasn't able to text or call me, although his mother could have broken her code of silence in such an emergency. As a matter of fact she sat there at his bedside for ten days and sent me no messages or notice of Sulo's illness and hospitalization. Regardless of my condition of course I would have been there in a heartbeat. A simple text saying Sulo is sick, or Sulo is in the hospital would have been reasonable notice, one would think. Or should I say any sane person would think that some contact or notice should be sent to the father. Who could understand such hatred, I cannot.

Did she not send me notice to avoid seeing me; from her reaction to my presence at the memorial service that could be the case. Regardless, after sitting at his bedside for ten days she finally sent me a two word text message; "Sulo died." Just typing it I feel all the shock, surprise and pain that I felt when I received it from her. Is that what she wanted? Would she be happy to know that her two word message keeps playing in my head very day? So out of the blue I got that message from her. How would you feel going about your daily routines and getting such a message about your only living child? For the first time I considered how much that woman, Sulo's mother really hated me. To sit there for ten days watching our son die without a word to me took extreme hatred. Yes 2016 was a horrible year. Like so many of us I got married bought a house; had two children; raised them, watched them grow attend school; play soccer, swim, basketball; graduate and start their adult lives. Then the most horrible thing that can happen to a parent; my youngest child died. Needless to say I barely survived that tragedy, but after a divorce and years of loneliness somehow life goes on. Although he hadn't spoken to me for many years I still had one child. I followed his activities and his life from afar until 2015 when we began a shaky new relationship and barely a year later on November 4, 2016 I received that text from his mother; "Sulo died." All those years we sat at the kitchen table for homework, watched Mr. Rogers Neighborhood, Sesame Street, Electric Company and did all those things parents do. But who in their right mind would ever consider the possibility of a parent's worst nightmare happening to them not once but twice? After all the pictures places, activities and memories, just like that I am no longer a parent; I am childless, I have no children. All of that past, all of those memories are meaningless; like they never happened, what proof do I have that they did happen? I have NO children to show for it! That first time; the death of my first child I had a very angry intense conversation with God.

I still talk to God but this 2nd time around the anger is gone, to be replaced by a daily overwhelming sadness. After the memorial service; for several weeks I maintained a conversation with Sulo's mother, mainly checking to see if she was still alive each day. She mumbled some nonsense about she and Sulo having an agreement that when one died the other would also die. What kind of crazy crap is that? I reminded her that her death like Sulo's would bring sadness to many others who are still trying to deal with the death of Sulo, especially our grandson. After a few weeks she was strong enough to handle life without my help. I now live in an over 55 retirement community where weekends and holidays are the hardest times. Children and grandchildren come to visit and wander the halls and recreation areas with their parents and grandparents, I can't help reflecting on what I no longer have when seeing them. But I do have my writing.

This part of the story about the death of my last child I have been putting off for weeks because I didn't know how or whether I could tell it. Well I did, but not without reliving every painful detail. Even the part where I saw Sulo's mother for the first time in over a decade at the memorial service put together by his Hollywood friends. Out of respect and not wanting to make a scene; I didn't know what to say to her. Both there for the formality; after her sitting for 10 days with my dying son without telling me he was even sick; there I said it again. What could I say to a person who hated me so much that she would do such a thing? Nothing. Maybe I could have asked why, but the why was obvious, the woman really hates me more than anyone else I know. I divorced her, I left her; reckon that is reason enough. And beyond all those why thoughts other than a brief hello, the woman refused to look at me or speak to me during the time we were at the service. Cool with that, but it seemed strange behavior for the mother and father of the deceased son. But what do I know; daily I am misreading and failing to understand simple interactions with folk.

Imagine after a family experience of more than forty years realizing you didn't know the person with whom you shared that experience, at all. Your lack of awareness and perception is scary. What else did I miss; even today do I habitually miss things when dealing with people? Have I suffered from such an affliction all of my life. Must I mentally go back and reevaluate a lifetime of interactions? Or maybe this lack of awareness of others and their actions and reactions is a part of aging. But then too I've felt this way all of my life. I have always felt that I was standing off to the side watching many personal interactions. What did I miss?

But with my children, and my family I was fully engaged at all times, forever looking, observing and participating in all aspects of their lives. When you do all that you can do for the ones you love and give all you can give everything is supposed to turn out all right, isn't it? What if it doesn't, "turn out all right" is it something that you did or did not do? If you could do it over again, what would you, should you change? Was there a specific time or event in their past or yours which created the conditions for this sad, sad ending. If you could turn back the clock; which age, time or events would you choose?

Yes, much to think about but thinking doesn't change a damm thing; it's all still what it is. Writing about past events is as close as one can come to reliving those events which can be a good or bad thing depending on the events you're writing about. Find happiness by writing about the happy times; even when the sad realities try to intrude; block them out and enjoy those happy memories. Annnnnnd remember so long as there is life it is possible for you to make new memories.

Goodbye

How does one say goodbye to yesterday's forever, quickly fading away?

Words, just a sick reminder of what will never again

be.

But to live within a silence, one wonders, is there something I didn't

see?

Busy, busy, doing the things that must be done; all the necessaries to raise two

sons.

How was I to know, that they wouldn't be around when it's time for me to

go.

Sitting here with the memories from birth to the last day; in the midst of endings

one wonders, was there another

way?

We Really. Really tried our best!

No free throws, every shot counts

I have been working on this my third and final book since 2014. Much life happened from its beginning to the end; parts I have included. Some folk who at the beginning were very close friends, by the end they were not. In the beginning I lived in an isolated beach community on the central coast of California and by the end I found myself living where my California residence began in the late 1960's, Los Angeles. How I ended up here again is quite another story in itself. Feeling a responsibility and knowing that we must tell our own stories or others will tell them and fit your/our stories into their perceptions of life and their reality I put the words on the pages. Sounds simplistic, but no one knows your story better than you, although you may meet folk who will foolishly argue to the contrary. They claim with absolute certainty that they know your story and the stories of your parents, grandparents and children better than you. We owe it to all those who came before and to those who will follow to speak and publish our truths to be forever enshrined in the library of congress. Otherwise we must accept the 'truths' written by whites from a white perspective to fit the stereotypes and beliefs of their white readers. When we write we tell stories about who we are, not who the white privileged think we are.

Thinking about this story and its writing, all the things I left out comes to mind. Knowledge of those things would destroy families and hurt many people who have worked hard to create positive images. I too have worked to create and maintain a positive image; is that not called life and living? So again I close by saying enjoy and appreciate every second of every day surrounded by the folk you love. Tomorrow, who knows? Peace and understanding to you all.

D. Williams 2017

www.ingramcontent.com/pod-product-compliance
Lightning Source LLC
Chambersburg PA
CBHW050853160426
43194CB00011B/2138